W9-BJD-979

PUBLIC
BUDGETING
IN
AMERICA

PUBLIC BUDGETING IN AMERICA

THOMAS D. LYNCH

Department of Political Science
Mississippi State University

Prentice-Hall, Inc.
Englewood Cliffs, New Jersey 07632

Library of Congress Cataloging in Publication Data

LYNCH, THOMAS DEXTER,
   Public budgeting America.

   Includes bibliographies and index.
   1. Budget—United States I. Title.
HJ2051.L93   353.007'22   78-31170
ISBN 0-13-737346-5

Printed in the United States of America

10 9 8 7 6 5 4 3

Editorial/production supervision
   and interior design by Penny Linskey
Cover design by Edsal Enterprises
Manufacturing buyer: Harry P. Baisley

PRENTICE-HALL INTERNATIONAL, INC., *London*
PRENTICE-HALL OF AUSTRALIA PTY. LIMITED, *Sydney*
PRENTICE-HALL OF CANADA, LTD., *Toronto*
PRENTICE-HALL OF INDIA PRIVATE LIMITED, *New Delhi*
PRENTICE-HALL OF JAPAN, INC., *Tokyo*
PRENTICE-HALL OF SOUTHEAST ASIA PTE. LTD., *Singapore*
WHITEHALL BOOKS LIMITED, *Wellington, New Zealand*

Contents

Preface

When I started teaching public budgeting, I found it quite difficult. I had worked in the federal government for six years as a program analyst. I left that experience with strong feelings that skill development as well as thorough "feel" for budget behavior were essential for a budget course. In preparing for the course, I felt there was no adequate book, so I created a budget game and held seminars on topics such as debt administration. Within two years, I realized that my teaching strategy was incorrect because the students were not getting enough of the vast basic knowledge essential for budgeting. My solution was to write and use this book.

My educational strategy is that you must first give the student basic knowledge and concepts. Next, you can provide the skill development. Without the former, they are lost in a fog of public budgeting activities in which they do not know the vocabulary and concepts. The purpose of this book is to give undergraduates and graduates those basics. I teach the course over two semesters with skill development and exercises concentrated in the second semester. In teaching with the book, I merely ask many detailed questions on each chapter. When the questions are finished, the students know the material. I find this technique quite successful, for it permits excellent discussions and development of why certain details are important. The review questions at the end of the chapters serve as a pool from which I select the mid-term and final questions for graduate students.

The book is designed with students in mind. The first chapters provide the historical, political, and economic context for the course. The material tends to overlap some with other college courses. Thus students should feel more comfortable, but still challenged by the material. The other chapters cover the array of material in specific topic groups. This book is not a cookbook on budgeting, but it does help students read and even write such a cookbook for their governmental context. The intended audience for the book is primarily the prospective professional manager, and secondly the non-public manager who wishes to understand what is or is not happening in our governments.

My hope is that this text will provide a focus for the study of public budgeting and financial management. There has been a lack of direction and focus in this area for many years. Many have felt we need more skill development, model procedures and forms, economic models, political and behavioral strategies. Frankly, I agree with most of the arguments. I find fault with those who feel that only their "thing" is worthy of serious attention. In writing this book, I felt a need to stress that our subject is applied social science and the focus must be on the *user*—the public manager. Given that perspective, the efforts of the social scientist can be understood as contributions to the larger society. My hope is that others will share the underlying belief in this book and that we build from this point. Rather than economists (or political scientists) talking to economists (or political scientists), I hope we all direct our ultimate attention to the users so that our contributions can be better applied to improve today's and tomorrow's world. Theoretical arguments are important, but so is applied social science.

When an author puts pen to paper, the product is said to be that of the author. That is wrong, especially in the case of this book. Evidence of my students, graduate assistants, former professors, colleagues, friends, secretaries, and, of course, family are present throughout this effort. Unfortunately, only I can fully appreciate their contributions, but the credit (if any is to be given) belongs to all. My students (Maxwell School, Syracuse University and Mississippi State University) were my guinea pigs who were fed the early lectures and eventually the draft chapters. I was blessed with excellent unofficial and official graduate assistants: Lutu Nsaman assisted in preparing bibliographic references; Philomene Makolo and Glenda Owens assisted in the drafts, galleys, and page proofs. Professors Sydney Duncombe, Joseph Zimmerman, Lewis Welch, Ronald Stout, Donald Axelrod, Jesse Burkhead, James Carroll, Dwight Waldo, Howard Ball, Morris W. H. Collins, Walter Broadnax, and especially James Riedel are all thanked. Thanks also to Ray Pethel, Stan Wakefield, William Medina, Carl Stenberg, Philip V. Cortese, and R. Ken Hedrick, Jr.

Hopefully, this book will be used in many places. Professors and students, please tell me what you think of this text. Your comments—orally or in writing—will be appreciated.

THOMAS D. LYNCH

PUBLIC
BUDGETING
IN
AMERICA

ONE

Budgets and Evolution

Public budgeting is a mystery to most people—even to many professionals working in the government. People are aware that chief executives propose budgets to legislative bodies and that these groups in turn make decisions on taxes and what programs will receive financial support. If they work in government, they know that material is prepared to justify "the budget" and that detailed controls exist which often prohibit simple management decisions. In the personal lives of most people, the family budget is a source of tension because of the need to live within one's income. Most people assume that public budgeting must deal with similar matters but that it must involve much more complex accounting techniques.

This chapter examines public budgeting and reflects upon its significance in the larger context of public administration. Some attention is given to explaining what knowledgeable people define or characterize as public budgeting. Because we can often better understand today by looking into the past, some attention is given to examining the evolution of public budgeting in the United States. Particular attention is focused on the critical issues which shaped the evolution of public budgeting. This chapter should help the reader understand:

1. the interrelationship of policy and budgeting;
2. the major historical reforms which have shaped public budgeting in America, especially how the issues implicit in those reforms are still influencing what we perceive the "proper" role of budgeting to be in our government.

1

What is Public Budgeting?

It is money. The one common subject in any budget discussion is money. Other subjects are important, but they are mentioned in relationship to money or are translated into money. Budgeting involves dollars and cents often expressed in the millions and billions.

Mayor Beame of New York City fiscal crisis fame is purported to have said that "the budget is everything." Henry Maier, Milwaukee mayor, said, "The budget is the World Series of government." Political leaders are all too often painfully aware that many of the most important policy decisions are made in the budget process. Mayor Beame was aware of the financial crisis of his city and the resulting policy dilemmas. Mayor Maier was aware that many—if not most—of the major political decisions were made when he proposed and the city council adopted Milwaukee's budget.

Budgets are always created within a restricted financial environment. Every budget decision involves some potential benefits which may or may not be obtained. Also every decision involves opportunity costs. If the money is spent for one program, then another program is not funded or funded at a lesser level. In other words, opportunities are lost in every budget decision. There never seems to be enough money to finance every project. Choices have to be made by someone with some appreciation of the benefits received from a particular choice as well as the opportunities lost because of that selection.

Choices must be made among competing and alternative programs. Analysis can help make the choices, but competition is the significant factor. People within and outside government are requesting more money than is available to spend. Someone must and does decide among programs. Those choices are policy decisions and the arena in which to make those decisions is called public budgeting.

The budgetary process is a political process conducted in the political arena for political advantage. The process is complex and often the complexity obscures the significance of the accompanying political battles. Politics in its best and sometimes worst sense is a part of budgeting. In some instances, key politicians or major companies are seeking money for "their" people. In other instances, the political advantages sought are to uphold some ethical position. Motivations differ but the seeking of political advantage is constant.

Budgeting means different things to different people as illustrated by Exhibit 1-1. This exhibit paraphrases a variety of statements heard in the practical and academic experience of one of the most knowledgeable persons working in public budgeting. Sydney Duncombe has been author, teacher, and budget director of two states. One should notice in reading this text how each individual view is acceptable but still limited in perspective.

EXHIBIT 1-1[1]

What are the Main Purposes of Budgeting?

I view the budget system as a *means of balancing revenues and expenditures*. Our constitution requires a balanced budget and in preparing our budget we first make careful estimates of revenues for the next year. We then reduce agency budget requests to our revenue estimates for the next year.

I look on the budget process as *a semi-judicial process* in which state agencies come to the Legislature to plead their case just as I plead the case of my clients in court. Our job as a legislative committee is to distribute the available funds equitably among state agencies.

The main purpose of the budget system is *accountability*. The people hold the Legislature accountable through the electoral process. The Legislature holds state agencies accountable by reviewing their budgets, setting the appropriation levels the people want, and letting state agencies know how the people want their money spent through statements of legislative intent.

The most important single reason for a budget system is *control*. State agencies would spend the state bankrupt in two years if there weren't an adequate means of controlling their spending. The appropriations are the first line of defense against over-spending. Important second lines of defense lie in allotment systems, position controls and controls over purchasing.

The executive budget document should be *an instrument of gubernatorial policy*. When a Governor comes into office he has certain programs and policies he would like to see accomplished in his term of office. Many of the program and policy changes he wants cost money and he will have to either raise taxes or cut expenses to pay for these changes. The people expect the Governor to show accomplishments and the budget is a major means of showing these accomplishments.

Budgeting is *public relations*. I write my budget justifications in the way I think will best gain the appropriations I need. If the budget examiner likes workload statistics, we'll snow him with statistics. If a key legislator would be influenced by how the budget will affect his constituents, we put that in the request.

A budget is *an instrument of good management*. Careful use of workload statistics, performance accounting, and standards of performance will tend to insure that personnel are effectively utilized.

A budget is really *a work plan with a dollar sign attached*. As an agency official, I am committing myself to certain levels of program which I promise to attain if I receive my full budget request. When the Governor and the Legislature discuss cutting my budget, I describe as accurately as I can the reduction in program level that will result.

The budget is an instrument for *planning*. A good budget system requires agency officials to project costs and program levels at least several years ahead. Such a system requires agency officials to examine the costs and benefits of alternatives to present programs in order to plan changes in programs where necessary. In short,

---

[1]Prepared by Sydney Duncombe, 1977.

budgeting should be an annual means for agency heads to reexamine the objectives of their programs and the effectiveness of the means used to accomplish these objectives.

Budgeting is *the art of cutting* the most fat from an agency request with the least squawking.

A Public Manager's Perspective

Viewed from a public manager's perspective, the budget is often the principal vehicle for developing government plans and policies. There can be a separate planning process, but often such a process develops vague statements without stressing relative priorities. The budget states specific dollar amounts relative to proposed government activities and these decisions reflect the government's plans and policies much more accurately than most planning documents.

The budget also represents the chief executive's legislative program. It states which programs are to be active, emphasized, or ignored given the limited resources available to the government. Other public statements may be made which discuss a mayor's or governor's legislative program, but the comprehensive and detailed presentation is presented in the budget.

There are several different ways to categorize the request for funds to finance a government, but they all outline planned functions, programs, and activities. Program and performance budgets more clearly explain the relationship of money requested and government activities. However, even line item budgets, which focus upon specific items to be purchased with the budget, provide the knowledgeable reader with a detailed outline of planned government activities.

Most budgets present the planned program for the year against a background of past experiences and future needs. Even zero base budgets normally cite past experience to demonstrate the type of activities likely to be funded in the planned year. In some instances, budgets project future needs beyond the planned budget year in order to suggest the future year implications of budget year decisions. This past and future information is highly useful to decision makers: The past gives them an impression of what the program can accomplish and the future gives them warning of the long-run implications of current budget year decisions.

Strictly speaking the budget is a request for funds to run the government. The request is normally made by the chief executive to the city council, legislature, or Congress. It also states the revenue and other sources of resources (e.g., debt financing) needed to balance the suggested expenditures. Once the budget is modified or approved, the executive branch develops operating budgets for the budget year. Traditionally, the document sent to the legislature by the chief executive is called *the budget*. In the federal government, Congress receives the budget but passes several appropriation bills which constitute the modified approved federal budget.

An Operational Definition

As can be noticed from the previous discussions, the term "budget" is used in a variety of ways. Each may be quite correct given the perspective of the user of the word. In public administration, the following definition is normally an excellent operational definition:

> "Budget" is a *plan* for the accomplishment of *programs* related to *objectives* and *goals* within a definite *time* period, including an estimate of *resources required*, together with an estimate of the *resources available*, usually compared with one or more *past periods* and showing *future requirements*.

The budget always represents what someone wishes to do or have someone else do. It is a tool to help us control our affairs. Once the money is spent, it can be contrasted to the plan but it no longer represents something called a budget; rather it represents actual obligations or expenditures. Prior to that time, the budget may change many times. The document sent to the legislature by a chief executive is normally considered to be "the budget," whereas the plan used by the bureaucrats during the budget year is normally called the "operating budget."

People writing budgets have programs and program accomplishments in mind. Admittedly, those people may have rather vague notions of the exact nature of each program and their desired goals and objectives. Dealing with and avoiding vagueness is one of the major challenges of public budgeting. But in spite of vagueness, people preparing budgets do believe that the requested funds will be used for some set of activities and that those activities will result in accomplishments.

Budgets are focused upon a specific time period called the budget year. In some instances, the year used corresponds to the calendar year, but normally an arbitrary year called a fiscal year (e.g., October 1 to September 30) is defined. The money is planned to be spent or obligated in the budget year. Years prior to the budget year (BY) are called prior or past years (PY) and the current time period in which the government is operating is called the current year (CY). Future fiscal years beyond the budget year are referred to as budget year plus one (BY + 1), budget year plus two (BY + 2), and so on. For example, let us say we are preparing the budget for the fiscal year 1980 but we are actually in FY 1979. The BY is 1980. The CY is 1979. The PY is 1978. The BY + 1 is 1981.

Budgets are planned for a specific time period and an estimate is always made on the resources required during that time period. The estimates include the revenue as well as the expenditures. Estimating is another challenge of budgeting as one can never be certain that a specific dollar sum will be raised or that the government can live within its proposed expenditures. The latter is more easily controlled, but unexpected emergencies or problems do occur.

In order to facilitate a better understanding of the requested resources, the budget usually compares the BY requests against the PY and CY actual obligations

5

or expenditures. This provides a basis for comparing and permits the decision maker to focus upon the difference or increment between the CY and the BY. This is called incremental budgeting. In zero base budgeting, one ignores the differences and demands that the whole BY amount be justified. As will be explained later in more depth, this distinction between incremental and zero base budgeting is overstated. Increasingly, budgets also go beyond the BY and show BY + 1, BY + 2, BY + 3, BY + 4, and BY + 5. This showing of future requirements helps the decision maker realize that BY decisions have an effect beyond one budget year. Thus, a policy maker may decide that a given set of decisions may be affordable for the budget year but not wise, given the likely future requirements. Unfortunately, policy makers often ignore future implications and this situation represents yet another challenge of public budgeting.

Budget Realities

If you examine a budget, there will be many tables and charts. If you work in government, there will be many forms that must be completed so that a budget can be prepared, executed, and evaluated. The details in the forms and tables are an essential part of budgeting, but you can never understand public budgeting by examining those forms and tables *per se*. The numbers and the formats used to present the numbers are merely some of the means and not the ends of public budgeting.

Budgeting is a good reflection of actual public policy and often a better reflection than formal speeches or written statements. Politicians must get elected to hold office, and clarity of expression may be dysfunctional because it makes needless enemies. Also, it is often difficult to verbalize policy. The budget states the planned priorities and the programs in a meaningful way to the people who must carry out the policy. This is not to say that all policy is reflected in the budget because some important policy matters have no fiscal implications. Nor is it to say that all budgets clearly present policy, but an expert can read the message which will be operationalized by the bureacracy.

A budget focuses upon a given year (the budget year) but its preparation, execution, and evaluation takes place over a period of several years (the budget cycle). Going back to the FY 1980 example, the preparation and approval of the 1980 budget year should have been finished just prior to the beginning of the fiscal year (October 1, 1980). In order to have an approved budget on time, the preparation and approval process must begin much earlier. Sometimes the preparation begins a full year or more before the beginning of the budgeted fiscal year. During FY 1980, the operating budget is used to guide obligations and expenditures, but after FY 1980 no more money can be obligated but some money can be spent to fulfill the FY 1980 obligations. The period to fulfill obligations can be open-ended, but sound practices place a one- or two-year limit so that the books can be closed. The final stage in the budget cycle is auditing and evaluating the program resources obligated in the earlier budget year. This can take place one to several years after the completion of the fiscal year. In other words, the FY 1980 budget cycle can start as early as 1979 and end as late as 1983.

Budgeting is highly emotional, detailed, and a great deal of work. When policy makers decide to fund or not fund programs, people are profoundly affected, lives are changed. Not surprisingly, budget decisions evoke strong emotions because the stakes are high and the consequences are important. Budgets are also detailed. The one cardinal sin for a budget officer is to make an arithmetic error because that is one mistake everyone can catch and criticize. The budgets are often hundreds and thousands of pages long, filled with tables. Each number is usually important to someone and mistakes are not treated lightly. The preparation of this mass of information requires much work. Deadlines drive the process and require intensive 50- to 60-hour-plus work weeks, especially prior to a major deadline such as submission of material to a legislative committee. The work is consuming and requires almost complete devotion. The work is also extremely interesting because of the interrelationship of budgeting and politics.

Students of public budgeting must use concepts developed in political science, economics, accounting, the behavioral sciences, finance, and other disciplines. Political science helps the budget person understand the political nature of government and the public policy-making process. Economics provides useful analytical tools and highly influential theories. Accounting provides the means to keep track properly of the complex array of dollars. The behavioral sciences help the budget person understand the human as a part of the budget process. Finance gives the practitioner some conceptual tools to use especially relative to the revenue aspects of budgeting. Public administration helps bring this information together and adds some concepts of its own. Students of public budgeting should be able to draw upon a broad interdisciplinary background so that they can more easily deal with their challenging problems.

Public budgeting does require highly specialized knowledge, critical behavioral patterns, and important skills. These can be learned through experience and the learning process can be facilitated through formal education. This text sets out the primary knowledge useful to those involved in public budgeting as well as those wishing to better comprehend government by understanding public budgeting. Public budgeting requires more than knowledge. To be effective, certain important behavioral patterns should be mastered and that requires a learning laboratory or experience. Also certain skills must be acquired such as being able to translate possible policy positions into dollars and cents almost instantly in order to deal effectively in active political bargaining situations. Public budgeting is one of the most professionally challenging and often most emotionally rewarding activities in public administration.

Budgeting is a constantly changing field and some of the significant public administration reforms took place in the 1970s. In later sections of this chapter and in chapter 2, the history of budgeting will be examined in more depth. A major congressional budget reform took place in 1974 and two years later another major reform was considered. In the federal executive branch, Presidents Johnson, Nixon, and Carter each have sought major budget reforms. Debates at the highest level continue to occupy public attention in spite of the complexity of the subject.

One last public budgeting reality should be stressed. Public budgeting is very big money. The 1979 federal budget was over $500 billion. The public sector is 34 percent of the Gross National Product. State and local government is also huge today. For example, in 1929, the combined federal, state, and local expenditure was $10.4 billion; in 1977, the New York State budget alone exceeded that combined 1929 amount. Bureaucra:s often round off their working tables in the thousands, and they commonly prepare and execute budgets for billions of dollars.

Political Realities

Budgets are decided through politics; analysis is only ammunition in the decision-making process. Sometimes the politics are crude and unethical; sometimes reason and ethical views prevail. Often the decisions involve complex conflicting values supported by minimal analysis, but they are decisions which must be made. The analyses used in public budgeting are only significant to the political actors if those actors use the analyses in their deliberation. Even when used and not ignored the analyses are merely some of the ammunition used to persuade other political actors. In some cases, an appeal such as to the nation's pride may be more significant than an elaborate analysis. In other situations, an analysis can be the key to persuading political actors on how they should vote on a major policy matter.

Budgets are proposed plans. The budget presentations sometimes can make the difference for a program but in some instances the presentation will make no difference because the program is politically weak. In other instances, the program may be so politically strong that even a bad budget presentation will not defeat the program. Often the proposed plan or budget of the executive is a significant factor in the public decision-making, and the quality of the presentation is considered to be a reflection of the managerial competency of the program.

Sacred political cows do exist. An influential congressman or political executive can successfully demand a specific project or program. The appropriateness of the project or program is irrelevant, but the power of the political actor is very relevant. In public budgeting, the professional must learn to tolerate this unless a moral or legal question is involved. The nature of the American political system almost insures the existence of sacred cows. Some of them are prompted by campaign promises and some by less desirable motivations. The percentage of programs and projects that are sacred cows will vary, but normally they are the exception. If the program decisions are dominated by sacred cows, then public management will suffer as foolish programs or projects cannot be stopped except by highly political and time consuming debate.

Public budgeting is strongly influenced by the political causes of the day. The causes vary over time but some contemporary causes include national security, energy, environment, poverty, recession, and inflation. Policy makers, who decide on budgets, are keenly aware of the political causes because their positions on those causes influence the way people vote for or against them. Therefore, politicians wish to know how budgets relate to those causes. Not surprisingly, budget justifications are often cast in terms of those causes or, at a minimum, the agency is prepared to answer questions involving the program and the politically sensitive topic. For example, in a time of recession with large numbers of people unemployed, a major defense project will be justified first on the basis of providing jobs and secondly on the basis of national security.

Approaches to the Budgetary Process

Three approaches to the budgetary process are important. One is control. The stress in budgeting can be placed on insuring that money is spent according to established policy and that no resources are used for illegal purposes. The second approach is management. This approach uses the budget process to direct the people in the bureaucracy and to achieve as much efficiency and economy in budget programs as possible. The third approach is planning which emphasizes the improvement of the political decision-making process of which budgeting is an important segment. These three approaches are not mutually exclusive and they almost always exist in every budget process. This three-approach distinction is conceptually useful to understand. Reformers can stress certain features of budgeting and envision budgeting as a tool for one purpose while ignoring the other purposes a budget can serve. This is not to say that the other approaches disappear. They are merely not stressed in the reform.

If reformers are stressing control, they wish to guarantee fiscal accountability. They are fearful of corruption and public employees being unchecked in their decisions. Those arguing for greater control are supported by arguments to increase the strength of the chief executive (which will also achieve greater economy and efficiency in government). Strong chief executives can enhance their strength through improved budget control mechanisms. Strong control can also mean that inefficient and uneconomical activities are increased because not enough management flexibility is permitted to deal with changing situations. The added procedural requirements can result in more workers and less productivity.

Early American public budget literature stressed the control function. Given the well publicized political corruption of the era, the stress on control is certainly understandable. The reforms included such well-known budget features as the following:

Annual budget: revenues and expenditures presented for one fiscal year period;

Comprehensive budget: all revenues and expenditures included in the budget;

Detailed line items: presenting the exact amount planned to be spent for every separate thing or service to be purchased;

Identification of all transactions: recording every obligation and transfer of money, and liquidation of obligation;

Apportionments and allotments: an executive branch mechanism to regulate the rate and actual spending of authorized funds.

Stress on budget control comes with a price tag. Extreme control limits management flexibility which might be essential in many situations. Interestingly, the reform for efficiency can lead to inefficiency because management cannot easily adapt to more efficient procedures. Budget control is a high administrative cost activity. Recording all transactions and every line item requires many people even in this era of the computer. Another cost of budget control is more subtle in its effect upon government. By stressing control, the emphasis is upon detail and the big policy decisions tend to be ignored. Thus government becomes less responsive to the problems of society.

If reformers are stressing management, they view the budget as a tool of the executive to achieve effective operational direction with greatest efficiency. The budget can be used as a mechanism to guide the massive bureaucracy. Reforms like performance budgeting (i.e., categorizing the planned activities to stress the relationship of money to achievement) and productivity improvements (i.e., getting greater results for relatively fewer resources) are stressed. Often reformers decentralize the details to the agency level while stressing means to achieve greater centralized direction. Normally those reforms are more conservative and business oriented, and, not surprisingly, these reforms were stressed more in the 1920s, early 1930s, and the 1970s when conservative Republicans were President.

If reformers are stressing planning, they view the budget as a way to bring greater rationality into the public policy-making process. These reformers are appalled at the poor decision-making situation of top policy makers and the noncoordinated nature of many decision-making processes. They believe that coordinated and rational decision-making is important and more planning and greater use of analyses is the way the decision-making process should be improved. Those reformers stress the importance of analysis, data, and categorizing the budget to facilitate analysis. In the 1960s, PPB (planning–programming–budgeting) and the use of analysis was stressed in public budgeting.

Evolution as Prelude

Parliament Versus the King

Public budgeting in the United States is very much influenced by early English history. The word "budget" seems to have originated from the Middle English "bouget" meaning bag or wallet. A great leather bag was used by the king's treasurer—later called the exchequer—to carry the documents explaining the king's fiscal needs. That bag was called the budget. Over time the document and the system used to prepare and execute the document came to be called the budget and budgeting. The bag was used primarily when the king's treasurer went to Parliament seeking funds for the king.

English history is largely a struggle between the king and the Parliament over control of the nation. Not surprisingly, the budget was central to that struggle. In 1215, King John signed the Magna Carta and the twelfth article of that document stated that no taxes could be imposed "unless by the common council of the realm." The council of the realm was made up of the elite nobles and it evolved into the Parliament. In 1688, the English Bill of Rights established that no man could be compelled to pay a gift, loan, or tax "without common consent by Act of Parliament." The King was losing the struggle to unilaterally control the budget and by 1760 the King agreed to an annual specified grant controlled by the Parliament.

This struggle or tension between the legislature (the Parliament) and the executive (the king) is also one of the most important characteristics of public budgeting in the United States. At the time of the American Revolution in 1776 and the drafting of the Constitution in 1789, the English experience influenced American leaders. The tension was considered good. Power, they thought, should be separated, especially between the legislative and executive branches. The separation helped prevent executive abuse of power but still enabled strong leadership to exist. Almost every American budget reform tends to address or affect this intended tension.

Colonial America

In colonial America, the revenue was generated within the colonies and the various state houses had a great deal of control over revenues and expenditures. The king's representatives administered the government. The legislatures became the place where the leading colonists gathered. They became accustomed to exercising power with a separate group actually administering the government programs. The separation from England, caused by the primitive means of trans-oceanic transportation, fostered an independence. But the need to live within their own resources and to decide how to apply their own resources using a locally elected legislative body were the important factors leading to self-reliance.

Many of the causes of the American Revolution relate directly to public budgeting issues. England decided to impose taxes (e.g., the Stamp Act) on the colonies largely due to the expensive French-Indian War. This unilateral act seemed unfair given the legislative authority over tax matters and the reasoning of such documents as the Magna Carta and Bill of Rights. Of course, many other reasons as well explain the emotions leading to the American Revolution, but issues concerning public budgeting were some of the most emotionally charged subjects of that era.

Not surprisingly, those strong feelings helped shape the U.S. Constitution. For example, Article I, Section 9 of the Constitution requires that all matters dealing with revenue must originate in the House of Representatives. The founders of the United States were not content to say that Congress had to act on revenue matters as did the English Bill of Rights a century earlier. Rather they stated that this matter had to start with the chamber of Congress which was to be *the* representative of the people. Today, the president presents his budget somewhat like the king's treasurer. The House passes the appropriation bills first. The Senate often acts as an appealing body and eventually the two chambers agree upon the appropriations. However, the House is still considered the leading chamber on matters concerning revenue and appropriations.

Budgeting in the 1800s

For the first few years of the federal government, Alexander Hamilton was the influential Secretary of Treasury. He viewed his role much like the English Exchequer, and his department was the most significant nonmilitary department. The national government's revenue source was custom duties, and the Coast Guard was an important force to ensure proper collection of the customs. Hamilton also effectively had the very large Revolutionary War debt retired.

Thomas Jefferson came to be the leader of the anti-Federalist faction which opposed Hamilton. The Federalist view was influenced by contemporary England which had the ministers dominating the Parliament and the executive activities. Jefferson thought the separation of powers was critical, and his and later administrations stressed that budgetary decisions were largely the dominion of the Congress. Executive leadership on comprehensive budget matters was considered improper by some presidents, but interestingly, Jefferson's administration was characterized by strong leadership by then Secretary of the Treasury, Albert Gallatin.

Congress started with a unified and comprehensive approach to public budgeting. The Ways and Means Committee was extremely powerful as it made decisions on revenues and appropriations. With few exceptions, the executive branch did not have a unified approach. The Treasury department did compile the expenditure estimates from all the agencies, but it did not edit or analyze the estimates. Such activities were considered to be legislative in nature.

As the century evolved, the Congress eroded its unified approach to the budget. By 1865, a separate House Appropriations Committee was established so that revenue and expenditures were considered separately. By 1885, there were eight separate committees which recommended appropriations. This disunity lessened the budgetary focus of power; but except for periods of war or depression, the federal government was not concerned about tight budgets. In this era, there was a constrained view of what government should do in society, so budgets tended to be small. Also the major revenue source—the customs—was providing more revenue than demands for expenditure so that Congress had the unusual problem of dealing with "large" surpluses.

Municipal Budget Reform

The modern reforms in budgeting started with reactions against corruption and not concerns for government efficiency. The reforms were addressed more to the municipal level largely due to the efforts of popular newspaper and book writers called "muckrakers." They reported noted examples of municipal corruption and called for government reform. The most effective reformers were the National Municipal League (founded in 1899) and the New York Bureau of Municipal Research (1906).

The latter group is one of the most remarkable in American history. One of the leaders was Charles Beard who was a noted historian and founder of the academic discipline of political science. Luther Gulick and other members of that Bureau were also instrumental in founding public administration as a study and practice. The research arm of the League moved to Washington, D.C. and evolved into today's Brookings Institution. The training arm was moved to Syracuse University in 1925 and became the Maxwell School of Syracuse University. The Bureau served as a model and "mother house" for many other bureaus throughout the country. The members of the bureau led and staffed almost every major governmental reform committee between 1910 and 1950.

Not surprisingly, the New York Bureau of Municipal Research was highly influential in budget reforms. One year after its creation, it prepared the first detailed report demonstrating the need for adopting a municipal budget system. In that same year, the Bureau produced an object classification budget for the New York City Department of Health. By 1912, the reforms of the bureau were reflected in the Taft Commission report calling for object (line item) classification budgeting in all federal departments and agencies. By the 1920s, most of the budgets of major American cities were reformed. In 1929, A. E. Buck, a staff person of the bureau, wrote the first and very influential text on public budgeting.

Budget reform was stimulated by social contract political thought. Influential reformers believed that democracy could be strengthened if citizens could vote for someone who had the power to carry out his promises. Therefore, the chief executive should be strong and budget reform was one of the best ways to strengthen the executive. They also argued that a political-administrative dichotomy existed thus permitting the professionalization of the administrative class while still permitting popularly elected leaders. This dichotomy has been discredited, but it served an important conceptual function for most of the personnel and budget reforms from the 1890s to today.

Budgeting in this Century

Prior to 1921

In the early 1900s, the federal government started to experience large federal expenditures and budget deficits. The customs revenue was not adequate and a federal income tax was passed. This new tax solved the fundamental revenue problem since the tax rate could be increased to provide the necessary revenue. This tax also attracted the keen attention of the business community as they now had a vested interest in minimizing the money that the government took from them as corporations and individuals. Business interests dominated the times. Business and many citizens stressed the importance of economy, efficiency, and government retrenchment. Many felt that the least government was the best government.

President Taft issued a report prepared by the Commission on Economy and Efficiency Goals titled "Need for a National Budget." The report stressed that the president should be responsible for preparing a unified executive budget. The rationale was motivated by two themes: (1) economy and efficiency, and (2) strengthening democracy. A president's budget would be better able to plan government activities so that maximum economy and efficiency were achieved. A president's budget would also strengthen his power—thus citizens could vote for or against a person who had the power to fulfill his promises. President Taft was not successful in his reforms and Woodrow Wilson's income tax temporarily took the pressure off.

Prior to 1921, agencies still followed the Jefferson tradition of preparing their estimates and transmitting them to the Treasury department which passed them on to Congress. Treasury conducted no analyses. The various Congressional committees considered the estimates with minimum coordination among themselves. The agencies did sometimes overspend the appropriations and Congress felt obligated to appropriate the overspent amount. The president did not participate in the budget process and there was no overall Executive Branch Plan.

Budgeting and Accounting Act of 1921

President Taft's reforms were largely enacted in 1921. Pressures for budget reform continued especially with the expense of World War I. The Budget and Accounting Act of 1921 provided for a national budget and an independent audit of government accounts. The law specifically required the president to submit a budget including estimates of expenditures, appropriations, and receipts for the ensuing fiscal year. The new legislation created the Bureau of the Budget (BOB) in the Treasury department. Section 209 of the legislation states:

> The Bureau, when directed by the President, shall make a detailed study of the departments and establishments for the purpose of enabling the President to determine what changes (with a view of securing greater economy and efficiency in the

conduct of the public service) should be made in (1) the existing organization, activities, and methods of business of such departments or establishments, (2) the appropriations therefore, (3) the assignment of particular activities to particular services, or (4) the regrouping of services. The results of such study shall be embodied in a report or reports to the President, who may transmit to Congress such report or reports or any part thereof with his recommendations on the matter covered thereby.

This landmark legislation greatly strengthened the president and created the powerful BOB as an arm of the president. The agencies were required to submit their estimates and supporting information to BOB. Agencies were not allowed to initiate contacts with Congress. Also legislation established that all recommended legislation from agencies had to be sent to BOB for review and clearance. This clearance function greatly increased presidential power because it allowed the president to insure the executive branch was in step with presidential policy. The Bureau could and did prepare the president's budget which was the executive branch (president's) proposal to the Congress. The agencies and departments in the executive branch were and are required to support the president's budget.

Budgeting is largely a story of relative legislative-executive strength. With Hamilton, executive strength was asserted but short-lived. After Jefferson, legislative strength in the budget area dominated but was diminished by the nonunified approach which evolved in the Congress. With the passage of the 1921 legislation, executive branch strength started to grow in spite of the fact that the Congress largely initiated the legislation. The power of the Congress was not diminished, but the 1921 Act did increase the power of the president.

The Budget and Accounting Act of 1921 also created a Congressional agency called the General Accounting Office (GAO) to audit independently the government accounts. This agency is headed by the Comptroller General who is appointed to a 15-year term by the president. The purpose of the audits is to verify that government funds are being used for legal purposes. The independence of the agency prevents improper pressure being exerted upon it by members of the executive branch.

The president's 1937 Committee on Administration Management (Brownlow Committee) recommended the strengthening of BOB's management activities. The 1921 legislation had given the bureau certain managerial responsibilities, but they were not exerted. The Brownlow Committee's report eventually led to the Reorganization Act of 1939. This in turn led to the establishment of the Executive Office of the president and the transfer of BOB to that new office. President Roosevelt defined the duties of the Bureau as follows:

1. to assist the president in the preparation of the budget and the formulation of the fiscal program of the government;
2. to supervise and control the administration of the budget;
3. to conduct research in the development of improved plans of administrative management, and to advise the executive departments and agencies of the government with respect to improved administrative organizations and practice;

4. to aid the president in bringing about more efficient and economical conduct of the government services;

5. to assist the president by clearing and coordinating departmental advice on proposed legislation and by making recommendations as to presidential action on legislative enactment, in accordance with past practices;

6. to assist in the consideration and clearance and, where necessary, in the preparation of proposed executive orders and proclamations;

7. to plan and promote the improvement, development, and coordination of federal and other statistical services; and

8. to keep the president informed of the progress of activities by agencies of the government with respect to work proposed, work actually initiated, and work completed, together with the relative timing of work between the several agencies of the government, all to the end that the work programs of the several agencies of the executive branch of the government may be coordinated and that the monies appropriated by the Congress may be expended in the most economical manner possible with the least possible overlapping and duplication of effort.

The Bureau became the right arm of a strong president.

Post-1940 Reforms

During World War II, the Bureau became even more important with all activities directed toward the war. Taxes were increased and record deficits were incurred. The Bureau assumed added duties including supervision of government financial reports and establishing personnel ceilings. In 1945, the Bureau's budget function was extended to include the government corporations. Also accounts had to be maintained on a program basis and full cost information was required. The Government Corporations Act of 1945 also directed the GAO to appraise the corporations in terms of their performance rather than mere legality and propriety of their expenditures. This provision was eventually extended to all GAO reviews.

The Full Employment Act of 1946 called for economic planning and a budget policy directed toward achieving maximum national employment and production. More about this Act and fiscal policy will be discussed in chapter 3.

The late 1940s saw the addition of more duties to BOB. The Classification Act of 1949 required the director to issue and administer regulations involving agency reviews of their operations. The Travel Expense Act of 1949 assigned the director regulatory functions on travel allowances.

President Truman appointed the Hoover Commission in 1947 and a report was submitted in 1949. The Commission recommended that

1. a budget based on functions, activities, and projects, called a "performance budget," be adopted:

2. the appropriation structure be surveyed and improved;

3. the budget estimates of all departments and agencies be separated between current operating and capital outlays; and

4. the president's authority to reduce expenditures under appropriations "if the purposes intended by the Congress are still carried out" be clearly established.

Several reforms resulted from the Hoover Commission but the Budget and Accounting and Procedures Act of 1950 was particularly important. It recognized the need for reliable accounting systems and the president was given the authority to prescribe the contents and budget arrangements, simplify the presentations, broaden the appropriations, and progress toward performance budgeting.

The Second Hoover Commission (1955) led to more technical but equally important budget reforms. Agency accounts were to be maintained on an accrual basis. Cost-based budgets were encouraged. Synchronization between agency structure and budget classifications was encouraged. The President's Commission on Budget Concepts in 1967 did not address any fundamental budget reforms but concerned itself with smaller technical issues. In summary, the post-1940 period saw many reforms which continued to strengthen the executive budget process.

REVIEW QUESTIONS

1. Explain how budgeting is policy or a reflection of policy. Why is this fact significant?
2. Explain the various perspectives one can have with public budgeting and how the definition of public budgeting can be affected by each perspective.
3. What budgeting reforms are particularly important to public budgeting today?

REFERENCES

BAKKER, OEGE. *The Budget Cycle in Public Finance in the United States*. The Hague: W. P. Van Stockum, 1953.

BARTIZAL, JOHN R. *Budget Principles and Procedures*. Englewood Cliffs, N.J.: Prentice-Hall, 1940, 1942.

BEAUMOUNT, ENID. "The New York Case From a Public Administration Perspective," *The Bureaucrat*, 5, 1 (April 1976), 101–12.

BENSON, GEORGES et al. (eds.). *The American Property Tax: Its History, Administration and Economic Impact*. Clairmont, Calif.: Institute for Studies in Federalism, Clairmont Men's College, 1965.

BLACK, GUY. "Externalities and Structure in PPB," *Public Administration Review*, 31, 6 (November/December 1971), 637–43.

BREAK, GEORGE F. *Agenda for Local Tax Reform*. Berkeley: Institute of Government Studies, University of California, 1970.

———. *Intergovernmental Fiscal Relations in the United States*. Washington, D.C.: Brookings Institution, 1967.

BRUNDAGE, PERCIVAL FLACK. *The Bureau of the Budget*. New York: Praeger, 1970.

BUCK, A. E. *Public Budgeting*. New York: Harper & Row, 1929.

BURKHEAD, JESSE. *Governmental Budgeting*. New York: John Wiley, 1956, 1965.

CLEVELAND, FREDERICK A. "Budget Idea in the United States." *The Annales*, vol. 62 (November 1915).

FISHER, LOUIS. *Presidential Spending Power*. Princeton, N.J.: Princeton University Press, 1975.

GROSS, BERTRAM M. "The New Systems Budgeting," *Public Administration Review*, vol. 29, no. 2 (1969).

LEE, ROBERT D. and RONALD W. JOHNSON. *Public Budgeting Systems*. Baltimore: University Park Press, 1973.

LEWIS, V. B. "Toward a Theory of Budgeting," *Public Administration Review*, 12, 1 (Winter 1952), 42–54.

MOAK, LENNOX L. and KATHRYN W. KILLIAN. *Operating Budget Manual*. Chicago: Municipal Finance Officers Association, 1963.

MOAK, S. S. and KATHRYN W. KILLIAN. *Manual of Techniques for the Preparation, Adoption and Administration of Operating Budgeting*. Chicago: Municipal Finance Officers Association, 1973.

Municipal Performance Report, vol 1, no 4 (August 1974).

NISKANEN, WILLIAM A. *Structural Reform of the Federal Budget Process*. Washington, D.C.: American Enterprise Institute for Public Policy Research, 1973.

NOVICK, DAVID. *Origin and History of Program Budgeting*. Santa Monica, Calif.: Rand Corp., Oct. 1966.

SCHICK, ALLEN. "The Road to PPB: The Stages of Budget Reform," *Public Administration Review*, 26, 4 (December 1966), 243–58.

SHARKANSKY, IRA. *The Politics of Taxing and Spending*. Indianapolis: Bobbs-Merrill, 1969.

TRUMAN, DAVID. *The Governmental Process*. New York: Knopf, 1951.

TWO

Modern
Budgeting

In the 1960s and 1970s, public budgeting in the United States experienced significant change. The emphasis in the middle 1960s was on planning-programming-budgeting (PPB). In the middle 1970s, the stress was placed upon using management-by-objectives (MBO) in the federal executive branch and creating a unified Congressional approach to budgeting in the legislative branch. In the late 1970s, the reform was zero-base budgeting (ZBB) in the executive branch and sunset legislation in the legislative. Each reform is significant and shall be discussed in this chapter.

The last portion of this chapter addresses various topics designed to put modern budgeting into context. Subjects like ideology, federalism, and decision-making models are briefly explained in terms of their significance to budgeting. Also some of the contemporary emphases in budgeting are briefly identified.

This chapter also discusses:

1. the significance of ideology in influencing how we approach public budgeting as well as the significant normative theories of decision-making;
2. a commentary on the approaches to public budgeting;
3. the contemporary reform topics associated with public budgeting;
4. PPB, how it was operationalized and its implications for public administration;
5. the weak attempt to institute MBO into the federal government and the potential of linking MBO with budgeting;
6. ZBB, how it has been operationalized, and its implication for public budgeting;
7. the factors that motivated the passage of the 1974 budget reform act and the essential features of that landmark legislation;
8. sunset legislation and its implications.

Context of Modern Budgeting

Ideology

Ideas are powerful especially when shared by many people. Ideas can guide people by discouraging certain types of activities and encouraging other activities. Ideas can be and often are used to place a value on people, things, activities, and even other ideas. Ideas can be consistent with other ideas forming belief systems. These systems in turn can be shared by many people and can guide entire civilizations. These belief systems are called ideologies and every culture has them.

This section sketches the American ideology and its influence on budgeting. The sketch is simplified. Many important belief systems and subsystems are not discussed as they are not central to the purpose of this section. The two major ideologies influencing public budgeting in the United States are democracy and capitalism.

Democracy in the United States evolved from a desire to have representative government in the agriculturally oriented colonies. Certain rights, like freedom of the press, were considered essential and were built into the Constitution. In time, the definition of "voter" extended from male landholder over 21 to the universal suffrage of today. The democratic government system also evolved as was explained in the 1780s Federalist Paper No. 10. Parties and groups interact in a government designed to have a separation of powers. People can influence government policy best by acting as a group and directing their influencing efforts at partisans in the political process. The partisans interact and adjust policy based upon the relative strength of the lobbying forces. The strength is sometimes due to economic interests but it can be due to shared and effectively argued belief systems.

In America, the notion of partisan bargaining, minority and fundamental rights, diffusion of power, and influencing partisans through collective action over time all constitute the meaning of democracy. In public budgeting, this means that one can anticipate that the agency's clientele groups (i.e., those affected directly by the agency's activities) can and will lobby the legislature (Congress) and the executive (the president). The agency's actions will be influenced by the executive, the legislature, and the clientele group. Subjects like freedom of information and sunshine legislation will be taken seriously, thus opening up much budget detail documentation to the media and public. Budget decisions will be made by both the executive and legislature. Public hearings will be considered important additions to the budget process. The belief system called democracy greatly influences the way Americans think public budgeting should be conducted.

A second major ideology in the United States is capitalism. The United States does not have capitalism in the strictest sense of the term, but capitalism as a belief system is quite apparent. Unlike democracy, there is an effective challenge to capitalism which has led to a blending of sometimes logically conflicting belief systems. Strict capitalism evolved from a reaction against English mercantilism of the 1760 era and was reinforced by social Darwinism of the mid-1800s to the 1930s. The desire was to limit the role of government in the economic activities of society. Government did have a role such as dealing with strict public goods like national defense, and possibly the government role could be extended to include:

1. coping with public allocations for the general good, like public education and pollution control;
2. avoiding private inconvenient monopolies like highways, bridges, and water systems.

Advocates of capitalism raise severe protests when subjects such as redistribution of wealth and the use of government control to achieve economic stabilization and growth are raised. The dispute is between inhibiting private economic freedom and activity versus using government to prevent abuse by private enterprise as well as having the government be an active agent in the society and economy.

From the 1890s to the present, a contrary belief system arose from earlier thinking. Its proponents advocated a total role for government in society. Government would have to run society and curb the natural economic abuses of the wealthy elites. The most visionary advocates of the belief system seriously stated that a classless society would evolve and there would no longer need to be a government acting as the people's trustee. In many nations of the world, this belief system is now dominant. In the United States, the belief system has served to raise the social conscience and the earlier forms of capitalism (e.g., child labor and shorter work week) have been greatly modified. Especially after 1932, the federal government has come to play an active role in society on such matters as consumerism, environment, inflation, recession, and safety. However, the debate continues on what should be the role of government in society and in the economy.

Capitalism, as modified in the United States, has influenced public budgeting. The very decision of what activities should be budgeted is related to the debates over capitalism. Macroeconomics is extremely important in deciding the desired effect of the federal budget on the economy. Regional economic theory also plays an influential role in state and local budgets. The stress on economy, efficiency, and productivity arise out of the tensions over capitalism. The very approach of budgeting—line item, performance, or program—is influenced by the debate over capitalism.

Decision-Making Models

Public budgeting is a decision-making process. Not surprisingly, there are several theories as to the way public policy decisions should be made. These theories or conceptual models are important because many people take them seriously and try to reform public budgeting using one of the theories as their guide. To better understand contemporary public budgeting reforms, these theories must be understood. But first, a criterion must be developed to judge the conceptual models, and the concept of conceptual models itself must be explained.

A conceptual model can be viewed as a tool which enables the user to understand and deal with complex phenomena. A tool can be judged "good" or "bad" in terms of the user's purpose. A hammer, for example, may be a good tool for building a shed, but it is bad for chopping wood. Professionals should judge conceptual models or theories in terms of the model's usefulness in helping them accomplish their tasks. Those tasks must be accomplished within a decision-making context largely induced by the ideologies of the culture.

Public budgeting in the United States must be conducted in a political, human, and often practical environment. The democratic ideology has helped to define the political environment. Consensus and partisan adjustments best explain the political context. Public budgeting is conducted by humans and it affects humans; thus emotional drama, error, pride, and other human characteristics help define the context of budgeting. In public budgeting, the practical is often a significant factor because decisions must be made. Even a so-called nondecision often represents an allocation of resources in budgeting. If the data or analyses are not available, then the decision-maker must make do with conventional wisdom or personal biased judgment. Thus the "do–able" or practical is significant.

Decision-making models can be judged in terms of their applicability to the decision-making environment of the public budget person. If the model is not in harmony with the decision-making environment (which is unlikely to be changed) then the model is "bad." That is, the model is not appropriate to the user's purposes. This value judgment must be limited to the decision maker discussed here.

Some major and commonly noted decision-making models are the incremental change model, the satisficing model, and the ideal-rational model. To this list, a provocative but little cited model called the "stages of problem solving" can be added. The incremental model is used for descriptive and normative purposes, but just because something exists in a certain way does not mean that it should continue to exist. The focus in this and subsequent paragraphs shall be on the normative use of the model. In the incremental model, major public policies evolve through cautious incremental steps; political forces mutually adjust their positions and, over time, public policy changes. This is an inherently conservative approach and it biases the decision makers against more radical innovative alternatives.

Aaron Wildavsky's *The Politics of the Budgetary Process* develops a model similar to the incremental change model. An agency develops and advocates a budget to its department, to the Office of Management and Budget, and to Congress. In the major phases of the budget approval process, the agency takes the role of an advocate; the reviewer (e.g., Office of Management and Budget) questions the wisdom of the proposal; and the reviewer makes a tentative decision, which is often appealed to the secretary, the president, or the Senate. This model is consistent with the incremental change model in that policies are mutually adjusted because someone advocates and someone accommodates. Wildavsky merely points out the roles taken by the various actors in the incremental change process.

The satisficing model points out that decision makers develop a criterion to judge acceptable policy alternatives for a given problem. They then search the alternatives and select the first acceptable alternative they discover. Time is significant in the satisficing model. Alternatives are considered but the ideal is not sought. The acceptable is the standard for judgment. Like the incremental change model, the satisficing model is used for both descriptive and normative purposes; but the consideration here is only on the normative use. The reasons for the limited search are the lack of time for an exhaustive search and the opportunity costs of such a search.

The rational model is most commonly cited as the ideal way to reach decisions, especially major public policy decisions such as those in public budgeting. Its assumptions are deeply rooted in modern civilization and culture. The model systematically breaks decision-making down into six phases:

1. establish a complete set of operational goals, with relative weights allocated to the different degrees to which each may be achieved;
2. establish a complete inventory of other values and resources with relative weights;
3. prepare a complete set of the alternative policies open to the policy maker;
4. prepare a complete set of valid predictions of the cost and benefits of each alternative, including the extent to which each alternative will achieve the various operational goals, consume resources, and realize or impair other values;
5. calculate the net expectations for each alternative by multiplying the probability of each benefit and cost for each alternative by the utility of each, and calculate the net benefit (or cost) in utility units;
6. compare the net expectations and identify the alternative (or alternatives, if two or more are equally good) with the highest net expectations.

In fewer words, using the rational model is merely defining one's goals, analyzing the available alternatives, and selecting the alternative that best meets the goals.

Although similar to the rational model, the "stages of problem solving" model is amenable to observation and analysis, but it too can be a normative model. Figure 2-1 presents the model visually. The starting point is the perception that a problem exists—not the formulation of goals. Perception permits the possibility of multiple value perspectives whereas goals tend to ignore the possibility of multiple or conflict of values. Either formally or informally, the decision maker defines the problem, considers the solutions, and analyzes the alternatives in a manner similar to someone using the rational model. A key decision is then made either to reconsider the nature of the problem or to plan to resolve the problem. (This reconsideration step is not a part of the rational model.) If the decision is to proceed, the necessary action steps are taken and outcomes are

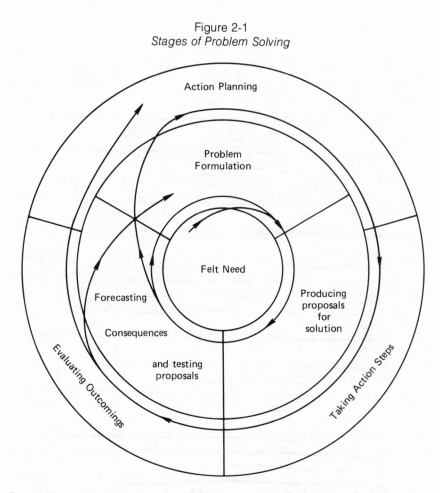

Figure 2-1
Stages of Problem Solving

Action Planning

Problem
Formulation

Felt Need

Forecasting

Consequences

Producing
proposals
for
solution

Evaluating Outcomings

and testing
proposals

Taking Action Steps

Source: Richard Wallen in Edgar H. Schein, *Process Consultation: Its Role in Organization Development* (Reading, Mass.: Addison-Wesley Publishing Company, 1964) p. 46.

evaluated. (This second reconsideration is also absent from the rational model.) From evaluation, the decision maker may either start over by reconsidering the problem or replan his or her action steps.

The incremental change model and the Wildavsky model are excellent tools for understanding the political environment of public policy making, but they are not useful for explaining the more technical difficulties associated with analysis. On the other hand, the rational model helps us comprehend the technical difficulties of analysis, but is relatively useless in explaining the highly important political environment.

With the incremental change and Wildavsky models, the public budget person can better understand how the budget process is dominated by the strategies employed by and the conflicts that arise among the participants (clientele groups, agencies, departments, the Office of Management and Budget). Definable strategies exist that require such practices as agency cultivation of an active clientele, the development of confidence among other reviewing government officers such as budget examiners, and skill in following tactics that exploit temporary opportunities. Analysis in the budget process must serve to aid the key actors involved in making public policy. Reasoning from the incremental change model, program and budget analysis must be timely, must be able to be used to seize political opportunities, and must be comprehensible to those who must use the analysis in partisan bargaining situations.

The satisficing and ideal rational models are useful for understanding the difficulties associated with decision making. The satisficing model dramatically emphasizes that decisions are made under pressure, and severe limitations make achieving even a satisfactory alternative a significant accomplishment. The problem with the model is that one is often not satisfied that the best alternative has been selected. On the other hand, the desire for deciding on the best alternative is reflected in the ideal rational model. The problem with that model is that the best alternative can often not be achieved because of practical concerns such as a lack of time. We seem to be trapped between our desire for quality and the necessity to cope with our daily pressures.

The stages of the problem-solving model can be contrasted to the ideal rational model. In the problem-solving model, the starting point is the perception that a problem exists, thus permitting one to consider the significance of culture, time, and perspective. By contrast in the rational model, the starting point is defining one's goals. Next in the problem-solving model, the person formulates the problem, defines alternatives, gathers information, and tests proposals. In the rational model, the next steps cited are defining alternatives and gathering information. In the problem-solving model, the last steps are planning action, taking action steps, and evaluating outcomes. Again in contrast, the rational model is limited to deciding a given matter based upon maximizing goals. The rational model does not extend to taking action steps and evaluating outcomes. Another distinction is that the rational model does not have reconsiderations as a factor whereas the problem-solving model does.

The problem-solving model can help people working in public budgeting understand the nature of analysis. The rational model serves as the primary theoretical explanation of how analysis should be conducted, but the rational model cannot be attained. The problem-solving model serves as an alternative theoretical explanation of how analysis should be conducted in the budget process. The problem-solving model permits cycles of defining one's problem, producing alternatives, and testing alternatives. It implicitly recognizes that any given analysis will depend upon the ingenuity of the analysts, the kind of data available to them, the amount of resources at their command in undertaking the analysis, and other factors. Also the problem-solving model helps the public budgeting person relate budgeting, management-by-objectives, progress reporting, accounting, auditing, and program evaluation.

None of the models by themselves is adequate. The problem-solving, the incremental change, and the Wildavsky models help the bureaucrat to understand the role of program and budget analysis in the budget-making process. They can be significant but there are some constraints in using them. The problem-solving model helps the bureaucrat to understand the context in which intelligence, knowledge, and analytical techniques must be used. Together, the models meet the criteria.

The rational model, the theoretical basis for some budget reforms, can lead individuals to make false and naive expectations. That model ignores the political context and demands the impossible in terms of analysis. This can encourage some individuals in the budget process to neglect timeliness, seek needlessly expensive data, search for needless alternatives, and quest for clarity in objectives which will not be forthcoming. The rational model can be useful, but not in the manner commonly assumed. Its usefulness is more to point out the impossible rather than serve as an ideal for the possible.

Approaches to Budgeting

A discussion of public budgeting normally leads to contrasting and judging the relative merits of various approaches to budgeting including line item, performance, program, MBO, and ZBB. Line item or object approach was developed in order to enhance the ability of top officials to control the bureaucracy. Performing budgeting stresses economy and efficiency. It relates money requests to organizational output. Program budgeting has the advantage of arraying the budget information to aid decision makers in resolving major program policy questions. MBO and budgeting approach stresses achieving and monitoring progress toward the planned objectives. ZBB blends both the concern for economy and improved policy-making.

Often the discussions on the budget approach degenerate into arguments over which is the best approach. Government is complex and no one single approach is best for all government programs for all times. If the problems in government primarily concern an "uncontrolled" bureaucracy, then line item budgeting might be appropriate. If the government programs involve providing routine service or products, then performance budgeting seems best. If major alternative systems are being debated, program budgeting may be the best approach.

Each approach is not exclusive of the others. Performance, program, and ZBB use similar information and overlap significantly. For example, each uses the concept of program output. The approach or approaches selected should depend upon the circumstances of each government or section of government. Thus, designers of specific budget reforms must have a detailed understanding of budgeting, the circumstances in which the government operates, and the nature of the programs. Simple one-technique budget approaches applied to all government programs should be judged carefully.

An unfortunate byproduct of the debate over approaches to budgeting is the stress upon format and procedures. One begins to believe that good government results from good public budgeting and that good budgeting exists if the correct procedures and format are followed. Public budgeting is not that simple. Government is challenging and requires top talent, well-intended ethical people, creative ideas, and procedures and formats designed to be useful instruments of public policy and management. Circumstances are always changing and our public budgeting instruments must be adapted to deal as best we can with today's and tomorrow's challenges. Tailoring procedures and formats is essential.

Federalism

The United States is a federated government and budgeting differs on each level. The scope, size, and different nature of programs lead to the differences in budgeting. In public budgeting, the similarities are more striking than the dissimilarities. However, the differences are important and are discussed here.

In the national government, most effort is focused on the expenditure as opposed to the revenue aspects of budgeting. Taxes are important, but more effort is channeled into controlling, managing, and planning expenditures. The state of the economy and the role of the budget in stimulating the economy are actively debated and are very significant in shaping both presidential and Congressional budgets. The revenue side of the budget is considered in terms of its influence on the economy. The typical agency budget officer does not consider the revenue aspects of the budget. At the highest levels in OMB and Congress, attention is addressed to macroeconomics and the analysis of proposed expenditures. There is a strong desire to improve the analysis associated with public budgeting; productivity is considered important.

The national government manages many of its programs in cooperation with state and local government. Sometimes the federal government interacts directly with citizens such as with veterans' programs. In many programs, categorical and block grants are provided to state and local governments with the latter managing programs. The government also has a significant revenue-sharing program with local governments. The result is that many federal activities are really intergovernmental in nature with the actual services being provided by local government.

Unlike the federal government, state and local governments must balance their budgets. Sometimes that legal requirement is not met, but it does exist. Revenue and expenditure forecasts are thus important for state and local governments in developing balanced budgets.

State governments have a great deal of potential power over local governments. States commonly focus their efforts upon highways and education with increasing interest being addressed to health, environmental control, and welfare. Like the federal government, state governments provide assistance to local governments, often acting as pass-through agents for the federal government. Unlike the federal government, state governments can directly control local governments. Many local budgeting requirements are established by state law.

The form of local government varies from large cities to small villages and townships. Each unit of government has a budget process. Each is concerned with balancing revenue and expenditure. Local governments provide direct services including public safety, education, and sanitation. Many local government activities require large expenditures for capital items like schools and roads, thus debt administration is an important aspect of local government. Transfer payments in the form of grants and revenue sharing are an important source of revenue.

The complex overlapping jurisdictions, economy of scale, and the growth of suburban areas and decline of cities are important to local government budgeting. The overlapping of jurisdictions means that tax collection is more complex and coordination of services is difficult. The existence of small governments means that many services are provided without the advantage of economy of scale. The declining tax base for cities is putting extreme pressure on city budgets. The increased population of suburban areas has strained the expertise and capability of the suburban governments to cope with the challenge. They must develop budgeting expertise while dealing with massive program growth. Each problem is significant and helps explain the challenge of local budgeting.

States Improving Local Government Budgeting

The Advisory Commission on Intergovernmental Relations (ACIR) has strongly advocated the need for state governments to be more concerned with improving local government budgeting. The ACIR has argued that a state agency should exist to monitor and assist local financial operations. Many local governments employ people who are inadequately trained in the complexity of public budgeting. A state agency could help local governments improve some of their procedures. For example, in Tennessee a state agency has instituted a computer accounting procedure in several small cities, thus providing less expensive but more comprehensive accounting service. The ACIR also recommended that a statewide system of standardized fiscal reporting, accounting, and auditing be established. This would provide the state and local governments as well as the general public with current, accurate, comparable, and intelligible information on local government fiscal conditions.

The ACIR was also concerned that the states are not doing enough in the area of local debt administration. They argued that state legislative restrictions on debt should be substituted for state constitutional limitations. States should be regulated on short term debt. States should provide assistance through (1) the review of bond prospectuses, (2) assistance to local governments in arranging for bond issues including marketing, and (3) providing pooled borrowing and other means to assist in the aggregation of bond issues. They should also be willing to intervene in local financial emergencies including acting in a capacity resembling that of a receiver in bankruptcy until the local fiscal crisis has passed.

The ACIR has made the following additional recommendations to state governments:

1. assist in the enforcement of local taxes and the interchange of tax information among localities and other states;
2. regularize and consolidate the administration of state financial aid to local governments;
3. establish a process for citizen participation on local budgets;
4. permit local governments to invest idle funds, join insurance pools, and permit local government self-insurance.

Other Budget Reforms

Other contemporary budget reforms are building the budget expertise of state and local legislatures and councils, state technical assistance to local government fiscal management, and linking program evaluation to budgeting. More state legislatures and some local councils are starting to recognize their handicap in dealing with budgets because they lack budget expertise. As they recognize the significance of this disadvantage, more state and local legislative bodies will hire their own staff experts to facilitate better legislative budget reviews.

Increasingly, small local governments are recognizing how little they know about budgeting and the resultant costly administrative errors. Especially in the areas of accounting and risk management, significant local savings are possible. In the area of debt administration, most local governments do not have the capability to pool debts and effectively deal with an increasingly complex bond market. Local governments often can increase their productivity, but again expertise is lacking to define and implement needed improvements. State technical assistance, such as that advocated by the ACIR, could provide the expertise. Reforms in this area should be the subjects of continuing debate.

Reasoning from the problem-solving models, there is a relationship between budgeting and program evaluations. The linkages are weak and attention can be expected to be focused upon strengthening those linkages.

An Executive Focus

Planning and Analysis

Planning-programming-budgeting (PPB) was an attempt in the federal government and is an attempt in some state and local governments to institutionalize analysis in the executive branch decision-making process. The advocates of PPB believed public budgeting was the key to most of the important decisions made in government and that public policy-making lacked enough analysis for top level decision makers. They believed that procedural reforms could insert essential analysis into the public budgeting process, thus improving public policy making.

PPB was not a new creation in the 1960s. In 1907, the New York Bureau of Municipal Research developed the first Program Memorandum. The Hoover Commission advocated performance budgeting and budgets were organized into programs in the 1940s. In the 1930s, welfare economics developed many of the same techniques later associated with PPB. In the 1950s, operations research and systems analysis also developed techniques later associated with PPB.

PPB was popularized by then Secretary of Defense Robert McNamara and spread by President Johnson to the whole federal government. Secretary McNamara had a strong analytical background and asked Charles Hitch to apply the concepts developed at Rand Corporation to the defense department. Most people, and especially President Johnson, were impressed with the McNamara management of the Department of Defense. In 1965, President Johnson ordered that PPB be used in every federal department and agency. In time, PPB also spread to many state and local governments as well as to governments around the world.

The era of PPB was one of guns and butter. The United States was fighting a war on poverty and a war in Vietnam. There were strong, intelligent (then called the "best and the brightest") people running the country, but the goals outmatched the available talent and resources. This was true with PPB because the goals were visionary, but the resources, including talented people, were inadequate for the challenge.

PPB was an attempt to embody the rational model of decision-making into the executive branch's policy-making process. The attempt and PPB were declared dead in the Nixon administration, but the verdict was too harsh. PPB was officially deleted from the U.S. Office of Management and Budget (the renamed Bureau of the Budget) official guidelines, but federal agencies continued to use it. In some federal agencies PPB worked, in many others it was never really tried, and in some agencies it just didn't work. PPB does continue to exist in some state and local governments.

A common misunderstanding of novices about budgeting is to equate PPB and analysis. PPB was and is an attempt to institutionalize analysis into the public budgeting process. PPB is not analysis or a form of analysis. It does encourage the application of marginal utility analysis, cost-benefit studies, cost-effectiveness analysis, sensitivity analysis, pay-off matrix, present values, and other techniques.

Analysis can be characterized as various art forms—many would argue sciences—which examine alternatives, view them in terms of basic assumptions and objectives, and test as well as compare alternatives. All this is done with a purpose of finding "useful" information or conclusions concerning policy questions. The techniques vary and were developed in several different disciplines.

PPB was operationalized through the use of several mechanisms. The use of analysis was stressed particularly in the early stages of the budget cycle. A categorization of government programs called a "program structure" was required to facilitate analytical comparisons. The greater use of data associated with the programs was encouraged. Output measures and five-year projections beyond the budget were considered essential. Analysis was further encouraged by the use of mandated special studies and analyses addressed to specific major program issues.

What are the lessons which can be learned from the PPB experience? They can be summarized as follows:

Theoretical and Conceptual Issues

1. Program budgeting, policy analysis, and other related concepts are vague, and thus present a difficult challenge to the practitioner who wishes to apply the concepts. A great deal of effort and creative talent is necessary to tailor and operationalize these concepts.

2. The rational model, as an ideal for practitioners, can result in serious mistakes. More about this will be discussed later in this chapter.

3. The use of one program structure does not strengthen but rather limits policy analysis. Subjects of analysis vary and one categorization greatly limits the necessary range of analysis.

4. Government programs often do not have and will never have logical, consistent operational objectives. Policy makers recognize the value of vagueness in achieving necessary political consensus, and that vagueness often hides conflicting views on the proper direction of a program. Public administrators inherit this confusion and must deal with it even though most analytical techniques cannot work with such ambiguity.

5. Analysis normally is helpful only for relatively narrow but often important policy questions. The use of analysis is constrained by such things as the ability of the analyst and the nature of the subject being examined. Analysis is often most useful on technical questions.

Implementation

1. A significantly large amount of money and many talented people must be devoted to making a reform like PPB work.

2. A phased implementation plan should be adopted so that agencies and portions of agencies most likely to accept the change can be introduced to the innovation first, and resisting agencies can be introduced to the change last. As a matter of realistic strategy, one can expect resistance from some top management which will effectively prevent successful implementation. Training and hiring policies can minimize the problem, but such effective resistance cannot be avoided entirely.

3. The key person for insuring effective policy analysis is the agency head. A desire and ability to effectively use policy analysis should be one criterion for hiring a person for this position. Then a tailor-made brief orientation course could be given new agency heads which could include the use of policy analysis in public policy making.

4. One particularly difficult problem is to achieve coordination of policy among the

policy analysts and planners, the budget officer, the accountants, the lawyers, the public affairs officer, the analysts preparing the agency's progress reports, and the program managers within an agency.

Political Factors

1. The use of plans covering five years does not appear to limit the political options available.
2. Policy analysis rarely addresses the political costs and benefits of a program to specific key individuals such as legislators, but good analyses do address analytical questions which set out political costs and benefits in general.
3. The political advantages of not using analysis with explicit objectives may be critical to reaching some decisions in some specific political situations, but there is no reason to believe there is a common circumstance.

Human Factors[1]

1. People in an agency must believe that the reform is a significant and legitimate undertaking. The real test for them will be how seriously key people (like the agency head) and key agencies (such as the Office of Management and Budget) treat the reform. If these people and groups continually demand and use the products of this reform, then significance and legitimacy will be established.
2. Positive and politically practical recommendations must be the products of the reform. If they are not generated, the people directly responsible for operationalizing the reform in the agency will lose effectiveness both among organizational peers and also among the key decision makers who use the products.

Management

1. Systematic attempts to institutionalize policy analysis do tend to centralize governmental decision-making.
2. Reforms like PPB do not greatly influence government reorganization.

Management by Objectives

At the beginning of the second term of the Nixon administration, the White House and the Office of Management and Budget strongly encouraged the federal departments and agencies to use management-by-objectives (MBO). The technique called MBO is the setting out of specific objectives for agencies and requiring regular high level periodic reports on the progress toward achieving those objectives. The Nixon administration's use of MBO varied from the conventional MBO, especially by not stressing lower level participation in the formulation of objectives. Also the adoption of MBO was not done through OMB regulations like PPB, but was required through the use of the informal memorandum from OMB to the various departments and agencies requesting information to a specific MBO format.

---

[1]Some items were covered under "Implementation."

Serious government-wide presidential use of MBO was short-lived and died with the Nixon administration. The reform did have a significant influence on many federal departments and agencies as the technique was integrated into their standard operating procedures.

In a few agencies, there was an attempt to link MBO and public budgeting. Such a linkage is theoretically possible but is rarely done. The linkage is accomplished by using a matrix table with MBO objectives and budget activities. The matrix table squares contain the amount of money needed to carry out the objective during the budget year. A given program may have multiple objectives, therefore the money cited would not be placed in mutually exclusive categories. Also, not all program activities would be covered by the objectives used in MBO. The advantage of the linkage is to insure the resources are available to meet the high priority objectives of the government.

Zero Base Budgeting

Zero base budgeting is an approach to public budgeting in which each budget year's activities are judged in a self-contained fashion, with little or no reference given to the policy precedents of past years. ZBB is contrasted to incremental budgeting in which the budget justification is focused upon the difference between the current year (CY) and the budget year (BY). In making the distinction between ZBB and incremental budgeting, a false impression can be given to both concepts as they are practiced. In ZBB, the analysts normally will want information on past funding levels and past accomplishments, but the analysts could also ignore such data. In incremental budgeting, the analysts normally will want information on all activities being planned in the budget year but their focus will be upon the program changes from the current year. The analysts already know much of the program information from reviewing last year's budget.

In 1964, the U.S. Department of Agriculture used a ZBB approach to prepare their budget. It was an additional exercise on top of the normal budget process. ZBB required voluminous documentation and a great deal of departmental time and energy. Critical evaluators of the approach concluded that, except for a few small decisions, the department reached the same conclusions as it would have reached with the less expensive incremental approach. The higher level officials did feel that they gained a much fuller understanding of their organization because of the ZBB experience. However, ZBB was abandoned.

Peter A. Pyhrr used ZBB in the private sector and popularized its wider use. Mr. Pyhrr used it successfully in Texas Instruments and wrote a book titled *Zero-Base Budgeting*, and also authored an extremely influential 1973 article in *Harvard Business Review*. The then governor of Georgia—Jimmy Carter—read about ZBB and invited Mr. Pyhrr to help him apply the approach to the state of Georgia. Presidential candidate Carter talked a great deal about the virtues of ZBB and President Carter has required its adoption by the federal government.

The use of ZBB in the private sector has been confined primarily to overhead activities (i.e., expenses needed to maintain the organization versus producing the product). There is a great deal of difference between public and private budgeting, but they are the most similar in the area of overhead. In private budgeting, revenue comes from sales which can fluctuate due to a variety of factors. If sales are up and unit costs are constant or lower, then the company has more money to spend or give back to the investors. In public budgeting, revenue comes from taxes which normally are intended to buy certain services. The focus is upon the services which are sometimes difficult to define, such as national defense preparedness. In the private sector, overhead is meant to be a service to the organization much as government is a service to the society. Not surprisingly, the private sector has had little difficulty budgeting for its major functions, but has had greater difficulty budgeting for its overhead functions. ZBB has proved to be a useful budgetary approach for the private sector's overhead activities.

The use of ZBB in the public sector is a recent development with the exception of the Department of Agriculture experience. ZBB has been adopted by a few cities, and several states (including Georgia, New Jersey, Idaho, Montana, and Illinois) have applied it. The assessment of its success and failure is premature, but its initial advocates are enthusiastic. Problems have arisen similar to the ones experienced with PPB but even preliminary conclusions are inappropriate until some hard empirical data have been gathered.

There are several different ZBB approaches. This is appropriate as ZBB should be tailored to each government's unique circumstances. Normally, the ZBB consists of preparing budget proposals and alternative levels of spending grouped into "decision packages." Program and higher level managers then rank those decision packages in the order of priority. The lowest levels don't get funded.

Decision packages are self-contained units for budget choice containing input and output data (i.e. resources needed to operate the program and the products of the program) as well as the expected levels of performance for each defined level of expenditure. These packages are prepared by the responsible manager for each discrete activity at the lowest level of an organization capable of formulating a budget request. Alternative decision packages are prepared and ranked, thus allowing marginal utility and comparative analyses. Often the guidelines stipulate that a package should be prepared for the minimum cost essential to carry out the activity effectively, but some guidelines recognize the extreme latitude given the manager using that type of guidance. Some states have selected arbitrary percentages to insure that less than last year's request is considered. They do this by stipulating that one alternative must be 50 or 80 or 90 percent of last year's request.

Decision packages are then ranked by managers and executives by priority. Other lower cost packages within each activity are necessarily given higher priority over the more costly packages. The packages are ranked by the managers preparing the packages and by executives at each level above the manager. A chief executive can and does establish a cutoff point for the government as a whole, as well as for each agency. Only the packages above the cutoff are included in the executive branch budget submitted to the legislature.

There are some serious problems in using ZBB. The most obvious is that ZBB can be a paper monster which buries executives in an avalanche of documents. ZBB necessarily means thousands of decision packages. For example, in Georgia there were 10,000 decision packages, and no chief executive can review each one. Mechanisms must be created to manage and limit the paper to only the critical decisions. Another problem is dealing with programs which are effectively uncontrollable in the budget such as veterans' benefits, social security, interest on the debt, retirement, and food stamps. ZBB cannot address them, yet they represent over 75 percent of the federal budget and are significant in many state and local budgets as well. The technique does not help judge priorities between budget activities such as defense, welfare, and environments. Also the technique does not lend itself to demanding responsive grant programs (e.g., grant-in-aid programs) which are designed to let communities largely define objectives and priorities. Marginal analysis of the budget packages cannot be used in those programs because the granting agency cannot accurately forecast benefit. The agency does not know who will qualify or what the funds will be used for and therefore what benefits should result. Also a very serious question still exists: Are government decisions different and does that difference mean more effective or efficient decisions?

There are some apparent advantages to ZBB. In programs involving clear operational missions, such as highways, recreation, and public works, the technique is analytically relevant to the program analysts and decision makers. The approach shifts budget attention away from adding to the current year program and focuses consideration upon increases to the minimum level of operational support. The approach is successful in educating higher level executives and their staffs on the nature of government programs. Also the approach may stimulate redirection of resources within budgets and programs into more productive activities.

A Congressional Focus

The 1974 Budget Reform Motivations

The Congressional Budget and Impoundment Control Act of 1974 is one of the landmark pieces of budget reform legislation in this century. The law's passage is dramatically related to the events surrounding President Nixon's resignation. The 1974 legislation created a unified congressional budget reform and it made the Congress a coequal branch with the executive on budgetary matters.

President Nixon and the democratically controlled Congress were constantly in battle. Nixon wished to decrease the role of government in society and Congress passed legislation seeking government action to redress various societal problems. Nixon had the advantage because it is much easier to defeat programs than it is to initiate them. One tactic employed by President Nixon was to use the disputed presidential impoundment powers on a wide range of programs including those he had vetoed with the veto being overridden. Another tactic was to stress that the Congress was acting in an irresponsible manner because of its piecemeal and uncoordinated approach to appropriations. As Herbert Jasper—an important actor in developing the legislation—pointed out, the Congress was most upset at Nixon's charge of reckless congressional spending.

The Watergate crisis weakened President Nixon and strengthened the Congress. The 1974 Act was one of several reforms directed toward strengthening the legislative branch. The Congressional Research Service and the General Accounting Office were expanded. Various reforms were passed to improve the congressional oversight activities. The important legislation was to achieve a unified congressional budget approach and neutralize the presidential impoundment. In 1974 the legislation was passed after a great deal of drafting difficulty because it affected the strength of some of the most powerful legislators in both the House and Senate. Congress was able to overcome its internal struggles so that it could deal more effectively with President Nixon.

The 1974 legislation should be viewed in context of the historical tension between the executive and legislative branches built intentionally into our system of government. After the Jefferson administration, the purse strings were clearly controlled by Congress, but Congress itself fractionalized the power over the years. This was not particularly significant as the executive did not attempt to exercise leadership in this area. With the passage of the 1921 legislation and a series of strong presidents, the power of the executive greatly increased against a fractionalized Congress. With the 1974 legislation, Congress once again focused its purse string powers and could deal with a strong executive.

Unified Congressional Budget Reforms

The 1974 legislation made several changes. It created the new Senate and House Budget Committees, created a new Congressional Budget Office, required a current services budget, and required various reforms addressed to the presidential budget. The new Congressional committees' duties included drafting overall budget targets. They could prepare reconciliation bills between the budget passed resolutions and appropriation bills. Also the new committees were intended to, and have, put pressure on Congress to meet established budget deadlines.

Linda Smith, a former House Budget Committee staffer, pointed out in *The Bureaucrat* that the committees were challenged but the process worked. In one House vote, the margin of victory for the Budget Committee was thin. But both chambers have supported the reforms on every challenge and have voted to support a unified budgetary approach in spite of powerful legislators seeking exceptions to the approach. The reform will work only if the Congress has the desire to make it work, but the initial tests were passed. The Budget Committees have strongly urged the Congress to meet its deadlines, and Congress succeeded in spite of extreme reservations from most observers.

The new Congressional Budget Office (CBO) is a source of nonpartisan budget expertise for both chambers of Congress. The new office is charged with presenting the Congress with respectable and viable alternatives on aggregate levels of spending and revenue. The office must also make cost estimates for proposed legislation reported to the floor and provide cost projections for all existing legislation. The Act requires CBO to prepare an annual report covering "national budget priorities" and "alternative ways of allocating budget authority and budget outlays." One last important duty is to keep score on administration and congressional actions related to the budget.

Thus far, the CBO has been successful. The Congress was slow to appoint the first CBO director and there were some beginning controversies. However, most concur that the CBO is making useful contributions especially in the score-keeping area. CBO is not the congressional counterpart to the executive branch OMB. That type of power rests with the budget and appropriations committees. CBO provides essential information so that the Congress knows the fiscal implications of various proposals and can act in a deliberate manner on fiscal policy matters.

Another innovation of the 1974 legislation was to require a "current services budget." In judging budget requests, normally reference is made to how much money was requested or spent for the same item in last year's budget. This is useful information, but it is still difficult to assert what exactly is the change in the budget. Last year's expenditures do not reflect accurately how much the program will cost in the budget year, given a maintenance of current services. To get that information, Congress has required the executive branch to prepare a current services budget. Some argue that the effort involved is not justified, given the small analytical advantage over merely using last year's expenditures. This still remains an open question.

The 1974 Act changed some of the previous requirements in the presidential budget development. The president's budget is still due in mid-January but the detailed backup information supplied by the agencies is due with the presidential budget. Given the normal habit of the president's delaying decision until the budget is distributed and the time needed to prepare the agency backup material, this requirement is unrealistic but it does accelerate the agency submissions by several weeks. This earlier information is made available to CBO, the Budget Committees, and the Appropriations Committees, thus providing them with more time to conduct essential analyses. The Act also stipulates that the following data is required:

1. a list of existing tax expenditures including revenue lost through preferential tax treatment and proposed changes;
2. funding projections on all *new* legislative proposals of the president;

3. budget figures presented in terms of national needs, agency missions, and basic federal programs;
4. five-year projections of expected spending;
5. requested authorizations (procedures for obligation including ceilings) for legislation a year in advance of appropriation (budget year specific guidance on obligations and expenditures) legislation.

The required data in the 1974 legislation reflected a thorough knowledge of the budget process. By requiring a list of tax expenditures and projecting funding of new added legislation, presidential surprises can be minimized. The requirement that budget figures must be presented by national need, agency mission, and basic federal programs permits the congressional analysts to conduct program analyses. The timing for authorization is essential to prevent preferential treatment to new presidential legislation rather than the desired Congressional comprehensive and unified approach to the budget.

The drafters of the legislation carefully designed budget procedures and timing to insure a unified appropriations consideration. The final action on appropriations is prohibited until after the budget committee action. Not one of the thirteen appropriations bills can be considered until all have been marked up in committee. A deadline is established on final action for the appropriation bills. The deadlines and other requirements establish clear Congressional standards for responsible committee action, and the budget committee chairpersons have not been reluctant to use that standard in prodding Congressmen and Senators. There is a two-stage budget reconciliation: The first stage sets initial targets by resolution; the second stage permits reconsiderations and face saving. The use of House and Senate resolutions places a heavy burden on both the Appropriations and Ways and Means Committees to act within the consolidated-unified approach or appear irresponsible. In the House, the Budget Committee uses an interlocking directorate with the other key powerful committees in order to facilitate consensus. Finally, the 1974 legislation guarantees a unified approach by calling for a reconciliation bill on all spending and revenue measures with the second concurrent resolution.

The congressional budget reform also changed the federal fiscal year from July 1 through June 30 to October 1 through September 30. This was realistic. The Congress always had difficulty approving a budget by the beginning of the July 1 fiscal year and the new reforms anticipated even more congressional deliberation. Everyone agreed that public management would be improved if Congress were timely in its passage of appropriations, so the fiscal year had to change.

Backdoor Spending

One of the concerns of the advocates of the 1974 reform was the use of backdoor spending (the commitment of federal funds outside the effective control of the appropriation process). Reformers argued that backdoor spending is contrary to the concept of a unified consolidated Congressional budget because some activities cannot be balanced against the competing claims from other activities. The 1974 legislation outlaws or tries to control backdoor spending with some major exceptions. The major exceptions were necessary or the legislation would not have passed.

There are various forms of backdoor spending. One is permanent appropriations where the program is allowed to spend whatever is necessary. This blank check is theoretically possible but is not found in practice. Contract authority is when government officials can obligate the government through legal contracts, and Congress must pass subsequent appropriations to fulfill the obligation. Borrowing authority is similar except the government official can borrow money and the Congress must pass subsequent appropriations to liquidate the debt. Yet another method is mandatory or entitlement spending such as unemployment compensation, welfare, food stamps, payment on the national debt, veterans' benefits, and so on. The payment levels are established by programmatic rules set down in legislation and administrative regulation. If there is a recession, the government will *automatically* pay more in unemployment compensation, welfare, and food stamps, and the Congress must pay appropriations to fulfill the obligation. Earmarked revenue is considered by some to be backdoor spending because funds from a specific source (e.g., gasoline tax) can be spent only for a specific activity (e.g., highways). This earmarking prevents a unified consolidated consideration of the budget. Use of the unexpended balance (i.e., money appropriated but not spent in the last fiscal year) by carrying it over to the budget year is also contrary to the unified approach, but it is allowed in many programs.

The backdoor spending exceptions cover about 75 percent of each year's budget. The 1974 prohibition applies only to *new* contract authority, budget authority, and entitlement programs. Other major exceptions are as follows:

1. all Social Security trust fund programs;
2. all trust funds that receive 90 percent or more from designated taxes rather than the general revenue (e.g., highways);
3. general revenue sharing;
4. insured or guaranteed loans;
5. federal or independent public corporations;
6. gifts to the government.

Impoundment

As was pointed out earlier, the extensive use of the impoundment by President Nixon was quite upsetting to the Congress. Nixon impounded large sums of money because he did not favor the programs which Congress had enacted and funded. The impoundment was not used because the executive branch found it could accomplish the Congressionally mandated purpose with less money. Impoundment became a type of veto which could not be overridden by Congress.

Interestingly, in some cases the Nixon administration impounded funds for programs which had been preserved by the Congress only by overriding a presidential veto. Congress felt that Nixon violated the spirit if not the letter of the Constitution.

The judicial branch concurred with the majority of Congress. In every instance that someone took the expense and time to battle the Nixon administration on impoundment, the president lost and was forced to spend the money. Court challenges take months and often years, so the delay tended to *de facto* establish the impoundment. The program administration was crippled by this executive-judicial decision-making process because of the extreme delays.

The 1974 legislation redefined the impoundment powers. The Congress and the courts pointed out that neither the Constitution nor the law granted the president the impoundment power. The executive branch argued that ample precedent existed over the many years of the nation's history. Congress recognized the best solution was to redefine the impoundment powers so that the president could not cripple a program regardless of the true validity of the impoundment powers. Congress pragmatically wanted to prevent a president from overruling the will of Congress on government spending issues.

Today there are two types of impoundments, each handled somewhat differently. If the impoundment is to defer the spending appropriated by Congress, then *either* the House *or* the Senate can force the release of funds by passing a resolution calling for their expenditure. If the impoundment is to cut or rescind the the appropriations, then *both* House *and* Senate must pass recession resolutions within 45 days of the recession or it is not valid.

One technical problem for Congress was how to deal with a president who might not inform the Congress of an impoundment. The threshold of trust between the Congress and the president was at a low ebb in 1974. The legislation required the president to send a message to Congress requesting impoundment and setting forth his rationale. The legislation then stated that if the president did not comply with the law, then the comptroller general (a congressional branch employee) would report the impoundment to the Congress. If the president did not comply, the comptroller general was directed to go to the courts to get a court order forcing compliance.

The ultimate strategy involved is complex. The Constitution provides for a means to impeach the president and requires the president to faithfully execute the laws of the nation. If the courts rule against the president after the new procedure has been applied faithfully, then the president has an extremely weak defense against the argument that he refuses to execute the law faithfully. Under the procedure, both the Congress and the judicial branch would have said he must comply. The Congress would be in an excellent position to impeach the president under such circumstances.

There has been only one minor test of the new impoundment process. President Nixon resigned about the same time the law became effective. President

Ford did send the required impoundment messages to Congress and did comply with the will of Congress except for one situation. On April 15, 1975, the comptroller general of the United States filed a lawsuit in the United States District Court for the District of Columbia. Named as defendants in the suit were Gerald Ford, President of the United States, James T. Lynn, Director of the Office of Management and Budget, and Carla A. Hills, Secretary of Housing and Urban Development.

The new legislation was being tested. On October 4, 1974, President Ford transmitted his impoundment messages including the deferment of approximately $264 million in contract authority for the section 235 housing program, but the legislation was due to lapse on August 22, 1975. The comptroller general reasoned that this would permit only 52 days to obligate the money, thus it was a *de facto* recession, and under the law the comptroller general reported the error in a formal message to Congress. This meant that Congress had 45 days to act or the money had to be spent; they did not act nor did the president release the funds. The comptroller general then notified Congress of his intention to bring a lawsuit and the Senate passed a resolution in support of the comptroller general. The Ford administration challenged the 1974 legislation on the grounds that (1) the comptroller general was improperly carrying out an executive function by instituting the law suit, and (2) the Constitution provided means other than the courts for resolving disputes between the branches of government. The legal arguments continued, but the case came to an abrupt end without a court resolution. On October 17, 1975, Carla Hills announced that the section 235 program would be reactivated and there was no longer a need for the suit. The Congress had won.

Successful Legislation

The Congressional budget reforms of 1974 have been successful. The new impoundment process has been followed by only one test. The results of this test supported the process. The new CBO has provided a useful service to Congress. The unified consolidated approach has worked. The budget resolutions are in effect guides to the Ways and Means Committee as well as to the Appropriations Committees. The biggest test was in the House on December 13, 1975, when that chamber voted 189 to 187 to limit spending to $374.9 billion as recommended by the House Budget Committee. This meant that any future legislation over the resolution amounts could be blocked by a point of order unless the limits were waived or a new resolution passed. Several liberal and conservative groups were among the 187 votes, but the House voted to use a unified budget approach with that critical two-vote margin. Since then, the margin of victory has grown as the concept has been accepted by the House members.

To the surprise of members of Congress and others, the deadlines are being met. The budget is more frequently being approved prior to the beginning of the fiscal year. This accomplishment, in itself, is considered a near miracle and should result in removing much confusion in public management. In earlier years, the bureaucracy had to operate with continuing resolutions (i.e., authority to spend at the past year's rate) until the budget was passed. This led to confusion as the public managers could not count upon the resources they were to manage. Timely congressional budget action will improve federal program management.

Sunset Legislation

In many states and in the federal government, sunset legislation is being considered and implemented. The sunset concept is that government programs should automatically expire unless positive action is taken to renew them every few years. The form of the legislation varies. In most instances, the sunset provisions permit the program to remain on the law books but the authorization for funds expires. In other words, the program technically exists but no money can be spent on the program unless the legislature reenacts the authorization section of the law. The cycle for renewal varies, but often a staggered five-year cycle is used.

The states of Colorado and Florida have taken the lead in sunset legislation. Colorado was the first state to enact major sunset legislation, but it is limited to the state's regulatory agencies. In June 1976, Florida also passed sunset legislation directed toward regulatory agencies, but it set termination dates for both the agencies and substantive laws.

The federal government is considering enacting sunset legislation. Sunset provisions exist on many federal government programs, but comprehensive sunset legislation has not existed. The proposed federal legislation calls for the automatic termination of statutory authorization over a five-year period. The termination schedule is staggered so that programs within a budget function can be reviewed at the same time. Some programs are exempt, such as interest payments on the national debt, retirement, health care, and disability programs. The review process is controlled on a day to day basis so that Congress can decide the form, scope, and time allotted for each review appropriate for the subject.

Sunset legislation is misleading. The title and the first explanation lead people to believe that there will be wholesale terminations of government programs. This is unlikely. If there is a strong enough reason to create and fund a program, then there is strong enough reason to reenact the authorization section of the legislation. Some programs will expire, but not on a wholesale basis. The legislation will mean a great deal more paperwork addressed to justifying the program, and, potentially, a situation where Congress may not be able to handle the generated volume of justifications.

The sunset legislation can be a significant opportunity for Congress to make periodic adjustments and corrections. Traditionally, Congress has not performed its legislative oversight function well; thus sunset provisions can improve the oversight function. A large unknown is the impact of lobbying activities under sunset provisions. One possibility is that the grouping of programs will weaken the efforts of lobbyists because they will have to compete with other lobbyists rather than focus their strength upon narrow issues.

REVIEW QUESTIONS

1. What political beliefs and ideologies are most significant in shaping public budgeting? In what way is that significance apparent in public budgeting practices?
2. Explain the 1974 Congressional budget reforms. Why is it important to be aware of those reforms?
3. Explain the federal context in which public budgeting is conducted.
4. What is PPB? Explain the role of analysis in PPB. Why is the rational model significant to PPB?
5. Contrast PPB and MBO. How does each relate to public budgeting?
6. Contrast PPB and ZBB. How are they similar? How are they different?

REFERENCES

Advisory Commission on Intergovernmental Relations. *ACIR State Legislative Program*. 4. *Fiscal and Personnel Management*. Washington, D.C.: Government Printing Office, November 1975.

ALYANDARY-ALEXANDER, MAND (ed.). *Analysis for Planning, Programming and Budgeting: Proceedings of the Social Cost-Effectiveness Symposium*. Washington, D.C.: Washington Operation Research Council, 1968.

ASPIN, LES. "The Defense Budget and Foreign Policy: The Role of Congress," *Daedalus* (Summer 1975), pp. 155–74.

BAKKER, OEGE. *The Budget Cycle in Public Finance in the United States*. The Hague: W. P. Van Stockum, 1953.

BARTIZAL, JOHN R. *Budget Principle and Procedure*. Englewood Cliffs, N.J.: Prentice-Hall, 1940, 1942.

BEAUMONT, ENID. "The New York Case from a Public Administration Perspective," *The Bureaucrat*, 5, 1, (April 1976), 101–12.

BEKER, JEROME. "Measuring Cost Effectiveness in Human Services," *Canadian Welfare*, 51, 1 (January/February), 5–6.

BLOCK, GUY. "Externalities and Structure in PPB," *Public Administration Review*, 31, 6 (November/December 1971), 637–43.

BRUNDAGE, PERCIVAL HACK. *The Bureau of the Budget*. New York: Praeger, 1970.

BUCK, A. E. "Performance Budgeting for the Federal Government," *Tax Review* (July 1949).

The Bureaucrat, vol. 3, no. 4 (January 1975); vol. 5, no. 4 (January 1976); vol. 6, no. 1 (March 1977).

CAPUTO, DAVID A. and RICHARD L. COLE. *Revenue Sharing.* Lexington, Mass.: D.C. Heath, 1976.

CLEVELAND, FREDERICK A. "Budget Idea in the United States," *The Annals,* vol. 62 (November 1975).

CLEVELAND, FREDERICK A. *Fiscal Issues in the Future of Federalism.* New York: CED, 1968.

COWART, ANDREW T. "Expanding Formal Models of Budgeting to Include Environmental Effects," *Policy and Politics,* 4, 2 (December 1975), 53–66.

DAHL, ROBERT A. *A Preface to Democratic Theory.* Chicago: University of Chicago Press, 1956.

DAVID, JAMES E., JR. (ed.). *Politics, Programs and Budgets.* Englewood Cliffs, N.J.: Prentice-Hall, 1969.

DEWOOLFSON, BRUCE H., JR. "Public Sector MBO and PPB: Cross Fertilization in Management System," *Public Administration Review,* 35, 4 (July/August), 378–87.

DOH, JOON CHIEN. *The Planning-Programming Budgeting System in Three Federal Agencies.* Washington, D.C.: Praeger, 1971.

DREYFUS, D. A. "The Limitations of Policy Research in Congressional Decision-Making," *Policy Studies Journal,* 4, 3 (Spring 1976), 269–74.

DROR, YEHEZKEL. *Public Policy Making Re-Examined.* San Francisco: Chandler, 1958.

DUE, JOHN F. and ANN F. FRIEDLANDER. *Government Finance,* 5th ed. Homewood, Ill.: Richard D. Irwin, 1973.

LINDBLOM, CHARLES E. "The Science of 'Muddling Through,'" *Public Administration Review,* 19, 2 (Spring 1959), 79–88.

LYNCH, THOMAS D. *Policy Analysis in Public Policymaking.* Lexington, Mass.: D. C. Heath, 1975.

MARCH, JAMES G. and HERBERT A. SIMON. *Organizations.* New York: John Wiley, 1958.

National Journal Reports, June 15, 1974. Congress Report/Conferees approve changes in budgeting procedures by Jall Hauemann, Vol. 6, no. 24, pp. 894–98.

ROSE, RICHARD. *Managing Presidential Objectives.* New York: Free Press, 1976.

WILDAVSKY, AARON. *The Politics of the Budgetary Process.* Boston: Little, Brown, 1964.

THREE

Economics
and
Government

The discipline of economics provides useful knowledge for budgeting, especially on fiscal and monetary policy. This chapter presents a brief review of fiscal and monetary concepts which greatly influence budgeting, especially at the federal level. At the completion of this unit, the reader should know the following:

1. the major tools of monetary policy, what aspects of the economy they primarily affect, and their significance to public budgeting;
2. the variety of ways in which the federal government can act to stimulte or depress the economy and the theory behind such actions;
3. an explanation of how fiscal policy did and did not work in the 1960s and 1970s.

Concern for the Economy

Twin Evils

One economic evil is severe unemployment and another is sustained increases in prices. The first evil is called recession. (A severe recession is called a depression.) The other is called inflation. Both result in significant hardships among the people of the world. Unemployment means many people in the economy who wish jobs cannot find them. Usually, during a recession, the economy is not growing or growing very slowly; but more significantly, families are not receiving any money or adequate money for a decent existence. Inflation often means that we are buying less with the same amount of money. People on fixed incomes or slow-rising incomes are more likely to be hurt by inflation.

EXHIBIT 3-1

Unemployment Rates Selected Years 1929–77
(% of Civilian Work Force)

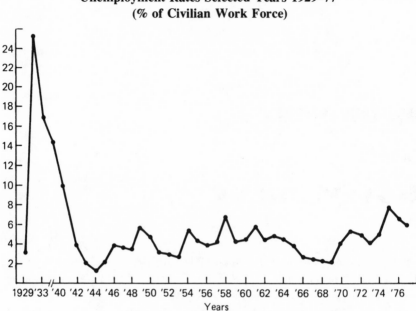

Source: U.S. Department of Labor, Economic Report of the President.

Exhibit 3-1 shows the U.S. employment rates from 1929 to 1977. The reader can easily understand why the 1930's are called "The Great Depression" since more than 5 percent unemployment is normally considered unacceptable, and the unemployment rate in that era reached a high of 24.9 percent. Some inflation is common, but the rate of inflation can rise to hyperinflation levels. Prices can rise so fast that no one is willing to receive or hold money. In the Germany of 1923, hyperinflation drove the people to use the paper currency as wallpaper. Barter reasserted itself as the principal method of trade. However, Western civilization has evolved to the point that it cannot sustain itself with a barter economy. Hyperinflation exists when a government enormously expands the money supply to finance large-scale expenditures. Mild inflation exists for reasons which will be discussed later.

Recession and inflation have been with us throughout modern society. Economic theory largely addresses these twin problems: How do they occur? What can be done to avoid them? In the middle of the 1900s, our tools to deal with these problems are monetary and fiscal policy. Both involve public budgeting.

Exhibit 3-2 is a Phillips curve which helps describe the relationship between the unemployment rate and the rate of inflation. Note that there is an inverse relationship. In the exhibit, as unemployment goes down, inflation goes up. Also note the odd locations of the points for 1970 and 1971 which reflect a different pattern than found in the 1960's.

EXHIBIT 3-2

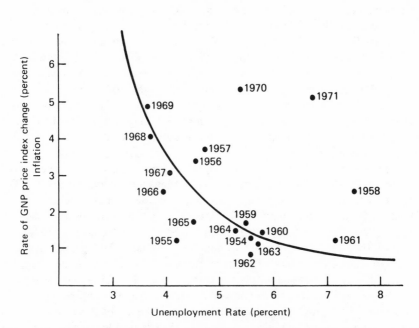

Source: Lloyd G. Reynolds, *Economics*, 4th ed. (Homewood, Ill.: Richard D. Irwin, Inc., 1973), p. 174.

Influence of Economics

When Franklin D. Roosevelt became president of the United States, the country was in The Great Depression. He advocated and the Congress strongly agreed that action was necessary and that jobs had to be created. FDR was not motivated or influenced by economic theory. He was influenced by the large number of unemployed people cited in Exhibit 3-1.

The Great Depression was a political turning point for the United States. Before that time, social and economic thinking called for minimum or laissez faire government. The words of Adam Smith, Herbert Spencer, and Charles Darwin were highly influential prior to 1929. The least government was the best government. Nature and business should take their courses without interference, as if they were guided by invisible forces or laws which would enable society to evolve into a higher, improved state. The Great Depression was a harsh awakening. In 1933, 24.9 percent were unemployed. This was not an improved state. Voters and many intellectual leaders felt the old theories were unacceptable.

Government could and should be used as a positive instrument in society. No longer was the least government the best government. FDR launched massive public works programs for the times. Today, most economists agree that he was not bold enough. The spending for World War II is probably what got the United States and the world out of the depression. FDR's New Deal programs convinced many Americans that a strong, active federal government was "a good thing." World War II and the subsequent Cold War convinced even more Americans that the United States must remain a strong military power. Thus, the view toward the role of government in American society has been greatly altered since 1929.

In the mid-1960s and 1970s, economic theory has guided some of our most significant government decisions, and a variety of governmental units have arisen as the institutional means to consider and implement economic policy. Especially at the national level, economic theory has become the context in which major decisions are made.

The institutional mechanism is complex. In the executive branch, there is the Council of Economic Advisors, the Office of Management and Budget (OMB), and the Department of the Treasury. Each helps consider economic policy, and the OMB is the major implementer of fiscal policy once decisions are made by Congress and the President. In the legislative branch, the Congressional Budget Office (CBO), the Joint Economic Committee, the House and Senate Budget and Appropriations Committees, the House Ways and Means Committee, and the Senate Finance Committee all play important roles. The CBO and the Budget Committees are particularly important in setting overall fiscal policy. Partly independent of both Congress and the president, the Federal Reserve System largely establishes the nation's monetary policy. The detailed workings of each group are beyond the scope of this text, and readers are encouraged to take economics courses to pursue these subjects.

For both the legislative and executive branches, the primary device to establish fiscal policy is the federal budget. The primary device to establish monetary policy is the Federal Reserve System.

Monetary Policy

Central Bank

The Federal Reserve System is the central bank for the United States. It attempts to control the economy's supply of money and credit. This supply in turn affects unemployment and inflation. The Federal Reserve will try to expand money and credit to foster greater employment and to contract money and credit to combat inflation. The Federal Reserve banks have tools which influence member banks, and they in turn influence business and the public. These tools are based on the facts that banks maintain a reserve-to-loan ratio and borrow money from the

Federal Reserve System banks. The three main Federal Reserve tools are as follows:

1. open-market operations
2. discount-rate policy
3. changing the legal reserve requirement of the member banks

Two other less significant tools are (1) moral suasion and (2) selective controls over "margin requirements" for loans made to buy stocks.

The most frequently used tool is open-market operations. The Federal Reserve's Open Market Committee frequently meets to decide to buy or sell government bonds or bills. Selling results in tightening, and buying results in expanding the money supply. For example, selling $10 million in government bonds depresses the overall money supply. The buyers of the bonds will draw a check at a member bank, and the Federal Reserve will present the check to the member bank for payment. That bank will then lose an equivalent amount of its reserve balance. This will contract the money supply often by $50 million. This anti-inflationary tactic results in decreasing the total money supply.

Another tool is the discount rate, which is the interest the Federal Reserve (Fed) charges member banks for short term loans. An increase in the discount rate increases interest rates which makes money more expensive, thus discouraging people from borrowing. This contracts the economy. The reverse Fed action will stimulate the economy.

A third tool, changing the reserve requirement, is the most powerful, but most clumsy, tool. In a previous example, a 20 percent reserve requirement was assumed. The Federal Reserve Board has the limited power to raise or lower that required legal ratio within Congressionally established limits. The Fed can tighten the money supply by requiring a greater reserve to be maintained, thus shrinking the loan amount available. The converse increases the money supply. Changing reserve requirements is the most powerful tool, but it is used infrequently because of its clumsy nature.

The minor tools are also useful. Moral suasion, (e.g., "jawboning,") might mean merely appealing directly to key banks. The appeal alone may be sufficient. Selected credit controls are another important tool as they involve stock marginal requirements. The Federal Reserve establishes how much credit a person is allowed to use in the buying of common and preferred stocks. This selective control acts in the same manner as the reserve requirement.

Effectiveness

The major advantages of monetary policy are as follows:

1. decisions can be reached and applied rapidly due to the less political nature of the Federal Reserve;
2. monetary policy does work if the proper vigorous action is taken, especially in combating some types of inflation.

The advantages are significant, but the use of monetary policy should be understood in terms of its effect on society. Federal Reserve policy hits companies such as the housing industries which depend heavily upon external credit. When banks are forced to restrict loans, the higher credit groups will have preference, thus smaller and newer businesses will suffer. Therefore, tight monetary policy will affect certain sectors of our economy more than others and certain groups (e.g., the young and the minorities) more than others. The fall of 1966 illustrated the dangers of restrictive monetary policy. At that time, the policy:

1. brought the capital market to the brink of crisis;
2. caused a radical decline in home construction;
3. threatened the solvency of intermediaries, e.g., banks;
4. left banks reluctant to make long-term loans.

Monetary Policy and Public Budgeting

Monetary policy is significant to public budgeting in at least two important ways. First, all levels of government borrow and invest. Monetary policy affects available credit and especially interest rates. The interest paid and earned is important to any government. This shall become more apparent in subsequent chapters. Second, many government programs (e.g., housing, environment) are heavily influenced by monetary policy. Budget justifications and intelligent budget reviews would not be possible without a thorough understanding of the effects of monetary policy on those programs.

Fiscal Policy

Policy Goals

The principal macroeconomic or fiscal policy goals are:

1. *Full employment:* Practically, this means about a four percent unemployment rate in the United States. At this rate, there are about as many people looking for jobs as there are jobs available.
2. *Maintenance of price stability:* Inflation is increasing prices. This brings a shift in the distribution of real income from those whose dollar incomes are relatively inflexible to those whose dollar incomes are relatively flexible. Thus, those on fixed incomes such as the elderly are hurt by inflation.
3. *Steady constant economic growth:* As the population increases, economic growth is essential not only to maintain the past standard of living but to improve that standard.
4. *An adequate supply of collectively consumed goods:* Some activities are public in nature and involve service to the good of the society. These include police protection, national defense, highways, schools, and so on.

In macroeconomics, there is an assumed relationship between the total spending level in the economy and the existence of either unemployment or inflation. Total spending can be thought of in terms of the gross national production of the society. The gross national product (GNP) equals personal consumption plus gross private domestic investment plus government purchases of goods and services plus net exports of goods and services. The GNP is the total productive activity in a country during a certain period of time.[1] If GNP is at the target level, then the unemployment rate and the inflation rate are at acceptable levels. In Exhibit 3-2, the reader will notice the inverse relationship between the unemployment rate and inflation. The best possible rates in the United States are debatable but many consider them to be about four percent unemployment and about three percent inflation. These optimal rates occurred in 1966 and 1967. All the macroeconomic or fiscal policy goals were being achieved. In the other years, the goals were not met.

Role of Government

How does a society reach these goals each year? This is the challenge of macroeconomics. Examine again the definition of GNP. Notice the key ingredients are both private and public. Exhibit 3-3 defines the ingredients of the GNP in billions of current dollars.

EXHIBIT 3-3

1976 Gross National Product

Personal consumption expenditure		$1,080.0
Durable goods	$157.0	
Nondurable goods	440.0	
Services	483.0	
Government purchases of goods and services		366.0
Net private domestic investment		240.0
Net foreign investment (net export of goods and services)		7.0
Net national product		$1,511.8
Depreciation		179.8
Gross National Product		$1,691.6

Source: Statistical Abstract of the United States, September 1977, U.S. Department of Commerce, Bureau of the Census, Washington, D.C.

Today, the GNP is well over $1 trillion, but the key relationships are the same. The private sector is the most significant (about 67 percent), but the public sector is large (33 percent). The key is total GNP. If the private sector is inadequate, then the government can act positively by changing its level of spending or influencing the private sector. If the level is too high, the economy will probably suffer inflation; and if the level is too low, the economy may suffer unemployment. The fiscal powers can be viewed as operating in pairs.

---

[1]Paul A. Samuelson defines GNP as "the sum of final products such as consumption goods and gross investment (which is the increase in inventories plus gross births or productions of buildings and equipment)."

Government Powers	Examples
1. Buy or sell	1. Buy as a consumer or sell stockpiles
2. Take or give	2. Taxes or rebates
3. Lending or borrowing	3. Surplus or deficits in the budget

The economy can be influenced by government action. Buying as a consumer stimulates the economy. Selling depresses prices. Increasing taxes will depress the income because consumers and corporations will have less to spend. Rebates stimulate the economy. A budget surplus will depress the economy, and deficit spending will stimulate it. Fiscal powers exist through government action because the federal government is a major actor in the economy.

There is no one fiscal policy solution to an economic problem. An examination of the above government paired powers implies that policy makers can disagree on the appropriate fiscal solution, but both will still be reasoning from macroeconomic theory. This does not imply that all methods or techniques will give the same results. For example, if faster consumer stimulation is desired, then rebates are probably better than deficit spending because the latter takes much longer to be felt in the economy. On the other hand, if the problem is chronic, then deficit spending may be the best solution. Possibly the economic problem is temporary and concentrated in one major product such as steel. Then the solution may be to stockpile the goods to stimulate jobs or to sell the stockpile to depress inflationary price increases.

Reasoning from macroeconomic theory, the existence of a public debt or a national budget deficit is not necessarily incorrect. If the debt can be easily serviced, then there is no difficulty in having a public debt (as pointed out in a later chapter). Having a chronic national debt may lead to serious difficulties. The debt payments may interfere with the government's ability to finance other useful projects. Also large interest payments can mean an equitable or nonprogressive redistribution of income. Note that these problems are manageable and do not speak against a deficit in one or more particular years. Also there are beneficial aspects of a large national public debt:

1. the public debt provides the means for the Federal Reserve to increase or decrease the money supply in connection with reserve requirements;
2. it provides needed liquidity for all the financial and nonfinancial businesses;
3. it provides a safe investment for the unsophisticated and unwary investor.

There are built-in fiscal stabilizers in the U.S. economy. Several fall outside the scope of this text, but one important set for public budgeting is transfer payments. These payments rise substantially during periods of recession and fall during prosperity. When people are unemployed, they receive unemployment compensation and eventually they may receive welfare and food stamps. Farm prices are likely to fall so agriculture price supports programs automatically start working. Today, emergency public works programs also begin automatically. During prosperity, these transfer payments shrink. These are commonly referred to as entitlement programs, and they constitute a large share of the national budget.

Using Fiscal Policy

In the early 1960s, the unemployment in the nation was excessive. In fiscal terms, the actual GNP was less than the desirable GNP level but prices were stable. The fiscal policy adopted was a tax cut. The Investment Tax Credit of 1962 and later the Revenue Act of 1964 were passed. The former stimulated the private sector to increase investment, thus stimulating income, employment, and the economic growth rate. The latter reduced tax liabilities thus stimulating consumption. The policy was successful. In 1965, further tax reductions were enacted and the fiscal policy seemed sound.

By early 1966 unemployment fell below four percent, and predictably (see Exhibit 3-2), the price level (inflation) was rising. Only modest steps were taken to increase taxes, but government purchases rose sharply. This was a period of guns and butter—a war in Vietnam and a war on poverty. In 1967 President Johnson did ask for a temporary tax surcharge, but Congress took no action. The Fed acted as noted earlier. The excessive use of monetary policy tools caused a credit crunch with high interest rates and a recession in the home building industry. In early 1968 the situation was getting worse. President Johnson requested another "war tax," but the Congress refused to enact this politically unpopular tax. Finally in June 1968, a compromise tax surcharge was passed, but it proved ineffective.

President Nixon inherited an economic problem. Monetary policy continued to be quite restrictive. The U.S. role in the Vietnam war began to diminish and government purchases were cut. The Vietnam war boom ended by late 1969, and a recession started by 1970.

The 1960s experience with using fiscal policy indicates that it is not a flexible policy easily applied. Quick action might be desired, but Congress is slow to act, especially on unpopular tax increases. Thus, a significant lag occurred.

Look again at Exhibit 3-2 and notice 1970 and 1971. Unlike the other years, they are not on the Phillips curve. We experienced both relatively high unemployment and inflation. The Phillips curve seems to have shifted to the right. In other words, we experienced a time in which both unemployment and inflation were at unacceptable levels at the same time. Economists call this staglation—stagnation accompanied by price inflation.

Economists and political leaders are arguing about this phenomenon. In August, 1977, a Treasury Department official was quoted as saying of President Carter: "I don't think that he understands why there's high inflation and high unemployment at the same time. But, then neither does anyone else."[2]

Some facts can help us to understand the phenomena, but confusion on this subject continues. The recession has fallen disproportionately on narrow groups—particularly the young and blacks. Monetary policy is curbing economic activity in the sectors of the economy dependent on borrowing, but the nation has

---

[2]Robert J. Samuelson, "The Enemy Among Us," *National Journal*, 9, 42 (October 15, 1977), 1619.

evolved into a service economy which is not as affected by monetary policy. Inflation originated most in food and oil price increases which rippled throughout the economy. The new labor and industry custom of applying automatic cost-of-living increases prevents the traditional groups from absorbing the inflation loss, thus lengthening the inflation effects. In other words, the American economy after 1975 is more complex, and the aggregate monetary and fiscal policy actions of the 1960s were apparently not as effective as they once were.

Fiscal Policy and Public Budgeting

At the national level, fiscal policy largely influences federal budgets. Once policy is determined using macroeconomics; then those decisions influence the following budget concerns:

1. the overall size of the budget including revenue and expenditure totals;
2. the types of spending such as capital investment versus direct payments;
3. the timing of spending programs;
4. the balance of activities—federal programs do work at cross purposes, and it must be decided which to emphasize and which to deemphasize;
5. the size of entitlement programs, and the amount available for the controlled programs;
6. the building or selling of stockpiles;
7. jawboning big labor or big corporations;
8. tax policy.

A federal budget professional and most state and local budget officers must understand fiscal policy. Macroeconomics is the theory used to make many key budget decisions. Budget justifications and reviews are often done using macroeconomics. With the new CBO and budget committees, Congress is likely to be more effective in using fiscal policy than it was in the 1960s, but political forces will still discourage the use of tax increases. Exhibit 3-4 is the summary from a CBO report titled *The Disappointing Recovery*. It illustrates the increasing influence of macroeconomics on Congressional thinking.

EXHIBIT 3-4

Summary of *The Disappointing Recovery*

The nation's output in recent quarters has fallen short of what forecasters expected last spring and summer. The report accompanying the Second Concurrent Resolution of the Fiscal Year 1977 Budget, passed in September 1976, assumed that output would grow at a 5.5 to 6.0 percent annual rate in 1976 and 1977 and that the unemployment rate would fall to 6.2 percent by the end of 1977. There now seems almost no chance of meeting these output and unemployment assumptions under current budget policy. The Budget Committees are consequently moving to consider a third budget resolution for fiscal year 1977 in advance of the initial budget resolution for 1978.

The mid-1976 forecasts assumed that the exceptionally long and deep 1974–75 recession would be followed by a faster-than-average recovery that would make up some of the lost ground. In fact, recovery since the bottom of the recession has proceeded at about an average rate, with the result that unemployment remains unusually high.

In the absence of policy changes, CBO's forecast for 1977 projects real output growth at 3.5 to 5.0 percent and an unemployment rate of 7.1 to 7.8 percent (7 to 7½ million workers) by the end of the year. Even by the end of 1978 the unemployment rate is projected above 6.5 percent. The rate of inflation is projected at 4.5 to 6.0 percent for 1977, well below 1973–74 rates but little changed from more recent experience.[3]

Other Economic Topics

In a text of this nature, all aspects of economics important to public budgeting cannot be covered in a single chapter. Subsequent chapters use various economic concepts, but the important contribution of economics to public budgeting is still not stated fully. Students are encouraged to read various economics texts, especially public finance books. The following subjects are worth investigating at greater length:

1. multiplier effect;
2. economic growth;
3. balance of payments;
4. regional economics;
5. public interest, including Rawl's "justice is fairness" implication to economics;
6. pareto-optimum;
7. welfare economics;
8. labor economics;
9. public goods theory;
10. public choice theory.

QUESTIONS

1. Explain why inflation and unemployment rates act in inverse relationship.
2. What happened in 1970 and 1971 which cast doubt upon macroeconomic theory?
3. Why does the shift in the American economy from an industrial to a service economy have significance to the effectiveness of monetary policy?
4. Why can liberals and conservatives disagree on fiscal policy but still base their thinking on macroeconomic theory?
5. Why is public debt not *ipso facto* bad?
6. Explain why entitlement programs are consistent with macroeconomic theory.

---

[3]Congressional Budget Office, Congress of the United States, *The Disappointing Recovery* (Washington, D.C.: Government Printing Office, January 11, 1977).

REFERENCES

BUCHANAN, JAMES M. *The Demand and Supply of Public Goods*. Chicago: Rand-McNally, 1968.
———. *The Public Finance*. Homewood, Ill.: Richard D. Irwin, 1970.
BURKHEAD, JESSE and JERRY MINAR. *Public Expenditure*. New York: Aldine-Atherton, 1971.
DORFMAN, ROBERT. *Measuring the Benefits of Government Expenditures*. Washington, D.C.: Brookings Institution, 1965.
DUE, JOHN F. and ANN F. FRIEDLAENDER. *Government Finance*, 5th ed. Homewood, Ill.: Richard D. Irwin, 1973.
HAVEMAN, ROBERT H. and JULIUS MARGOLIS. *Public Expenditure and Policy Analysis*. 2nd ed. Chicago: Rand McNally, 1977.
MAOK, LENNOX L. and ALBERT M. HILLHOUSE. *Local Government Finance*. Chicago: Municipal Finance Officers Association, 1975.
MUSGRAVES, RICHARD A. and PEGGY B. MUSGRAVES. *Public Finance in Theory and Practice*. New York: McGraw-Hill, 1973.
NICHOLS, DOROTHY M. *Modern Money Mechanics*. Chicago: Federal Reserve Bank of Chicago, 1975.
REYNOLDS, LLOYD G. *Economics*, 4th ed. Homewood, Ill.: Richard D. Irwin, 1973.
SAMUELSON, PAUL A. *Economics*, 10th ed. New York: McGraw-Hill, 1976.

FOUR

Budget
Preparation

This chapter addresses the topics of budget cycle, estimation, building the budget, and budget reviews. Public budgeting can best be understood in terms of a cycle of events which takes place over a time period of several years. The chapter explains the various phases in the cycle and the cycle variation found in different levels of government. One must project or estimate both revenue and expenditures in most phases of the budget cycle. This chapter describes estimation, stresses when accuracy is important, and comments upon the accuracy which can be expected from the various estimation techniques.

This chapter will explain:

1. the nature (i.e. phases, cycle variations, overlapping of cycles) of the budget cycle;
2. each phase of the cycle and the activities done in each phase;
3. the common differences in the budget cycles of the various levels of government;
4. the current simple and more complex techniques used to estimate expenditures and revenues;
5. the consequences of poor estimation and the setting in which estimates are made at the local level;
6. the role and work of the central budget office in initiating the process of building the budget;
7. the central role and tasks of the agency in preparing the budget;
8. the importance of and steps associated with executive and legislative reviews of the budget;
9. the use of executive budget hearing in the review process;
10. the ingredients and preparation of the executive budget document;
11. the Congressional budget timetable;
12. the legislative deliberative process on the budget.

The Budget Cycle

The Nature of the Cycle

The budget cycle takes place in four phases which can extend over several years. The first phase is *planning and analysis*. Here, the issues are explored and the agency budget is prepared. The second phase is *policy formulation* which involves extensive executive and legislative reviews and decisions. The third phase is *policy execution* and *reinterpretation* when the budget becomes operational. The final stage involves *audit and evaluation*. The beginning of the third phase is a key date. On that date, the operating budget goes into effect and ends in one year. Prior to that date, enough time must be provided to consider the issues, conduct analysis, prepare the budget, and permit various executive and legislative groups to modify the evolved budget. After the end of the operating budget, then time is needed to close accounts, audit and evaluate the programs. This latter phase can take place in a few months, but often involves several years.

Cycles vary from one government to another and from one agency to another. If the government or agency is small, then the smaller numbers of people normally result in a briefer budget cycle. In a large agency with many field units, coordination is difficult and more time is needed to prepare the document.

The federal budget cycle is particularly important because state and local governments sometimes use the federal government as a model and—more importantly—local and state governments are dependent upon federal transfer payments such as revenue sharing and grant programs. If the federal government delays, many other groups are affected.

One confusing reality of public budgeting is that the budget person and agency must operate with overlapping budget cycles. On the same day, a budget person may have to review the evaluations covering last year's program, prepare readjustments on the current year or operating budget, and answer Congressional questions on the budget year covering the next fiscal year. This can be and is confusing. Not surprisingly, people working in budgeting learn to refer to their work by specific fiscal years to minimize confusion.

Budget Phases

Planning and Analysis

The planning and analysis phase was popularized by PPB in the 1960s, but the phase was not original to PPB reforms. The New York Bureau of Municipal Research encouraged planning and analysis at the turn of the century. Almost all budget preparation did and does involve some analysis, but the amount and sophistication was greatly increased during the PPB reform era. Planning and analysis can take many forms, but most of the techniques were developed in the disciplines of economics, operations research, and systems analysis. Techniques including modeling, sensitivity analysis, and survey research are used, but are not covered in this text because they are not closely associated with budgeting. Other techniques like forecasting, cost benefit, cost effectiveness, and marginal utility analysis are introduced in various sections of this text.

The planning and analysis phase takes place at the beginning of the budget cycle, but analysis does occur at other periods in the cycle. In the policy formulation stage, time is a key factor so there is not the luxury of being able to prepare elaborate analyses. Only quick original analysis or reapplication of earlier analyses can be used in this phase. There is little analysis, except for forecasting, done in the policy execution phase. A great deal of analysis is done in the audit and evaluation phase. The techniques, analytical problems, and focus of analysis does change somewhat due to when this budget phase occurs relative to other budget activities.

Policy Formulation

In the policy formulation process, the budget is developed and approved. Policy positions become operationalized as the budget is prepared. The agency is the preparer and significant advocate of the budget. The agency's clientele group and elements in the legislative and the highest levels in the executive branch may also support the budget on aspects of an agency's budget, but the agency is the advocate. The reviewers and modifiers of the budget include the department, the chief executive and his or her staff, and the legislature. A variety of conflicting influences converges on the budget process from various levels in the executive branch, the legislature, clientele groups, the media, and even sometimes the judiciary branch.

The federal process is elaborate, but it does illustrate the complex steps in the policy formulation process. Prior to this phase, the agency has submitted quarterly program financial plans which give budget reviewers initial indications of likely fund requests five years beyond the budget year. At the beginning of the phase, the central executive branch budget office (i.e., Office of Management and Budget) issues guidance to the departments and agencies for the development of the new budget. Then the various agencies issue their budget calls to agency personnel in order to compile the necessary information for the budget. The agency uses this information to prepare its budget.

The remaining portion of the policy formulation phase involves budget reviews and eventually decisions on the budget. The agency submits the budget to the department budget office. The format can vary in style from a line item to program budget to decision packages. The department budget office and the highest officials review the budget and decide upon the department's recommended budget. The agency makes the necessary changes and the revised budget is submitted to the Office of Management and Budget. Again the budget is revised,

OMB arrives at its recommendations, and the president revises and eventually approves the budget. In some cases, the president permits an appeal from the department. In the federal government, a current services budget is submitted to Congress in November and the president's budget is submitted in January. The Congress then reviews the submission and passes appropriation bills prior to the beginning of the new fiscal year.

Policy Execution

In the policy execution phase, the budget is used as the guidance for specific decisions by bureaucrats. This phase takes place during the current year, and all obligations must be made in this year if they are to be attributed to the fiscal year. The executive branch can sometimes reinterpret policy during this phase by not spending the planned resources or by shifting funds from one activity to another. As a general practice, the latter does not occur at the federal and state levels, but does occur sometimes at the local level. The executive policy to not spend appropriated funds is an impoundment. The nonspending can take the form of delaying the spending in the intended budget year or recession from the budget. On the state level, some executives have the power of line item vetoes or impoundment, depending on the state constitution.

At the agency and department level, the rate of obligation and disbursement of resources can be controlled by allotment. This power is intended to assure that funds are available when needed for proper economic and managerial purposes. With the greater emphasis upon macroeconomics, the federal government is more carefully controlling the rates of both obligation and disbursement. Sometimes the allotment power is used for political purposes such as insuring maximum and timely obligations on key programs at the correct moment in a political campaign. The allotment power might be abused and treated like an illegal impoundment, but no evidence of such abuse has been publicly raised yet. Normally, allotments are used entirely for economic and managerial purposes.

Authorizations and appropriations are often phrased in technical budget language. The technical wording can be significant to the operating budget. The normal appropriation is for only the budget year, but the language need not be so limiting. For example, the appropriations may be for no-year funds, thus permitting the agency to obligate the funds in subsequent fiscal years if the money is not entirely obligated in the current year. Other technical devices are contract and bond authority. The Congress can also place special conditions on appropriations. For example, the appropriation can read that "$150 million is appropriated under section 204 of XYZ legislation but none of this money can be used to build a flag pole in front of the Bureau of Standards building nor can any money be spent on the ABC project." Often such detailed conditions are not included in the appropriation language, but are included in the nonlegally binding report which accompanies the appropriation bill. Agencies are sensitive to such requests and normally will comply unless some very unusual circumstance exists. Another technical budget device is for the appropriations committee to negate yearly contract authority by saying no more than a specific amount can be obligated during the budget year.

The federal and state government use of the authorization and appropriation distinction is extremely useful, given the complex budget decisions which are made. Many local governments do not make the authorization and appropriation distinction because a two-stage process is not as useful to them. There are normally fewer city counselors or county supervisors, so a more elaborate two-stage process is not needed to coordinate decision-making.

Once the allotments have been made, the agency can prepare its operating budgets. Normally, the operating budget is not the desired sophisticated managerial tool which has proper linkages to accounting, management-by-objectives and progress reporting, and program evaluation. The operating budget should inform the agency's units how much and at what rate resources can be obligated and disbursed. The operating budget should reflect the decisions made in the MBO process. Also, the recording of progress and accounting of actual obligations and disbursement should be used in a classification scheme so that management can verify the budget and MBO decisions were executed. Also, proper program evaluations can be done only if the program direction is understood and necessary cooperation exists among the evaluators, managers, and budget persons.

Audit and Evaluation

The final phase takes place after the current year is complete. Some audit and evaluation work can and should be started much earlier in the cycle, but the focus of the work and the preparation of the final reports take place in this final phase. Audit and evaluation activities are conducted by such groups as the agency, the department, the General Accounting Office, and the Congress itself through its oversight function. Audits are often addressed to checking if the agency properly recorded their transactions and obligated resources legally. Increasingly, auditing has been expanded to include program evaluation, especially by GAO. However, program evaluation is often done in separate agency and departmental program evaluation units. To a limited extent, legislative bodies conduct oversight hearings and investigations which can be considered program evaluation.

Laws are sometimes quite specific in requiring audits and evaluations. States have audit agencies, and states require auditing in and of local governments. States often require a local government to submit its annual audit to the state. The audit is often examined by the state itself. States sometimes have legislative review commissions which perform program evaluation. Often, audit agencies are staffed by accountants and those agencies are reluctant to perform program evaluations because they are not trained in that activity. However, the trend is for audit agencies to become more involved in program evaluation and for new evaluation groups to be established. In the federal government, many programs are now being required to set aside and use a portion of program funds for program evaluation.

Local Government Budget Cycles

There are some differences between federal and state government and local government budget cycles. Revenue estimation is very important in local as well as state government, particularly in the planning and analysis phase. The estimation is normally done by the finance or central budget office. Budget formulation practices vary in local government, but often there is a small central budget staff. Procedures are much more informal, but sometimes state law or local charters require more formal practices such as public hearings. Often the budget is prepared by a budget office receiving input from the city agencies and guidance from the city manager or mayor. The chief city executive sometimes serves as the person to see in order to resolve outstanding issues and as a court of appeals. The exact procedure depends upon each local government, with some having the agency heads reporting directly to the city council or county elected board of supervisors.

Local governments vary greatly in their review and power over the budget. Normally, budgets are detailed line-item documents which part-time nonexpert board members must review and approve in a short time. Not surprisingly, budgets are confusing and frustrating to board members. They usually focus their attention upon small comprehensible items or pet projects rather than conducting a comprehensive review of the submitted budget. Often, local governments conduct public hearings in connection with the legislative deliberations on the budget.

Once the budget is approved, the focus of the budget is upon control. In some local governments, almost every change in the line-item budget must be approved by the legislature. In other local governments, almost any change can be made by the city manager or department head. The money is controlled, but the ability to make changes in the budget during the operating year varies.

Estimation

Setting

Estimation for revenues and expenditures is done within a legal framework. Since a budget is a plan, all revenues and expenditures are either estimates or targets to be met. In the case of expenditures, some are required open-end obligations such as welfare and some are within the control of the government appropriation-budget process. Those expenditures outside the control are estimated. Even controlled expenditures are estimated so that a reasonable target amount can be established. There are various legal requirements and prohibitions which are considered in estimation.

The context of revenue estimation is quite important. For some revenue sources like income and sales tax, the changes in the economy are highly influential and data on the economy is essential. Often local governments are highly dependent upon intergovernmental transfer payments so an understanding of the certainty and high-low amount ranges of the transfer is necessary for proper budgeting. Another factor is the quality and likely yield of the taxes. Without such information, gross errors in estimation are possible. Politics is a factor and its implications are important. Sometimes the availability or timeliness of data is significant for accurate estimation. The tolerance of error and the state of the art of estimation together are important factors. For example, the state of the art might permit an accurate estimate with a 10 percent range but the government can tolerate only a 5 percent range. In such cases, decisions are still made, normally with a bias toward the conservative; but better decisions could result from using a more accurate estimation technique.

There are several occasions for estimating. An estimate of revenues and expenditures is needed to establish the overall dimensions of the budget in the early budget preparation stage. Estimates are updated for the final executive budget. The legislature needs estimates for its deliberations. Estimates are also needed to establish cash flow needs during budget execution. Estimation is also needed for deliberations on new legislation, especially tax legislation.

What happens if there are poor estimates? If the estimates were conservative (i.e., if the expenditures were lower or the revenues were higher), then the policy makers have the task of dealing with a surplus. If there is a continuing pattern of surplus, the government leader may be playing a game with the citizens as the budget document is phony. The budget total really is the amount less the built-in surplus. Another explanation is that the state of the art of estimation is inadequate for the needs of the community. If the estimates were "high" (i.e., the expenditures were higher or the revenues were lower), then the government must face a difficult challenge—often in the middle of the current year. The policy makers must cut the already budgeted, controllable expense items, pass an emergency tax, or borrow money. Normally a combination of cutting expenses and borrowing money is done. Cutting already budgeted money causes significant public management problems. Borrowing money is the least distasteful option, and is acceptable for the unusual fiscal year. However, continued practice of emergency borrowing for operating expenses can lead to a serious fiscal crisis for a state or local government. At the federal level, different economic factors must be considered as explained in chapter 3.

The need to borrow emergency money for operating expenses is a sign of poor management, but there may be understandable reasons such as an unexpected cold winter or other natural disaster. If a community is forced to use Tax Anticipation Notes (TAN), then this action may reflect an inability to face realities or poor cash management practices. Either situation is a serious professional mistake. A community is wiser to be conservative on its estimates, because the "surplus" can always be treated as revenue for the following fiscal year and the idle cash can draw interest income until that time.

Techniques of Revenue Forecasting

The techniques of forecasting range from the simple to the complex, but all should be used with the principle of conservatism (i.e., underestimate revenue and overestimate expenditures) in mind. One approach used in France is called the "rule of penultimate year." It calls for the forecaster to use the last completed year as a basis for the revenue estimate, assuming that there is growth in the economy and related revenue source. Another simple technique—the method of averages—is to average the revenue generated over the last three or five years. Again, the assumption is made that a growth trend in the tax source exists rather than a decline or an uneven tax yield.

Forecasting revenue calls for a separate treatment of each revenue source. Normally, the standard approach is first to determine the patterns associated with each revenue source. Next the base must be determined and then the forecast is made based upon assumptions and the determined patterns. Forecasting is merely more sophisticated guessing which depends on good data and good judgment often refined through experience.

Information is important to revenue forecasting and certain background information should be maintained. A copy of legislation, legal history, administrative factors concerning the tax or any change in the tax should be maintained. Charts should be maintained showing changes in the tax rate over time and the monthly tax yield with an explantion of an abnormal change in the trend line. Data should also be maintained on any significant variables which affect the revenue yield.

There are various more complex revenue forecasting techniques. One requires an estimate of the average tax collected per taxpayer and an estimate of the number of taxpayers. The two estimates are multiplied together and the result is a forecast of the income tax revenue. Various survey techniques can be used to determine the two estimates. Some communities use a payroll tax. To forecast the revenue, estimate the area payroll and tax rate and multiply. A variation is to calculate the tax rate by occupation groups. A third method builds upon the concepts of economics and is useful for estimating income tax revenue. First, the relationship between personal income and leading indicators is determined. Next, the leading indicators are calculated and simple calculations are then used to determine personal income. The tax yield is determined from the personal income. For sales taxes, the area sales are forecast and the tax yield from that level of sale is calculated. These techniques sometimes require the use of a computer.

Exhibit 4-1 is an example of a summary table of revenue estimates. This appeared in the city of Long Beach's budget. Notice the use of comparisons to aid decision makers.

EXHIBIT 4-1

Comparison of General Governmental
Revenues by Source
(000 Omitted)

| Source | Actual Revenues | | Revenues 1959-60 | | Estimated Revenues |
	1957-58	1958-59	Original Estimate	Revised Estimate	1960-61
Property Tax Receipts					
Real & Sec. Pers. Prop.	$ 6,631	$ 7,211	$ 8,166	$ 8,175	$ 8,877
Unsecured Pers. Property	1,017	1,042	1,075	1,052	1,030
Intangible Pers. Prop.					
(Solvent Credits)	30	12	12	11	12
Total Current Taxes	$ 7,678	$ 8,265	$ 9,253	$ 9,238	$ 9,919
Delinquent Taxes	52	73	82	69	72
Penalties and Interest	13	17	21	18	17
Total	$ 65	$ 90	$ 103	$ 87	$ 89
Total Property Taxes	$ 7,743	$ 8,355	$ 9,356	$ 9,325	$10,008
Other Local Taxes					
Sales Taxes	$ 4,565	$ 4,587	$ 4,600	$ 4,800	$ 4,900
Payment in Lieu of Tax	50	55	64	61	74
Tel. Co. Franchise	315	341	360	390	439
. . . .	. . . .	. . . .	. . . .	. . . .	. . . .
Total	$ 5,263	$ 5,350	$ 5,375	$ 5,667	$ 5,865
Licenses and Permits					
Bicycle Licenses	$ 4	$ 3	$ 8	$ 10	$ 3
Park. Meter Receipts	117	119	119	121	125
Market Stall Fees	9	9	9	9	9
. . . .	. . . .	. . . .	. . . .	. . . .	. . . .
Misc. Constr. Permits	18	30	29	32	34
Total	$ 1,094	$ 1,193	$ 1,190	$ 1,168	$ 1,208
Fines and Forfeits					
Mun. Ordin. Violations	$ 258	$ 298	$ 320	$ 310	$ 315
CVC Fines—Traffic	648	658	660	666	720
Total	$ 906	$ 956	$ 980	$ 976	$ 1,035

Source	Actual Revenues		Revenues 1959-60 Original Revised Estimate Estimate		Estimated Revenues 1960-61
	1957-58	1958-59	Original Estimate	Revised Estimate	1960-61

Source	1957-58	1958-59	Original Estimate	Revised Estimate	1960-61
Revenue from Use of Money and Property					
Interest Earnings	$ 114	$ 100	$ 102	$ 95	$ 95
Int. Earn (Gen. B.R. & I. Fund)	48	71	50	68	60
. . . .	. . . .	. . . .	. . . .	. . . .	. . . .
Auditorium	144	142	137	155	150
Stadium	45	36	37	42	43
Total	$ 664	$ 713	$ 676	$ 737	$ 705
Oil Sales and Royalties					
Sales of Oil—Gen. Bond R. & I. Fund	$ 1,891	$ 1,727	$ 1,556	$ 1,502	$ 1,246
Sales of Dry Gas— City Upland Wells (Gen. B.R. & I. Fund)	107	92	90	109	50
Total	$ 1,998	$ 1,819	$ 1,646	$ 1,611	$ 1,296
Revenue from Other Agencies					
State Motor Vehicle Lic.	$ 1,656	$ 1,567	$ 1,617	$ 1,560	$ 1,588
State Liquor Licenses	242	244	250	248	250
State Gas Tax	970	958	932	930	1,112
. . . .	. . . .	. . . .	. . . .	. . . .	. . . .
Total	$ 3,280	$ 3,193	$ 3,231	$ 3,178	$ 3,464
Charges for Current Services					
General Government	$ 9	$ 17	$ 17	$ 17	$ 17
Ambulance Fees	19	20	5	7	—
Police Department	3	15	4	5	5
Health Department	24	24	24	31	39
. . . .	. . . .	. . . .	. . . .	. . . .	. . . .
Total	$ 521	$ 1,476	$ 2,364	$ 2,237	$ 2,290
Sundry Revenues					
Refunds and Misc.	$ 41	$ 27	$ 107	$ 85	$ 84
. . . .	. . . .	. . . .	. . . .	. . . .	. . . .
Total-Sundry Revs.	$ 540	$ 69	$ 293	$ 138	$ 183

Source	Actual Revenues 1957-58	Actual Revenues 1958-59	Revenues Original Estimate	1959-60 Revised Estimate	Estimated Revenues 1960-61
Inter-Fund Charges, Contributions and Transfers					
Gas Dept. Surplus	$ 1,250	$ 1,250	$ 1,600	$ 1,400	$ 1,350
Water Dept. Surplus	—	95	111	111	94
. . . .	. . . .	. . . .	. . . .	. . . .	. . . .
Laboratory Services	8	11	10	7	7
Pavement Restoration	24	25	22	25	26
Utility Building Service	32	36	33	32	32
Radio Maint. Service	1	1			
. . . .	. . . .	. . . .	. . . .	. . . .	. . . .
Total	$ 3,394	$ 3,598	$ 5,800	$ 4,305	$ 5,432
Total Gross Revenue	$25,404	$26,723	$30,910	$29,343	$31,487
Less: Inter-Fund Revenue Transactions	− 904	− 1,095	− 1,109	− 1,104	−1,148
Less: Reserve for Future Debt Service	− 2,024	− 1,984	− 1,417	− 1,418	−1,104
State Health Assist. Fund-Unapp. Reserve	− 11	− 3	− 3	− 27	− 11
Net Total Revenue	$22,465	$23,641	$28,381	$26,794	$29,224

Source: Long Beach, California, *Operating Budget Document,* 1960-61, pp. IX-XI.

Techniques of Expenditure Forecasting

Sophistication Varies

The burden for estimating expenditures during budget preparation normally rests upon the agency. The techniques used vary from the sophisticated to the arbitrary. In some situations, an open-ended approach is used. The agency estimates the optimum program tempered by the economic and political climate. Such estimates can be based upon detailed work plans involving months to be prepared or quick judgment involving a few minutes. If such a technique is used, a particularly heavy burden is placed on the budget examiner to second guess properly the judgment of the administrator. An arbitrary approach is for the chief executive to declare a fixed dollar ceiling for each department and agency prior to the preparation of the budget. Such ceilings are normally based upon past experience and do not permit necessary administrative flexibility. The advantage is ease in keeping within desired expenditure limits.

There are several more sophisticated approaches. An agency can determine the unit cost to produce a service (e.g., cost per 1,000 gallons of water) and the desired number of units. Unlike the private sector, most government activities do not lend themselves to this unit cost approach to forecasting. Another approach is to prepare an item by item estimate for each program. Normally, each item is open to question but overall judgment is difficult to question.

The trend line approach is commonly used. The estimate is determined by using the activity's historical data, then preparing and extending a trend line into the desired forecast period. Judgment is used to determine any appropriate deviation from the trend based upon factors likely to cause unusual change.

In some agencies an incremental approach is used with the focus of discussion entirely upon justifying the budget increase. A more complex incremental approach is to use marginal productivity analysis to determine the optimum allocation of resources. In most activities there is a point of diminishing returns when the last added unit yields the same amount of satisfaction. When this point is reached, additional allocation of resources becomes much more questionable.

Two other approaches used in zero budgeting are the priority listing and the alternative budget proposals. The agency person's judgment is still used, but the material is presented in a way that gives the budget examiner greater opportunity to cut the request. The request can be presented with assigned priorities. Alternative budget packages can be prepared sometimes using arbitrary alternative levels like 50 percent, 90 percent, 100 percent, 110 percent of last year's totals. These packages should indicate what services will be performed for each level of service. The data lend themselves to analysis including marginal productive analysis mentioned previously. Some programs cannot be presented using this approach. When the approach is used, extra effort is needed to prepare the budget.

Technique Application

The application of expenditure estimating approaches during budget preparation is largely dependent upon the type of expenditure. If personnel needs are estimated, the unit cost or trend line approach is used. Potentially, economic modeling can be useful. The following information should be considered:

1. departmental staffing tables;
2. work load trends;
3. classification plan;
4. estimates of salary savings due to normal hiring lags and other similar conditions;
5. use of overtime and premium time;
6. management studies especially on improved performance;
7. sick and annual leave;
8. quality of the work force;
9. impact of new capital facilities.

Projecting activities can be done with in-house personnel or by contract. Both often use the open-ended approach, trend line, or unit cost depending on the uniqueness of the project, available information, and project objectives. Contracts can involve (1) professional and technical services, (2) maintenance and repair of physical facilities, (3) rental of both real and personal property, (4) utilities, (5) care of persons, and (6) other basic services performed directly for citizens.

Estimating for material and supplies is done with the trend line and unit cost. The following information should be considered:

1. present inventory;
2. price levels including inflation and bulk order savings;
3. changing patterns in the use of materials;
4. changing requirements in relation to methods of producing results;
5. balance of materials to manpower so that manpower is not idle waiting for material.

Estimating for equipment needs is often done for the agency by an imposed fixed dollar ceiling but an open-ended approach is also used. If equipment replacement is planned, the equipment life is weighed by identifying the work to be done, the inventory, the service record, the procedures for inspection, and the quality of repairs done. If equipment expansion is planned, careful consideration and justifications are given to equipment use and equipment need.

One of the more elaborate developmental efforts using sophisticated expenditure forecasting was done in New Haven and reported in 1972 by the Urban Institute. Like most projection processes, it divided the government's activities into definable categories. Three key variables were used: (1) population and subpopulation, (2) salary, and (3) service. Each category was projected in terms of the variables and test variables using sensitivity analysis. Projections were done for both personnel and nonpersonnel activities. An economic model and computer program were developed.

In summary, expenditure forecasting requires judgment. Various approaches and techniques are useful in the variety of forecasting situations which arise. Errors in forecasting can lead to difficult administrative situations such as layoffs or missing equipment resulting in expensive delays. Errors in forecasting less controllable expense items, like pensions or early retirement benefits, can result in extreme budgetary pressures in later years.

Building the Budget

Program Financial Schedule

On a quarterly basis, each department and agency can be required to transmit a program and financial schedule to the central budget office. This now fairly common budget requirement provides useful information to the budget office. On a quarterly basis, the central budget office can better forecast expenditure needs. The schedule categorizes the program by activity, method of finance, and fiscal year. Schedules commonly forecast five years beyond the budget year and include output measures associated with the desirable appropriation levels. The schedules are also divided into obligations and expenditures, thus providing useful information to economists and analysts concerned with the government's cash flow. Thus, the data can be used to estimate likely expenditure demands. This is useful data in preparing the budget call and issuing executive guidance on budget preparation.

These forecasts should not be viewed as extremely accurate, but merely as an indication of likely financial patterns given existing policy. In each quarter, policy can change and other factors evolve requiring the periodic updating. The program financial schedule is particularly significant prior to the development of the central budget office's budget call. The total of the schedules equals a reasonably high estimate of what all the departments and agencies will request. This intelligence is useful in framing budget office guidance for building the budget.

EXHIBIT 4-2

Budget Calendar, Los Angeles

Date	*Action to be Completed*
January 2	Mayor's Budget Policy letter requesting Department heads to submit proposed work programs and budget estimates for ensuing fiscal year. Necessary forms and revisions to budget manual are transmitted with that letter.
February 1	City Administrative Officer approves staff budget assignments which are thereafter distributed to the staff.
February 15	Current level work programs and budget estimates received from department heads.
March 1	Service betterment budget estimates, if any, received from department heads.
April 10	City Administrative Officer reviews tentative Capital Improvement Expenditure Program and, upon approval, transmits it to the Public Works Priority Committee by April 10.
April 10	City Administrative Officer submits annual salary recommendations to City Council by April 10.
April 10-30	Hearings conducted by the Public Works Priority Committee to determine final priority of capital projects to be included in Capital Improvement Expenditure Program for ensuing year.
April 10-17	Preliminary budget hearings held by City Administrative Officer and Budget Coordinator with the Assistant Budget Coordinator and staff analyst for each department.
April 18-28	City Administrative Officer assisted by Budget Coordinator conducts departmental budget hearings with each department head at which time the staff analysts' recommendations for that departmental budget are presented and department head is given an opportunity to express his viewpoint.

May 1[1]	Final date for submission by City Controller of the official estimates of revenue from all sources (other than general property taxes).
May 1[1]	City Administrative Officer submits his official estimate of revenue from general property taxes.
May 1-5	Mayor, assisted by City Administrative Officer, conducts budget conferences with each department head. Attended by Council members, press and taxpayer groups.
May 5-12	Final budget decisions made by Mayor assisted by City Administrative Officer.
May 12-31	Budget printed under supervision of City Administrative Officer.
June 1[1]	Mayor submits proposed budget to City Council.
June 1-20	Council considers Mayor's veto of any item and may override Mayor's veto by two-thirds vote.
June 20-25[1]	Mayor considers any modifications made by City Council and may veto such changes.
June 25-28[1]	Council considers Mayor's veto of any item and may override Mayor's veto by two-thirds vote.
July 1[1]	Beginning of fiscal year—Budget takes effect.

[1]Charter requirement.

Budget Call

Budget Coordination

Exhibit 4-2 presents a slightly modified budget calendar used by the city of Los Angeles. The calendar is important to the building of the budget because it establishes essential deadlines. Preparing a budget is a complex undertaking involving the whole government. Coordination is achieved by first deciding who must do what when. This is decided in the calendar. The budget calendar milestones of a local government include:

1. distribution of instructions and forms;
2. preparation of revenue estimates;
3. return of completed budget request forms;
4. completion of review and preliminary preparation work assigned to the central budget agency;
5. completion of executive review and executive determination of final budget content;
6. submission of the budget to the legislative body;
7. completion of public hearings;
8. preliminary legislative determination of the content of the appropriation ordinance or budget to be approved;
9. final action by the legislative body;
10. executive approval or veto of the adopted budget and legislative action;

11. completion of administrative actions, if any, needed to finalize budget appropriations;
12. beginning of fiscal year.

Once the preliminary estimates of expenditures and budget calendar have been prepared, the central budget office can proceed with preparing for the budget call. The call is giving guidance to all the departments and agencies on how to go about preparing the budget. In many governments, including the federal government, much of the guidance is standardized and established in official bulletins and circulars such as OMB Circular A-11. Agency budget officials need only refer to the established procedures and report forms. In addition to the standard operating procedures, each year special guidance is issued in the form of a "policy" letter, "allowance" letter, an executive policy message, or a statement on the budget. The "policy" letter is used in the federal government to convey executive guidance and budget ceilings. The "allowance" letter comes later to inform federal agencies and departments of presidential or OMB decisions after the executive review process.

Budget Guidance

The executive policy message or statement on the budget at the state and local level requests budget information and establishes guidance. For example, the policy may be one of "hold-the-line," retrenchment, or expansion. Also, programs and activities to be emphasized or deemphasized are announced. Common subjects discussed in municipal statements include:

1. mandated increases such as pension payments, salary increments, and debt service;
2. raise or change in taxes;
3. request to hold the line or identify inadequate services requiring expanded effort;
4. plea for economy;
5. explanation of local economic trends influencing the budget;
6. explanation of who must provide what information and when it is due (the budget calendar).

The detailed explanation call may be in the form of a budget instructions booklet which provides guidance to the agencies and departments. The booklet contains:

1. the preliminary statement of executive budget policy;
2. the table of contents including listing of forms;
3. the budget calendar;
4. general instructions;
5. specific instructions for each form including a sample form.

Budget office follow-through is essential. The instructions must be sent to the chief departmental officials. Each level of government will repackage the instructions and reissue them to lower levels. Eventually, the program managers receive the information requests. Meetings are useful at all levels to clarify and avoid possible confusion. Special care should be taken to explain any changes in the procedures. Every official involved should understand the current financial status and likely trends including personnel pay trends. Emphasis must always be given to the need for accurate, prompt, uniform replies. The types of forms required have been explained in Municipal Finance Officers Association publications cited in this chapter's references.

The budget call always asks for a statement of government functions, activities, work programs, or some narrative explaining what services are to be received for the tax dollar. The general instructions asking for this budget explanation normally stress the desirability of brevity, clarity, and comprehensiveness. The explanation should reflect any program changes and even emphasize those changes. Each level in the executive branch uses the information with the central budget and department levels focusing upon having a complete inventory of government activities keyed to specific units assigned to functions and activities. The descriptive detail is greater at the unit and agency level.

Agency Call

Exhibit 4-3 is a sample agency call for estimates used in past federal budget training manuals. The call draws attention to the executive policy and the required format to be used in the agency. The call points out that the agency is still operating under a continuing resolution for the current year. Reference is made to instructions which are particularly sensitive. The call states who should prepare the information (i.e., assistant directors and division heads) and when the information is due (e.g., August 20). Note that only 20 days are allowed to compile the information. Tight deadlines do occur in budgeting. If zero-base budgeting were used, the instructions would vary by requiring alternative decision packages and priority rankings.

Preparing a budget at the agency level is a difficult task. The material must be assembled from the units and the budget figures in particular must conform to agency policy set down by the agency head. Personnel statistics and cost information is normally calculated by the budget office to compute the salaries and expense portion of the budget. If the agency has field units, the process is more complex because more groups are involved. Extreme accuracy and consistency are important because their absence denotes sloppy preparation and poor management.

The format of the agency budget requests varies greatly depending upon which budget reform happens to be in vogue. The format can be a detailed line item presentation that permits greater control over the bureaucracy, a program budget that stresses policy issues and their budget implications, a performance budget that relates input to program accomplishments, a zero base budget that focuses on marginal value and prioritization, or incremental budget that stresses changes from past policy decisions. The format selected can be of some importance, but its role

EXHIBIT 4-3

AGENCY CALL FOR ESTIMATES (SAMPLE)

RESOURCE CONSERVATION AGENCY
Washington, D.C. 20550

August 1, 19PY

MEMORANDUM TO ASSIST DIRECTORS AND DIVISION HEADS

Subject: *Instructions for Preparation of the Budget Estimates for FY 19BY*

The 19BY budget submission to the Office of Management and Budget (OMB) will conform generally to the program and activity structure used for the 19CY budget estimate. The overall budget estimate will be prepared to reflect policy and program decisions which resulted from budget meetings held by the Director on the 19BY budget.

For purposes of the presentation to OMB, descriptive materials for the various programs should be brief statements covering the points outlined in the following format. It is expected that the submission to the Congress will be a more detailed budget.

Since no appropriation has been approved for the Agency for 19CY, the program estimates for that fiscal year will be the same as in the 19CY Budget to the Congress. Under item "C." of the instructions, supplenentary data is being requested for the preparation of staff salary estimates and travel and other administrative expenses that are spread among the activities shown in the Salaries and Expenses appropriation.

Estimates and drafts of the justification material must be received by the Budget Office by August 20.

Comptroller

---

is over-emphasized. The more important factor is the quality of professionalism devoted to preparing and reviewing the budget. Good professionalism calls for in-depth understanding of the agency and the related budget implications. How this is done is explained in chapter 6. Too often the format is established by some budget reform movement instead of tailoring the format to the type of programs administered by the agency as well as the needs of the central budget office.

Budget Reviews

Once the agency prepares the budget, the review process begins in the executive and legislative branches. The agency first meets with the department officials.

They conduct a complete examination of the budget request, often including budget hearings. Departmental budget decisions are made and the agency budget request is revised based on department level decisions. Normally, the department recommends cuts but is a more friendly reviewer than the central budget office. That latter unit next reviews the agency or compiled departmental budget. Recommendations are made by the central budget office to the chief executive and sometimes departmental officials make direct last minute appeals to the chief executive. Finally, the chief executive's budget is released.

Executive Budget Hearings

Normally, the agency submits its budget to the reviewing party who carefully analyzes the submission. Chapter 6 describes how program and budget analyses can be conducted. After the initial analysis of the submission and any other available material, the reviewing party, such as the department budget office, is prepared to seek additional information. Often this is done by formal written questions to the agency on specific inquiries and sometimes more informal inquiries are made. The reviewers—budget examiners—prepare an analysis of the material and prepare background material for a hearing. Hearings need not be held but they enable the budget officer and the executive to obtain a better understanding of an agency's request and reasons supporting that request.

Agencies also prepare for hearings. The depth of preparation varies but the agency is wise to prepare carefully. Anticipated questions from the reviewers can be developed, and responses can be written and studied by the agency's representatives. A plan of action or strategy can be prepared, keeping in mind the factors discussed in the next chapter on budget behavior.

The hearing itself is semi-formal with testimony rarely transcribed. The chief executive of the department should chair the meeting to ask questions and understand the budget request. The principal budget officer is present and plays an active role. Often questions are prepared for the chief executive to facilitate the process. The agency presents a statement and questions follow, or the review is handled entirely with questions and answers. Regardless of the style used, the agency should explain their program, especially any program changes. The questioners should probe for elaborations on vague points as well as potential political or management problems. The hearing is only for information purposes and this forum is inappropriate for tentative or final decisions because more deliberation is necessary.

After the hearing is completed, the budget analysts carefully review their notes and reconsider the submission and other material. Guidance from the departmental chief executive is also reviewed. Often the reviewers may ask some additional questions by phone or in writing. The departmental budget office then prepares its final analysis and recommendations.

The departmental chief executive is then briefed on the budget. The briefing depends upon the management style of the chief executives. Some delegate the entire responsibility to the budget office and others review the requests in detail. Normally, the pressure of time on the chief executive prevents long detailed reviews of requests. A set of briefing information usually includes:

1. summary of agency requests;
2. recommendations of budget office;
3. summary of the past year's chief executive's ideas relative to the budget;
4. added suggestions by the budget office;
5. preliminary budget (balanced for state and local government);
6. summary of policy issues.

A similar process exists at the gubernatorial or presidential level of government. This review takes place after the departmental reviews.

Executive Budget Document

Budget Message

Budgets sent to legislatures and city councils are almost always accompanied by a budget message. The contents vary depending upon the political situation. Normally, the messages include a discussion of the financial condition of the government and a commentary on the current year operating budget, such as "the current budget is and will continue to be balanced." Revenue highlights are mentioned, including revenue estimates, new revenue sources, and prospects on increased or new taxes. The government is usually put into perspective by citing major trends in finance, population changes, income level shifts, and so on. The principal elements of the proposed expenditures are explained, including the rationale for any major program changes. Sensitive topics like "mandatory" increases as well as pay and fringe benefit policy are mentioned. Problem areas not addressed by the proposed budget are cited, often with an explanation for that omission. At the local level, the message could also explain the relationship between the operating and capital budgeting. The message summarizes the highlights of the budget and blunts possible political criticism if possible.

Budget Summary

A summary of the budget is essential. It should present consolidated summaries of revenues and appropriations. At the federal level, various economic related information is presented. At the local level, the comparative statement of resources includes:

1. cash surplus at the end of the first prior year;
2. estimated receipts for the current year;

3. anticipated expenditures during the current year;
4. estimated cash surplus at the end of the current year;
5. anticipated income during the budget year;
6. proposed expenditures during the budget year;
7. projected cash surplus at the end of the budget year.

Additional information can be included in the local level budget summary. A statement on the tax rate and the assessed valuation of the property including amount of land, improvements, and exemptions are often included. A statement on other revenue sources is useful. The statement of appropriations by organization unit can be included. Finally, a summary of appropriation to various activities can be mentioned.

Budget Detail

After the summary material, the detailed revenue and expenditure estimates are presented. The revenue estimates are grouped by funds and presented by comparing the budget year estimates with the prior year and current year. Appropriate footnotes are added to explain tax rates, tax base, and nonrecurring humps or valleys in the estimates. All assumptions used in preparing the revenue estimates are explained. The detailed expenditure estimates often include:

1. a narrative explanation of the functions of each department, suborganization unit, and activity as well as a separate section for comments on the major changes proposed in each activity;
2. a listing by department and suborganization unit of the objects of expenditure and by activity with an identification of proposed resource changes;
3. a listing by position title for each unit and activity as well as any proposed changes;
4. an identification of the work load volume being undertaken in conjunction with each activity.

The executive budget document is often considered to be *the* budget even though the legislature may make some changes. In some jurisdictions, *the* budget is the final document passed and approved by the legislature. Regardless of the stress given the executive budget document, it is extremely influential in the decision-making process. The document is the chief executive's plan. Any modification must be done with the awareness that any changes cannot be simply additions or deletions. Even in the federal government, additions to the budget raise the question of either ''Where is the extra money going to come from?'' or ''What programs are going to be cut?'' If deletions are suggested, the easier but still difficult question raised is either, ''Where is the extra money going to be spent?'' or ''What taxes should be cut?'' These are not simple questions and the executive budget becomes the point of departure for legislative consideration of the budget.

Congressional Budget Timetable

Budget Milestones

In the earlier discussion of the budget calendar and in Exhibit 4-1, there are target dates set for legislative action on the budget. For many governments, the executive may be considered presumptuous to state target dates for the legislatures because of the separation of powers concept. In spite of that attitude, most budget people can estimate fairly accurately what the target dates are on the legislative budget process. Often the legislative body will state its own targets in its rules. The one forcing deadline is the beginning of the new fiscal year when everyone agrees the budget should be adopted. The other deadlines fall between when the legislature receives the chief executive's budget and the beginning of the fiscal year.

In the federal government, the Congressional deadlines were set by the 1974 Budget Act. These critical targets, coupled with serious prodding by the budget committees, encourage the Congress to pass timely appropriation legislation instead of the pre-1974 practice of passing appropriation legislation three to six months into the current year. Both the targets and the active pushing of the budget committees are essential. The targets set a standard. Budget committees use social and political pressure to achieve responsible Congressional action.

The seriousness of not passing timely appropriations is often overlooked. If no appropriation legislation is passed, then the government cannot pay its employees or anyone else. Government operations cease to exist because no one has the authority to spend money. If a decision has not been reached on appropriations prior to the beginning of the new fiscal year, then a legislative body passes a continuing resolution which normally says that the government can continue to obligate and spend at last year's budget levels. The wording of the continuing resolution could also say the government can proceed at the lower of either last year's budget or the approved version of the House or Senate bill. The wording is normally framed to permit spending at the lowest amount the legislature is likely to pass. Managing a program under a continuing resolution is no significant problem unless the final legislation either provides the manager with significantly less or more money than the continuing resolution. If less money is provided, the entire program may have to stop. If more money is provided, the program may have to obligate money recklessly in order to use it during the remainder of the fiscal year. Either situation is bad public management which can be compounded by repeated yearly use of the continuing resolution, as happened with Congress prior to 1974.

Congressional Budget Timetable

The new Congressional budget deliberative process starts with the presidential submission of the Current Services Budget on November 10. This budget alerts the Congress, especially the Congressional Budget Office, the budget committees, and the appropriation committees, that they should be anticipating specific revenue, expenditure, and debt levels unless current policy is changed. The Current Services Budget also provides a baseline of comparison to the later presidential budget.

The presidential budget is sent to the Congress 15 days after Congress convenes in the new calendar year (e.g., January 20). The budget normally follows the State of the Union Address to Congress by about one week. Presidents usually address Congress with a specific budget message which is more detailed and specific than the earlier State of the Union speech. The budget messages vary in content with a president's style, but the earlier discussion is a common pattern with the exception that more emphasis is often placed on the national economy.

By February 1, the Congressional Budget Office must send its annual report to the budget committees. This report analyzes the economy, the Current Services Budget, and the president's budget. Alternative levels of spending are suggested. Interestingly, the original legislation called for an April 1 submission, but the CBO realized this did not give the budget committees sufficient time to digest the CBO report so the date was changed by mutual consent.

By March 15, the various committees, like appropriation, must submit their respective reports to the budget committees. This is a tentative financial guess by the committees on revenue, expenditure, and debt. The committees use the CBO report, the president's budget, and the detailed backup information supplied by the agencies to help them arrive at reasonable budget estimates.

One month later on April 15, each budget committee reports its recommended budget resolution. This resolution represents the difficult compromise on the entire budget: the revenues, expenditures, debt, as well as targets for each committee important to the budget process. One month later, May 15, each chamber votes on its own resolution. An inability to reach a decision would destroy the process. Opposition can come from the conservatives for spending too much money and from the liberals for spending too little money. The resolutions need not be the same in each chamber. May 15 is also the deadline for reporting all authorization bills. The Congress doesn't want unanticipated expenses resulting from authorization legislation, so this deadline is essential.

Seven days after Labor Day in September final action on appropriation bills is required. This gives the appropriation committees several months to hold their hearings and make their difficult decisions.

By September 15, final action on the second budget resolution is required. This permits last minute changes possibly due to intervening circumstances since the first resolution was passed. Often, there may be no difference between the first and second resolution, but an opportunity for flexibility has been provided. By September 25, all final actions on budget reconciliation should be passed, thus providing a uniform consolidated Congressional budget in each chamber.

The remaining days in September are used to resolve differences between chambers, pass the legislation, permit a presidential veto, and reconcile or override the veto. All this can be done if there is perfect cooperation among the chambers and the president. If not, then delays will result and a continuing resolution may be necessary because the federal fiscal year begins on October 1.

Legislative Considerations

At all levels of government, legislative bodies consider budgets and budget supporting material. This information is key to proper legislative understanding of government operations. The considerations and the subsequent legislation permit the legislative oversight activity to exist. The purse strings are important. If weaknesses are identified, legislators can re-tailor policy often with their redrafted budget. The budget consideration in legislatures is a much more open process than executive reviews. Thus legislative budget hearings serve as a forum for better community understanding of government as well as a device to permit citizens to express their views on budget matters.

The time needed for legislative consideration of the budget varies with the size of government. Committees must have time to study the budget and related information, conduct hearings with public officials and possibly interested citizens, discuss policy internally, and finally enact the legislation. Normally, 60 days is a reasonable time for smaller local governments.

Legislative organization to deal with the budgets also depends largely on the size of government. Larger governments should have standing committees with highly competent professional staff support. Committees and staffs can be organized on partisan or nonpartisan basis. Given the complexity of government and budgeting, more smaller states and local governments should hire professionally trained and experienced public administrators. Exhibit 4-4 presents an illustrative page from a legislative analyst's review of a budget request. The reader will notice how a good analyst can focus attention upon the items which should concern the legislator.

The hearing is that standard method used to gather information and focus upon potential problems of concern to the legislature. Often those problems would be isolated with careful staff program and budget analysis. The legislative hearing is conducted differently from executive hearings. With legislative hearings, a transcript is often maintained and there are more co-equal questioners of the agency personnel. Some legislators are friendly and others are hostile. Just as in the executive hearings, the agency is wise to prepare for the hearings with briefing books, to plan strategies and tactics, and to have rehearsals. The hearings are usually scheduled more at the convenience of the legislative committee than the agency. Follow-up questions are common as in executive hearings. Decisions are not made at hearings, but rather at closed door "mark-up" sessions.

If public participation is part of the hearings, then the committee normally takes care to give due notice of the time and place of the meeting. Failure to give

EXHIBIT 4-4

Legislative Analyst's Review Sheet
Department of Hospitals and Institutions
1963 Budget Request

Newark City Hospital

The 1963 Budget request of $6,469,185.00 for the Newark City Hospital shows an increase of $229,131.67 over 1962 Operations as follows:

1963 Budget Appropriations	$6,453,424.00	1963 Request	$6,469,185.00
1962 Emergencies	115,149.96		
	$6,568,573.96		
Less Cancellations	328,520.63		
Net 1962 Operations	$6,240,053.33	1962 Operations	6,240,053.33
		Increase	$ 229,131.67

The request for 1,270 employees is 25 less than the 1,295 in 1962.

Page No.	Line No.	
4		There were 29,669 less patient days in 1962 than in 1961 resulting from a drop in admissions from 18,760 in 1961 to 15,460 in 1962, a net drop of 3,300.
5		The average day's stay per patient dropped from 9.5 to 9.1. The average daily admissions dropped from 60.9 in 1961 to 56.4 in 1962, a net drop of 4.5 admissions. The average daily census of patients in the hospital dropped from 575.6 in 1961 to 549.9 in 1962, a drop of 25.7 in 1962.
6	1 & 2	What is the status of the Medical Director and the Assistant Medical Director?
6	3	Will the Comptroller's position be filled? Is the present incumbent Joseph Rubino to remain on the hospital payroll?
10	12A	Has this position been filled?
19	37	Is this position going to remain in the hospital?
25		New employee, Director of Surgery. In accordance with policy followed in similar cases the appropriation for this employee will be deleted because there is no valid ordinance supporting it. The appropriation will be made after adoption of the ordinance and before final adoption of the budget by amending the approved budget.
41	103A	Bernice Lippe replaced the Director of Nurses on January 14, 1963 at the minimum salary of $7,500.00. Her salary as Assistant Director of Nursing Education on Page 112 was $6,460. One pay should be deleted from the Director of Nurses' appropriation and one pay remaining in the Assistant Director of Nursing Education's line on Page 112.

due notice or to notify all the likely interested "publics" can result in heated public criticism.

The legislatures normally have the power to modify the executive's budget, but that is not always the case in local government. Even if the power exists, modifications are difficult because of the interdependent characteristic of budgets. If our figure is adjusted upward, another figure must be cut if the budget is to balance. Exhibit 4-5 illustrates one city council's modifications.

The adoption of the budget can vary in terms of detail. Appropriations should be by department in order to fix responsibility. Some argue that it should be by major object classification and others by program or activity. There is no one correct way. Object classification is good for greater control especially when there is a low threshold of trust afforded the government's middle and lower level managers. Program classifications are good for situations which need management flexibility to operate effectively and efficiently. Detailed line item budgets are extremely inflexible. Necessary taxes and a formal resolution on the final official revenue estimate accompany or are passed at the same time as the budget.

EXHIBIT 4-5

Schedule Setting Forth Changes Made by City Council in
City Manager's Original Estimate of 1960-61 Budget

	Manager's Estimate	Revised Amount
Office of City Manager	$ 146,135	$ 138,246
Reason for Change—Reduced cost of annual report, reduction of .5 man year administrative analyst. Add cost of salary increase.		
Secretary-Treasurer	166,844	169,484
Reason for change—Add cost of salary increase.		
Accounting	77,686	74,751
Reason for change—Delete one accountant position. Add cost of salary increase.		
Data Processing	179,470	181,303
Reason for change—Add cost of salary increase.		
Purchasing	30,867	31,539
Reason for change—Add cost of salary increase.		
Tax	400,390	408,861
Reason for change—Add cost of salary increase.		
Legal	99,472	101,636
Reason for change—Add cost of salary increase.		
Retirement Administrator	22,731	23,043
Reason for change—Add cost of salary increase.		
Personnel and Civil Service	29,703	50,349
Reason for change—Add cost of salary increase. Add cost of salary and wage survey.		

REVIEW QUESTIONS

1. What is the budget cycle? How does the local budget cycle differ from the federal one?
2. What are the special contextual features of local budgeting?
3. Why is estimation important? What techniques are useful? Explain why.
4. Contrast revenue and expenditure estimation.
5. Why are the program financial schedule and budget calendar important preliminary steps to the budget call?
6. What budget instructions are important in building a budget? Why?
7. Contrast executive and legislative hearings.
8. Why is the central budget office "powerful"?
9. What information should be in an executive budget? Why?
10. Explain the significance of the Congressional budget timetable.

REFERENCES

ARONSON, J. RICHARD and ELI SWARTZ. *Management Policies in Local Government Finance.* Washington, D.C.: International City Management Association, 1975.

BURKHEAD, JESSE. *Government Budgeting.* New York: John Wiley, 1956.

FISHER, LOUIS. *Presidential Spending Power.* Princeton, N.J.: Princeton University Press, 1975.

JASPER, HERBERT N. "A Congressional Budget: Will It Work This Time?" *The Bureaucrat,* 3, 4 (January 1975), 429–43.

MOAK, LENNOX L. and KATHRYN W. KILLIAN. *Operating Budget Manual.* Chicago: Municipal Finance Officers Association, 1963.

Municipal Performance Report, 1, 4 (August 1974).

SMITH, LINDA L. "The Congressional Budget Process—Why It Worked This Time," *The Bureaucrat,* 6, 1 (1977), 88–111.

U.S. Civil Service Commission, Bureau of Training, The Management Science Training Center. *Budget Formulation,* 1976.

FIVE

Budget Behavior

Public budgeting is done by human beings and one can understand a great deal about budgeting by examining the factors which influence human behavior within this special context. This chapter first examines how the key actors in the budget process interact. The next major topic is an in-depth examination of the agency budget office and the perspectives associated with the office. The final major topic is a careful examination of the strategies associated with the game of budgeting. This chapter examines:

1. the political influence patterns among the key actors in the budget process;
2. means commonly used to cultivate an active clientele;
3. the duties of an agency budget office;
4. the perspective of a budget officer and typical behavioral patterns;
5. four common philosophic attitudes of budget officers toward the budget process;
6. explanation of how confidence in the budget officer is developed;
7. the significance of program results in budgeting;
8. the preparation process for hearings;
9. the review setting;
10. spender's strategies;
11. cutter's strategies;
12. strategies to support new programs;
13. some important cautions in public budgeting.

Politics and Perspective

Four Institutional Roles

Public budgeting can be understood in terms of four institutional roles. Each has a definable behavior. Exhibit 5-1 shows the interrelationship among the groups.

EXHIBIT 5-1

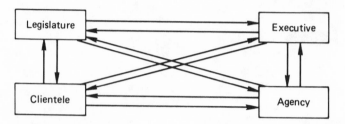

The four institutional roles are the agency, the executive, the legislature and the clientele. Two other groups, the courts and the media, are significant, but are not discussed here because their influence patterns are unusual. Discussion of their influence is outside the scope of this text. The agency is the institution with the responsibility for managing the programs and preparing the initial budget. The executive is loosely defined here to mean the chief executive, his or her staff, and the central budget office. The department, of which the agency is a part, plays an odd role of sometimes being an extension of the executive but often being a superagency depending on the stage of the budget process. The legislature above is the legislative branch of government such as the Congress in the federal government. The clientele is a group affected by the agency's programs and it takes an active interest in the agency's policy.

The double lines in Exhibit 5-1 represent several two-way influence patterns. The agency influences the executive through its budget request and the executive's budget decision is one form of executive influence on the agency. The executive influences the legislature through its executive budget requests and the passage of laws is one formal influence upon the executive. The agency's programs by definition affect its clientele. Clientele groups are well known for their lobbying (influencing) activity on legislators, but they also lobby and influence the chief executive and the agency. Less well known is that legislatures and executives can influence clientele groups directly. To make matters more complex, an influence pattern may involve more than two groups. For example, a clientele group influences Congress on appropriation legislation which ultimately becomes law and then the agency is influenced by the language of that appropriation legislation.

A case study involving the U.S. Maritime Administration illustrates the influence patterns. In the Nixon Administration, there was a strong desire at the highest levels in the U.S. Office of Management and Budget to phase out the operating and ship-building subsidies on an accelerated rate. OMB required the Maritime Administration to launch an analytical study on exactly how this was to be accomplished. Somehow, Mrs. Sullivan, who headed the House Appropriation subcommittee, discovered the OMB study. She was extremely upset that OMB wished to change policy clearly established in the law and phoned OMB Director Mayo. The substance of that conversation was not recorded, but the director withdrew the request for the study. This series of events illustrates the influence of the central budget office on an agency as well as the strength of a single legislator on a central budget office.

Clientele influence on agencies is not fully appreciated. In *Policy Analysis for Public Policymaking*, this author presented several case studies involving the budget process in the U.S. Department of Transportation. In February 1970, the Office of Management and Budget called for a special analytical study by the Urban Mass Transportation Administration on that agency's policy guidance for capital grants reflected in the published *Information to Applicants*. In time, the study and a revised *Information to Applicants* was prepared. Before it became official, a letter was formally sent (as required by OMB Circular A-85) to inform state and local government associations of the proposed new guidelines. The Circular A-85 standard OMB guidance requires an agency-to-clientele interrelationship prior to the time that the final government policy becomes effective.

In this instance, representatives of the transit industry and the cities were taken by surprise. They took strong exception to the "unrealistic data demands and planning analyses" that would be imposed. They felt that DOT committed a breach of faith because there was no informal consultation prior to sending the official notification. They reacted by developing a counterstrategy—they met with agency officials and tried to soften the most undesirable aspects of the new selection criteria. The agency officials felt that they came close to the clientele's feeling while keeping within the strict OMB policy prescriptives. This case illustrates the infrequently documented influence of a clientele group on an agency.

Legislative groups and chief executives can directly influence clientele groups. The most noticed such influence is at the large conventions of these groups when high ranking legislators or executives address the members. Less publicized meetings occur when legislative and executive officials request cooperation or seek lobbying support of key legislation.

End runs and finesses do occur in this complex four-way relationship. For example, an agency can influence its clientele group by pointing out the implications of existing proposed policy. The clientele group can then go to either the legislative or executive to kill the proposed policy. A more complex situation would be when the agency had to proceed with some action (e.g., conserve energy) which its clientele group may find distasteful. The agency might be able to counter likely pressure by having the chief executive lobby the clientele group and the legislature. This would strengthen the chances of success for the agency by minimizing clientele resistance.

In the budget process, the agency to clientele to legislature triangular relationship is a common pattern. The more sophisticated clientele groups recognize that the size of the budget and the individual programs are significant. In many cases, an informal communication network exists between the agency and the clientele group. Any formal publicly available information is monitored, analyzed, and communicated to clientele members. Sometimes active campaigns are launched to build a strong lobbying presence for particular budget issues of importance to the clientele.

State and local patterns normally are not as complex as those found on the federal level. However, large state and local governments have patterns more similar to the federal level. The seriousness of lobbying and clientele groups not surprisingly relates to the money or potential money involved; thus large governments with large programs tend to have the active clientele groups. In medium and small government, clientele groups can and do act less formally. Clientele interests are handled as nonpaid part-time activities via simple phone calls and meetings. Often, on the record views are expressed in public hearings, or possibly even a demonstration or media event might be organized. Highly emotional confrontations are rare on budget issues, but they do occur.

The agency, executive, legislature, and clientele each has a separate institutional role. Each perceives itself as a separate group although individual exceptions can be cited—for example, an agency political appointee may identify solely with the chief executive. Also, each group can be further subdivided, and subdivisions may come into conflict and threaten to harm the larger group. For example, the Maritime Administration is composed of maritime unions and operators. When they work together they are surprisingly powerful for their respective size, but the alliance can and does break down on specific issues. In the Congress, the substantive and appropriation committees sometimes are in conflict. In the executive, two staff agencies such as the White House staff and the Office of Management and Budget can also be in conflict on issues, but in the executive branch the chief executives can more easily arbitrate internal disputes than in the legislative branch.

Role Objectives and Enemies

The agency and its leadership almost always have pride or a sense that its programs are worthwhile. The career employee recognizes his job and income is associated with the agency's objectives. In some instances, an almost missionary zeal and self-identification with the agency can exist among the top agency leadership. In other instances, the zeal may be only a belief that what the agency does is a worthwhile function. Rarely do top agency leaders disagree with the mission or the fundamental value of the agency and its programs.

Another factor to consider is the budget process itself. The agency is always placed in the position of requesting and defending. Reviewers are always doubting the agency and demanding facts and better arguments. When someone is placed on the defensive and expected to argue "its" case, not surprisingly agency executives take on those roles. President, governors, and mayors sometimes act surprised when their agency appointees argue the agency position. Given the dual elements of self-worth and role demands, chief executives should be more surprised if their appointees don't speak for their agencies.

Given those circumstances, issues are viewed from the perspective of the agency's mission and the people in the organization. Does a change further or detract from the agency's mission? Will the people in the organization benefit or lose from a change? Programs are justified with these questions well in mind.

The chief executive plays a different role. The executive wishes to economize, cut requests, and coordinate programs. There is an arm's length relationship between the executive and the agency leadership in spite of agency political appointees serving at the pleasure of the executive. The executive must maintain the option of saying "no" to an agency request. Requests must be reviewed carefully and cuts are necessary for purposes of economy and better allocation of resources around the executive branch. When the executive decision is reached, the chief executive expects that the agency will formally support the executive decision even though the agency may perceive the decision not in their best interest. Discipline is maintained in several ways: formal statements are cleared by the executive's staff, budget requests must follow the executive's budget and allowance letter, the political influence of the chief executive is significant, and the agency head can be fired.

Another factor for state and local government agency heads to consider is that their chief executives sometimes can line item veto budget items or reallocate line item budgets. These powers vary greatly from one government to the next, but some chief executives can unilaterally reconstruct the council approved budget on line item veto. The only limit on the power is the likely political resistance the chief executive would receive from the legislature or city council. With this type of power, agency officials would be hesitant to challenge or to try to circumvent chief executives.

The legislature (sometimes called council, board, or commission) plays an entirely different role. They are the people's elected deliberative body normally composed of well-intended, intelligent individuals. However, on budget matters the legislature is confronted with often confusing information and little time to make decisions. At the federal level and in some large state and local governments the legislatures may even dominate the policy-making process, but this is often not the situation. Normally, legislatures are not the initiators, but rather play a more reactive role. Attention is given more to pet projects and issues of local popular concern rather than a unified comprehensive approach to the budget.

The clientele is interested in how an agency's program affects them. They meet and discuss in conferences the significance of existing legislation, chief executive's attitudes toward programs, and the policies of the agency. Sometimes the clientele works as a whole, but often various subgroups act with some coordination among the groups. Clientele groups vary with success often depending on clientele leadership, the stakes involved, the organizational network, the dedication of the members to the issue, and the strategies and tactics employed.

The paths of clientele influence vary. Often a special agency-clientele relationship occurs because a job rotation unofficial policy exists. Sometimes clientele groups support the winning president or congressman. This also can lead to a cordial climate. Lobbying is the standard path of influence. Also formal and informal relationships can exist between the agency and the clientele as illustrated in the earlier cited UMTA and Maritime case examples.

Agencies and clientele groups can have anticlientele groups. For example, consumer groups can oppose the manufacturing interests and government regulating bodies. In recent years, more groups from the political right-to-left, Nader, environment, antinuclear, and so on are becoming active. These groups are often significant.

The "good and bad" guys depend on values, issues, and perspectives. For some agencies, there is a pattern in which various actors tend to be allies on most issues. This need not be the situation. From the agency's point of view, the executive may be the stumbling block on an issue and the essential ally on yet another issue. From the clientele's viewpoint, the agency may be the enemy causing useless red tape or a vital agency necessary for the survival of the clientele members. Each situation must be examined separately. Rarely does a uniform and consistent pattern over time exist where there is a set of actors who are always friends and others always enemies. The patterns evolve and change, thus the actors must adapt to a dynamic environment.

Cultivation of an Active Clientele

For most government agencies, there is no problem identifying a clientele group. Highway departments are well aware of their clientele. The Veterans' Administration hears from its clientele. However, some agencies cannot easily identify clientele groups. For example, the United States Information Agency does not serve people in this country. What group is their clientele? The U.S. Bureau of Prisons does not have an active clientele group. In such cases, the nature of the organization or its mission precludes a clientele group, thus the agency is handicapped in the U.S. pluralist style of government.

The most obvious way to cultivate a clientele is to carry out the agency's programs, but some strategy is involved in building a supportive clientele. In the first place, the clientele should understand and appreciate the full extent of the benefits they receive from the agency's programs. In the second place, most legislatures represent the whole population so a breadth of clientele across the nation, state, or city is best if the clientele wishes to lobby the legislature. Thirdly, some clientele members may be in a better position to aid the agency such as a group in the House Appropriation Committee chairperson's home district. Lastly, mute clientele members are not that useful so they must be encouraged to be active politically.

Strategies of both expanding and concentrating the clientele are used. An agency can take care to provide grants or assistance across the country or build a balanced set of programs which appeal to several specific sectors of society. Agencies have their public information officers explain the programs and attendance at clientele conferences is considered very important. Some clientele members can be acquired by changing or adding attractive services for that group. For example, in an area where senior citizens are well organized, the parks department is wise to have programs for the elderly. Often the intensity of support is important so the program may be altered to be sure to benefit a particularly noted influential group.

The clientele must be heard by the legislature and the executive. In some instances, the clientele are poorly organized or not adept in dealing with the American democratic institutions. Congressmen, senators, and legislators often assume that if they do not hear supporters that no one cares. Given the need to cut, the tendency is to cut where no one cares enough to complain. Legislators do consider themselves to be guardians of the treasury, but they do not like the uncomfortable feeling when cuts can return to haunt the legislators at the next election. Even the problem of saying "no" to an impassioned plea is not pleasant. An agency rarely advocates lobbying the legislature, but they can explain the significance of lobbying and stress that the small budget is a problem which can be corrected by the legislature.

Sometimes agencies structure subunits to attract clientele. For example, the agency is broad-based but effective lobbying would be done by narrow focus groups. The agency can appeal to those narrow groups. For example, the National Institute of Health uses subunits focused upon specific diseases which correspond to the active health clientele groups. The result is a strong set of clientele groups. The hazard in this approach is that a glamorous subunit can lessen support for the other units.

Another approach is the creation of an advisory committee. Even the most conservative group of advisors tends to advocate the desirability of the agency's program. This can lead to increased and more effective clientele support.

Budget Office

Agency Budget Office

The place for developing and orchestrating the budget process is the agency budget office. The duties of such offices vary, as they sometimes include the accounting function and an analytical/planning unit. There are some common duties which describe what an agency budget office does. The following is an excellent list of duties from one agency budget office—the Budget Division of ACTION in the federal government:

1. In conjunction with the appropriate operating officials, develops budget estimates for programs and offices, conducts budget reviews, and recommends budget allocations.

2. In conjunction with appropriate operating officials, develops, presents, and justifies ACTION's budget submission to the Office of Management and Budget and to the Congress, including financial and personnel exhibits, budget narrative material, and budget back-up data. Prepares Agency witnesses for hearings before the Office of Management and Budget and the Congress.

3. Recommends budget priorities as the result of Office of Management and Budget and Congressional budget guidance for use within the Agency.

4. Prepares apportionments, allotments, and maintains overall control of Agency financial resources and position allocations.

5. Issues operating budgets with position and average grade allocations to all offices, regions, and posts and insures budget execution with legislative authority and limitations.

6. Conducts budget reviews and analyses during the fiscal year and recommends reprogramming actions and other funding adjustments.

7. Recommends and implements budgetary procedures, budget controls, and reporting systems and makes recommendations regarding the financial aspects of the management information system to improve financial management within the Agency.

8. Works with appropriate operating officials to coordinate the budget with Agency plans, objectives, and programs.

9. Acts as the Agency's primary point of contact with other governmental agencies on budget matters.

Exhibits 5-2 and 5-3 illustrate the variety of activities of budget execution responsibilities and the complex interrelationships which commonly exist in performing budget responsibilities.

Perspective of the Budget Officer

Much of the work of the budget officer is repetitive. Exhibits 5-2 and 5-3 point out the yearly routine. The budget process has an established pattern and after a few years the substantive issues of the agency also take on a familiar pattern.

Budgeting is largely repetitive and the filling out of reports tends to make the work mechanical.

The budget officer sees the world in terms of dollars, accuracy, and legality. The agency and its activities must always be translated into money. Budget officers will discuss new and old ideas, but eventually they ask, "What does this mean in terms of money?" Accuracy is essential. As will be discussed later, having the confidence of others is quite useful to the budget officer and confidence is not increased by making mistakes, especially in simple math. Care must be taken to establish procedures which double-check tables, insure final typing is error free, and verify the accuracy of stated facts. Legality is also a concern. If money is spent for reasons not permitted by law, then the budget officer may go to jail. There are few agency level decisions which the budget officer does not know about and often the law fixes responsibility for agency action on the agency head and budget officer. Wisdom dictates that the budget officer must be sure of the legality of questionable matters in order to avoid later problems.

Deadlines are the guiding force for a budget officer. Sometimes they seem impossible and often they are crucial. A common situation is to see a budget officer working late at night or on the weekends in order to meet some deadline. If a deadline is missed, then someone—usually the agency head—will be upset. More significantly, the agency may have lost an important opportunity or handicapped itself in a decision-making situation. Timeliness can mean even the survival of the agency's program. On the other hand, some deadlines are foolish and the wiser person will take the extra time to do a better job because timeliness is not significant. Ignoring deadlines should be done with judgment based upon knowing how and when the information will be utilized.

The budget can be used to minimize or surface disagreements. The budget officer is an artist who realizes that a budget can be presented in many ways in spite of the requirements of format. For political or internal management reasons, specific issues may best be hidden or minimized. This can be done by placing the issue within a larger, more dominant subject. In many situations, surfacing disagreement is a much better strategy. An issue can be surfaced by presenting it with some prominence in the budget document. This forces decision makers to deal with the problem and try to resolve it. In many instances, minimizing or surfacing a disagreement is mandated by outside forces, such as a major media story on the subject, which cannot be ignored. In some instances, these decisions are made by the budget officer, thus his political and management judgment are important.

Deadlines and other pressures force the budget officer to use the satisficing approach to many decision-making situations. When someone is demanding a budget submission, and the timeliness of that submission is important, then the budget officer may be pleased to find even a satisfactory answer. Budgeting is done under pressure and the budget officer must do the best that he or she can in the

EXHIBIT 5-2

Functions	Officials: Director/Deputy	Assistant Director for OPP	Budget Director
Apportionment request	Responsibility delegated to OPP	Submits request to GMB	Prepares request from sum of allotments; monitors
Continuing resolution	Concur with GC interpretation		Coordinates activity; issues instructions
Treasury warrant request			Prepares request
Allotment issuance	Reviews, approves	Issues allotments	Prepares allotment from sum of operating budgets
Operating budget issuance			Directs; issues jointly; monitors
Reapportionment	Request to the OMB	Concurs in request	Prepares request with backup
Allotment reprogramming	Final approval in cases of question	Approves reprogramming	Recommends; prepares documents
Operating budget reprogramming			Reviews requests; concurs in all decisions
Estimation of receipts/reimbursements		Concurs	Prepares; estimates; monitors
Allotment management			Monitors
Operating budget management			Monitors
Quarterly review		Approves new budget allocations	Directs review; recommends new allocation
Year end review		Approves new budget allocation	Directs review; recommends changes

Source: Budget Execution Responsibilities, ACTION, 1975.

Assistant Director for A&F	Allotment Holder	Intermediate Budget Holder (10 regions; Office)	Operating Budget Manager
Receive info copy apportionment monitor for pos. viol.			
Request to Treasury			
Receive info. copy of allot.; monitor for pos. violation	Receive allotment; monitor		
	Review and approve budgets; jointly issue	Review and approve subordinate budget request	Recommend operating budget totals
	Request reprogramming		
Insures account reporting compatible with format	Review request; approve if operating group budgets change	Review; approve if operating group budget totals unchanged	Request reprogramming
	Manage within budget totals and restrict		
			Manage within budget totals and restrictions
	Prepare data; recommend new levels	Recommend new levels for operating group	Recommend change in operating budget
Complete review of open obligations	Recommend changes	Recommend changes	Recommend changes

EXHIBIT 5-2 *(Continued)*

Functions	Officials: Director/Deputy	Assistant Director for OPP	Budget Director
Violation reports	Receive report; report to president and Congress		
Personnel and average grade ceiling	Reviews and approves allocation to 10 major offices	Develops/reviews allocation to 10 major offices	Recommends allocations to operating units
Review of past year performance			Analyzes; prepares report
Preparation of status of funds report			Provides budget input to reports

time available. Searching for ideal answers on all occasions is not compatible with budgeting.

Agency Budget Behavior

As explained earlier in this chapter, loyalty to an agency is a common behavioral phenomenon. This loyalty is similar to that found in professional athletes. When they work for a team, loyalty to the team is given. Budget officers believe in their agency's mission and feel that their role is important for the well-being of the agency. Blind loyalty does not exist because program weaknesses are well-known. A more balanced loyalty prevails which recognizes faults but believes the program is or can be essentially sound.

Individuals working in a public agency take pride in their work. This can lead to the desire to expand the projects and programs. Budget reviewers are often frustrated by agency desires to expand programs, but such expansion tendencies are positive indicators of the health of the program's management. Agencies should not be criticized for being enthusiastic. Reviewers should applaud positive attitudes while recognizing the reviewers' role may call for them to disapprove expansion.

Budgeting's political context often supersedes apparent rationality. What might appear to be the best solution is not necessarily the best position for the agency to take. Recall that agencies exist in a context of powerful interacting forces. When a person is sailing, the best sailing course may not be directly toward

Assistant Director for A&F	Allotment Holder	Intermediate budget holder (10 regions; Office)	Operating Operating Budget Manager
Instigate report to director with evidence			
	Recommend intermediate level totals	Recommend allocations to operating units within operating groups	
Generate reports and distribute			

the ultimate objective. Sometimes tacking into the wind is necessary due to the force of the opposing wind. In public administration, the budget game strategy may not be to advocate directly or oppose a position but rather wait for the clientele or legislature to react to circumstances. Judgment is essential.

There often is some flexibility in budgeting due to what some call gimmicks. How to employ those gimmicks is another important talent. For example, the timing of obligation and disbursements can be significant and this timing can be controlled by the budget officer. Another trick is that a given expense item can be assigned to one of two programs. This choice permits some often needed flexibility. Gimmicks exist because some discretion exists and a budget officer can use that discretion to ease the burden of managing the program. Skillful budget officers are aware of the available discretionary decisions and use them to ease the problems of public management.

Public budgeting requires decision makers. Even decisions not to act represent policy choices. If a budget reviewer delays a program or project for another year, that is a decision which often has important implications. Decisions may be based on sound reasoning, but they do affect people. Decision makers must be able to live with criticism because budget decisions often generate strong arguments. Also, decisions are often made on meager information thus contributing to the possibility of self-doubt in the minds of public budget officers. If the budget officer cannot emotionally deal with criticism and doubt, then he or she should consider a different type of work. Doubt and criticism are a part of public budgeting.

Public budgeting requires the highest professional characteristics. Later in

EXHIBIT 5-3

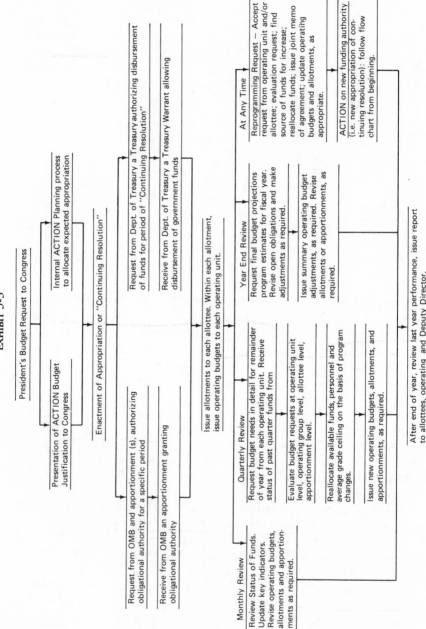

this chapter, the importance of confidence in the budget officer will be explained. Confidence is established through professionalism. Honesty and integrity are essential professional characteristics. This does not mean that the budget officer does not prepare the *strongest case possible* for a program, but it does mean that "possible" includes avoiding lies and misrepresentations. No one faults a budget officer for being sensitive to shifting political causes (e.g., environment, energy, inflation, unemployment) and framing budget justifications to take advantage of those shifting but temporarily persuasive rationales. This political sensitivity along with accuracy, legality, honesty, integrity, and other factors come together to constitute a professional.

One unfortunate characteristic of some budget officers is arrogance. This characteristic exists more in budget reviewers found in units like the department budget offices and the U.S. Office of Management and Budget (OMB). Lord Acton once stated that power corrupts and absolute power corrupts absolutely. Even budget officers and budget analysts possess some power due to the nature of their job; a few are corrupted but many more become intoxicated. They know they have power and they let others know it with their arrogance. For example, young OMB budget examiners may be mild mannered before they start working for OMB, but once on the job they can visit the "field" and act in a cavalier, flippant, or even bossy manner to people with much higher civil service rank and longer experience. Such behavior is not professionally wise because it often leads to needlessly poor cooperation from the agency, thus making the examiner's job that much more difficult.

Budget officers are almost always career civil servants who must work quite closely with politically appointed agency or department heads. This close rapport is sometimes influenced by the unusual position the agency head must face. Often they are expected to give their allegiance exclusively to the chief executive but the role of agency head strongly induces a loyalty to the agency. In some instances, these two loyalties are in conflict, thus presenting an agency head with an extremely difficult emotional dilemma. When such situations arise, the budget officer will become quite aware of the dilemma because the agency head's handling of that dilemma will influence the budget process. Understanding the dilemma is helpful, but there are no easy answers to this type of situation.

Public budgeting is an activity which requires responsible people. In the federal government, this responsibility is dramatized. If a budget officer over-obligates or permits to be spent an amount in excess of that apportioned by OMB, then a legal violation has occurred which can result in his being fired, fined, or sentenced to jail. Exhibit 5-4 is the quote from the Anti-deficiency Act which details the action required when violations occur. A fine or jail sentence results from willful violations. Such violations are rare.

One last important observation should be made about agency budget behavior. Good professionals love the game. They find it challenging and exciting. They love being important and having responsibility. They love the need to work under pressure and yet deliver quality work. They love knowing all the complexities of budgeting and being able to use their skills. They love the intrigue and excitement of both politics and public management.

EXHIBIT 5-4

Anti-deficiency Act
(Section 3679 of Revised Statutes, as amended)

Actions required when violations occur.

(1) *Administrative discipline; fines; or imprisonment.* In addition to any penalty or liability under other law, any officer or employee of the United States who shall violate subsections (a), (b), or (h) of this section shall be subjected to appropriate administrative discipline, including, when circumstances warrant, suspension from duty without pay or removal from office; and any officer or employee of the United States who shall knowingly and willfully violate subsections (a), (b), or (h) of this section shall, upon conviction, be fined not more than $5,000 or imprisoned for not more than two years, or both.

(2) *Reports to President or Congress.* In the case of a violation of subsections (a), (b), or (h) of this section by an officer or employee of an agency, or of the District of Columbia, the head of the agency concerned or the Commissioner of the District of Columbia, shall immediately report to the President, through the Director of the Office of Management and Budget, and to the Congress all pertinent facts together with a statement of the action taken thereon.

Four Views

In chapter 2, decision-making models and their importance were explained. People working in budgeting are often influenced by these normative theories and four ideal types can be used to describe typical reactions to those normative theories. The four ideal types are the true rational believer, the pure reactive person, the budget-wise person (the cynic), and the wise budget person.

The True Rational Believer

With the influence of PPB, there are people working in public budgeting who strongly believe that decision-making related to public budgeting should use the rational approach. If decisions don't follow that approach, then they consider the decision highly questionable and in error due to poor professionalism or the unfortunate intrusion of politics into proper decision-making. They try to insure that as many decisions as possible, especially significant decisions, should follow the rational approach: (1) set goals and objectives; (2) define alternatives; (3) analyze alternatives; (4) select the best decision or make the recommendation.

Such faith in the normative decision-making theory called the rational approach leads to unfortunate consequences in public budgeting. Many public organizations have vague multiple and sometimes mutually conflicting goals and objectives. Articulating specific goals and objectives may be impossible, but analysis may still be useful for the decision-making. If analysis is limited to the rational approach, then analysis cannot be conducted. This is an unnecessary constraint applied to circumstances where analysis could be useful. Thus the decision maker is unnecessarily handicapped. Another problem with the rational model is that it implies no limits exist to the defining of alternatives and the analysis of alternatives. As is pointed out in this author's book *Policy Analysis in Public Policymaking*, some individuals will proceed to spend large sums of money on analysis when the end results will be as useful as a much more limited analytical effort. Those individuals were motivated by the rational model to pursue the alternatives and exhaustively examine those alternatives. Another problem with the rational model is that its believers don't appreciate the importance of feedback in analysis, thus helpful feedback can be ignored.

A more subtle problem of the rational model is the inherent assumption that there is one overall perspective. A commonly cited fable involves several blind men and an elephant. The storyteller stresses how each blind man examines a different segment of the elephant and proceeds to argue with the other blind men over the nature of the beast. The ironical thrust to the story is that all parties including the storyteller were inherently limited by their perspective. Any object or series of events can be described in an infinite number of ways and there is no one description as the storyteller assumed. The rational model leads us to make the same mistake as the storyteller. One is wiser to recognize that there are only shared perceptions of felt needs which can be translated into formulations of problems and objectives. Unfortunately, the common use of the rational model does not encourage such sophistication.

The Pure Reactive Person

In contrast to the true rational believer is the pure reactive budget person. This type of person acts in a stimulus-response pattern. The budget calendar and the requests govern this type of person. Little thought is given to shaping events or somehow making a difference through the reactor's product. The job is merely a task to be done as defined in the job description or the demands of the job. Decision-making models mean little to this type of person. However, the political-administrative dichotomy is significant because this is used as the justification for his mechanical response. Using the dichotomy, political decisions should be left to the political appointee and civil servants merely respond to the wishes of the political appointees.

The hazard of this approach is that mindless or potentially foolish mistakes are not avoided. The budget person has a unique vantage point and can often understand both the political actors' viewpoints as well as the workings of government. By merely reacting, the government loses the important insight of the budget expert, thus more errors are likely to occur. An aggressive, outspoken budget staff can greatly improve government, but a reactive staff will permit policy makers to make unnecessary—often significant—errors. Most policy makers recognize the value of an aggressive, outspoken rather than a reactive budget staff.

The Budget-Wise Person

These people are aware of all the forms and tables, but discount them almost completely because the government's decisions are all political. They are often cynical about life in general and stress the public nature of "public administration." They can sometimes cite dramatic case examples of gross politically inspired decision-making sometimes involving corruption but often involving vote trading. Such decision-making often does preclude effective public management. This type of person stresses that such decision-making is inevitable and that all that a budget staff can do is react and watch events unfold. In some government settings, the cynic is right; but in many others, the political actors in the political process are influenced by well-prepared budget justifications, and professional budgeting does translate to effective public management. If a cynical view dominates where professional budgeting could make a difference, then a valuable opportunity for more effective government is lost.

The Wise Budget Person

People of this type recognize that politics is sometimes of overriding importance. They also believe that analysis has its limitations but can often greatly help in decision-making situations. Professional public budgeting can be extremely significant to the way government is managed. We hope that this text will help more people be wise budget persons.

Develop Confidence

Confidence of the budget reviewers, especially the appropriations committees, is extremely important to the budget officer. If confidence doesn't exist, any reviewer can ask hard questions and force the agency to justify every detail. If the appropriations committees lack confidence, they can write into the appropriation bill or committee report very specific special conditions, thus tying the hands of the agency and making program administration a nightmare. If confidence is established, the budget reviews are less difficult and greater administrative latitude is provided for public management discretion.

There is a natural tendency on the part of the reviewers to place confidence in budget officers because some facts and management judgment must be accepted on faith. The sheer complexity of the budget plus the lack of time to review budgets means that not everything can be reviewed in depth. Priorities of reviewers' efforts in examining are decided upon with the more questionable or politically sensitive topics receiving the greatest attention. Budget reviewers would like to trust the expertise of the best budget officer because valuable budget reviewer time can be saved. Thus, a budget officer is wise to establish a reputation as being highly professional.

The ideal model of a highly professional budget person is used by reviewers to "rate" budget officers. The criteria vary but a fairly accurate picture can be painted of the type of person most likely to be trusted. Such a person is

1. a master of detail;
2. hard working;
3. concise;
4. frank;
5. self-effacing and devoted to the work;
6. tight with the taxpayer's money;
7. capable of recognizing a political necessity when it is present;
8. conscientious about keeping key reviewers (e.g., congressmen) informed of sensitive changes in policy or important developments.

Budget officers find that a reputation of playing it straight is wise. Lying, covering up, and being tricky are highly undesirable characteristics for the career civil servant. Memories can be long among top reviewing staffs. If a reviewer, especially an appropriations committee, feels that it is misled, then strong punitive actions can be taken such as tying the agency into administrative knots with special appropriation language. On the other hand, a positive reputation can even mean securing emergency or supplemental funds on the basis of skimpy hearings: that is, getting funds almost entirely on the integrity of the budget officer.

Reputations are enhanced with professional friendship. A close personal relationship with budget reviewers, such as the agency's Congressional subcommittee staff, can ease tensions. Years of outstanding service are even more significant than friendships because such experience often builds a sense of integrity and trust which constitutes "professional friendships." In many cases, these professional friendships are built upon shared work experiences and service together in professional associations.

One of the characteristics associated with building confidence is being capable of recognizing political "necessity." However, judgment can differ on the question of "necessity." Some accommodation to favors and pet projects do occur, but such practices can move from the unusual to the expected. When this occurs, effective public management cannot be carried out. Part of building confidence is being able to turn down political actors so that requests are not considered a "political necessity." Techniques for pleasant turn-downs include:

1. "My hands are tied"—other factors may exist such as an executive mandate which precludes the favor.
2. "Maybe in the future"—the favor may be granted but the timing is simply not wise then.
3. "But look at the other positive actions we have taken"—stress that other decisions

were in their favor or to their liking and appeal to the notion that one should only expect to win a "fair share" of the time.

4. "It cannot be done"—economic, technical, or other reasons can be cited why the request is either impossible or extremely unwise to fulfill.

Other strategies can be employed to minimize granting favors. Action on the favor can be delayed. If they are truly serious, the political actors will pursue. Delay thus acts as a filter for the true "necessities." A parallel strategy is to give in on the most intensely sought favors and pet projects. Intensity can also be measured by means used to bring pressure upon the agency. Regardless of how intensity is shown, the strategy is to give in on the intense favors and resist on the less intense favors and pet projects.

Strategies and techniques can help, but in a few cases the consequences must be faced. Sometimes budget officers must face a no-win situation due to their professional or personal ethics or the need to support other persons in the bureaucracy such as the agency head. In some instances, the situation can be mitigated by allowing one political actor (e.g., a Congressman) to do battle with another political actor (e.g., a political appointee or the media); but such a ploy can result in making two enemies and losing rather than gaining their confidence. In other situations, the budget officer may merely have to use time to heal relationships or hope that key actors don't blame the budget officer but blame the deed. The consequence may be severe, but sometimes one's professional integrity requires action which ironically can harm one's professional reputation.

There is no developed contingency for establishing confidence. All that can be done is to be aware of the techniques and strategies available, to observe successful budget officers, and use careful judgment. No one approach is useful for all budget reviewers or all situations. Each set of circumstances must be considered separately before action is taken.

Results

Confidence in a government program often rests upon demonstrating results. Results are significant because the public and political leaders anticipate that some benefits will be evident from government programs.

There is an important distinction between an activity accomplishing its purpose and people feeling that they are being served. Politically, the latter is more significant. Often the distinction is only theoretical because accomplishment translates to people realizing their lives have been enhanced, but this need not be the case. The people—the agency's potential clientele—may be unaware of the importance of the program, may have come to take it for granted, or may not feel that the program is important. Earlier in this chapter, the significance of the clientele in the political process was noted. If the potential clientele is not an active supporter of the program, then the program may very well fail, given the normal political competition for funding support.

For an agency, serving an appreciative clientele is ideal. The best kind of result is one that provides services to a large and strategically placed appreciative clientele. They best type of clientele is one which brings its satisfaction to the attention of the decision makers such as the appropriation committees and the president. Not all agencies are blessed with such a happy harmony of circumstances, so attempts must be made to develop alternative means to build and maintain essential support of key decision makers.

If an agency doesn't enjoy overwhelming public support, a persuasive case can be made with tangible accomplishments. In the budget justification process, emphasis is placed on the accomplishments of the program. The criteria used to judge success are sometimes the subject of debate and sometimes semantic confusion is used to rationalize odd criteria for success. In such circumstances, the merits of the accomplishments are less persuasive. Nevertheless, the citation of accomplishment is normally highly useful in any budget justification.

If the listing of results is not sufficiently impressive, the agency can extend an invitation to the decision makers or anyone likely to influence the decision makers (e.g., the media) to visit the agency. Budget reviewers and other influential people are shown the need (e.g., the poor being helped), the activity (e.g., the production of a missile), or the heroic efforts by an overworked staff (e.g., emergency room care at a hospital). Often this technique is extremely useful. The U.S. space program used this approach quite successfully to maintain a high public interest in their efforts. However, there are significant risks. The reviewers may not be impressed and this can be translated into lower budgets rather than increased or sustained budget support.

A hazard of visits and other attempts to explain highly complex programs is the problem of explanation. Most political decision makers are not experts, so explanations and visits must be simplified to communicate the essential message without technical verbiage. If they are too simple, then the complex nature of the challenge is not understood and the level of funding seems unwarranted. If they are too complex, then the reviewer questions the clarity of the management direction and again the level of funding is reduced or the program is cut entirely. Selecting the exact visit format and explanation for complex programs can indeed be a challenge.

A hazard of demonstrating tangible accomplishment is that the program may be praised and then cut because the program objectives have been met. Government programs are designed to meet a problem and success may mean the problem ceases to exist. If that occurs, the program should cease to exist. The irony is that losing one's job seems like a punishment rather than a reward.

Some government programs are disadvantaged by not having tangible accomplishments which they can demonstrate. For example, unless civil defense is used there is no tangible accomplishment. Another example is the International Communications Agency which broadcasts propaganda overseas. How does one deal with such programs when tangible results cannot be shown? There are several ploys that can be used:

1. "Our program is priceless"—argue that results are not evident but what if the program did not exist? If we did not have civil defense, what cost would there be in human lives if disaster occurred?

2. "Results of our program cannot be measured"—argue that a demonstration of results is simply not possible given the nature of the program. This may be a truthful argument, but it is not very persuasive.

3. "Results will be evident in the future"—argue that results are not evident now because the program is new or the program's results are only evident when an emergency occurs. This is a more appealing argument, but skeptics can say that finding out a program is wrong in an emergency is too late.

4. "Figures show"—argue facts and figures show results in spite of the fact that they really are not relevant. This is a foolish ploy, given the potential loss of confidence that could result.

5. "In this complex situation, the figures confirm . . ."—argue by ignoring the questionable cause-effect relationship of a multiple causal situation. This is a reasonable ploy, but care must be taken in the wording so that the statements are positive but not false. Extreme claims, which cannot be tested, should be avoided.

6. "Please notice that we reviewed over 1,000 applicants"—argue not by focusing upon results but on the procedures and process measures of the organization. The critical observant reviewer can always ask, "So what?" but at least such a display of facts and figures is better than saying nothing because the information does demonstrate some activity did take place.

7. "You must appreciate that we cannot prove the relationship of this education to later achievement, but we know such a relationship exists"—argue that faith establishes the relationship between the program and the desired benefits in society. If the subject is something that is taken for granted, then such an argument might be successful.

Preparing for Hearings

Hearings often are important in building confidence in a program and program officials. In some situations, hearings only serve to brief decision makers or to create a record to be used to convince others. However, hearings can and often do affect decision makers given the competing pressures on their time and the inadequate preparation they give to review budget material. Hearings are particularly important in establishing confidence. Program officials who cannot answer or poorly answer questions create an impression that those running the organization don't really understand what they are doing.

Rehearsals for budget hearings are essential. The number of hearings vary by agency and government, but four hearings on the budget alone are minimal in the federal government. As noted in an earlier chapter, rehearsing, or holding mock hearings, is a standard practice. Agency administrators play the role of key reviewers such as appropriations committee chairperson. Tough questions are anticipated and answered before the hearing in order to avoid later difficulties. Mock hearings are an excellent device to expose weak justifications, to build effective agency coordination in handling questions, and to appreciate the perspective of the reviewer. Mock hearings also help the budget officer decide what subjects should be discussed and stressed in the traditional opening statement.

The key to preparing for budgeting hearings is to do sufficient research to avoid or minimize surprises in the hearing. A surprise normally makes the administrator appear to be ignorant and can rattle a person to the point of answering all the remaining questions poorly. A diligent search of past hearings and statements often indicates what the reviewers consider important. Also a review of the program itself and reactions to the program are essential in framing the tough questions. Often the rapport of the budget officer with others, such as people in the central budget office, can be a vital resource for intelligence.

Briefing books for hearings are useful. Normally, they include only the tough or standard questions and answers which are anticipated. They can include a brief discussion on the perspectives of each reviewer, but such information is normally common knowledge. Also such descriptions can fall into the wrong hands, thus leading to unnecessary embarrassment.

Questions in a hearing come from a variety of sources including the reviewer (e.g., senator), staff, clientele, and even the agency itself. Questions are sometimes planted with entire lists of questions supplied by the agency. Sometimes the planted questions are the most difficult so that the agency can go on record on a subject in the best possible manner. Planted questions rarely occur at the department and OMB hearings, but they are common in the Congress where friendly legislators wish to aid a program. In some instances, the rapport between staffs is so close that the effect is the same as planted questions.

Hearing presentations tend to create a portrait of the agency leadership in the minds of the reviewers. Hearings are an opportunity to paint a self-portrait of credibility and generate a favorable mood toward the agency. The leadership can take on such mantles as protector-of-the-public-safety, men-of-science, statesmen, guardian-of-the-environment, and so on. Effective hearing presentations tend to ward off unpleasant and time-consuming probes for an agency.

The best way to make a positive impression at a hearing is to know the budget. There is no adequate substitute for being knowledgeable, but knowledge can be coupled with a good organized presentation. Normally presentations and answers which are brief and to the point, but which offer an opportunity to go into more depth on follow-up questions, are most effective. Care can be taken not to give the impression that important subjects are being slighted. An administrator can be forgiven for not knowing a detail and in fact such data are often supplied for the record after the hearing. Administrators are sometimes not forgiven for not knowing the answers to questions involving management direction. Questions—

even on detail—often can be anticipated and answered or transmitted at the time of the hearing. Such action is extremely impressive and builds confidence.

Hearings are a game with certain taboos. Agency officials recognize that they have two masters—the legislature and the executive—but agency officials cannot challenge the chief executive's budget even though they may wish more support. Therefore, agency officials always say they support the executive's request, but everyone present knows that the officials mean otherwise. This communication is achieved by:

1. exhibiting a marked lack of enthusiasm;
2. being too enthusiastic to be true;
3. refusing to answer questions in a form of a protestation of loyalty to the chief executive;
4. yielding to sharp pointed questioning.

This taboo is significant. If the central budget office or the department feels the agency is not adhering to the established executive branch policy, then the agency head and other political appointees can be fired. "Speaking against the administration" can be taken extremely seriously; but in a few instances, the central budget office or department may not wish the agency to resist legislative desires to increase the budget over executive branch requests due to political strategy. Each situation must be judged separately.

Another taboo is that the agency should not admit yielding to clientele pressure. The agency is accountable to all the people, thus yielding to one clientele is an admission of favoritism. It also admits the pressure can be successful. Instead, language is carefully phrased to indicate the agency wishes to receive advice from citizens and does act upon suggestions which have intrinsic value. The agency does respond to sound advice but the decision is made only on the merits of the advice. Pressure is not influential according to this taboo and should not be admitted to openly.

Strategies

Reviewers versus Reviewed

The budget game requires advocates and reviewers. The agency is the advocate, but clientele groups and sometimes even legislators can also be called advocates. The reviewers are the department officials, the central budget office (e.g., OMB), the House appropriations subcommittee, and the Senate appropriations subcommittee. As the budget moves through the budget cycle, reviewers change roles and become advocates. For example, after the central budget office has reviewed the budget requests and final executive branch decisions are made, then that former reviewer is an advocate to the legislative appropriations subcommittees. The primary advocate, however, always is the agency. If the game is played well, there always exists an arm's length relationship between the advocate and reviewer. Each plays the role with caution, care, and an awareness of the natural tendencies associated with each role. A requirement for a good game is that each party know the rules and strategy. Ideally the game should be played by professionals. An uneven game results in unreasonable cuts or unreasonably high budgets. Both results are undesirable.

One budget strategy failure illustrates the gamesmanship. Occasionally, an agency will resubmit the previous year's budget with the only change being the fiscal years mentioned in the text. When this occurs, the reviewers question the budget request because intervening variables since last year must cause some program changes. The possibility of an *exact* budget request approaches zero because administrative environments always change. A distinct likelihood exists that another reviewer may have ordered the agency to use the same budget level as the previous year's budget, but to use the *exact* budget request seems to imply lack of adaptability to changing conditions. Part of the game is to at least give the appearance of managing the program, and this is not done by using last year's budget.

Budget requests are rarely approved intact and reviewers normally reduce (cut) the request. There are several common rationales given for cutting budgets:

1. a climate of opinion existed which was against spending;
2. strong views by influential decision makers necessitated the cut;
3. spending on your program became a political football;
4. there was an overriding need to balance the budget.

The reason cited may address the management capability or fundamental objectives of the agency's program. However, such statements are more difficult to rationalize against the superior expertise of the agency on those topics. The reasons cited above are less subject to dispute and appeal, thus they are the more likely rationales to be cited.

Some ironies can exist with budget cutting. An agency may wish to be cut or even cut its own program. For example, maybe the agency leadership lost faith in a program, internal discipline called for cuts, or higher priorities in other programs meant cuts in some programs. Interestingly, cuts can stimulate mobilization of the agency clientele, thus eventually resulting in even higher budgets than would have occurred without those earlier cuts.

Another phenomenon which can occur is intra-legislative conflict. One obvious area of conflict is between the two chambers (House and Senate). Conference committees are intended to resolve such disputes, but strategies can be used so that one chamber's position dominates. For example, the Senate may raise the amount in order to achieve the desired amount through compromise. Another tactic is to have a chamber pass a resolution supporting its conferees, thus permitting them to cite the solidarity and intensity of feelings in their arguments.

Conference committees are often unpredictable and most agencies would prefer to avoid this uncertainty unless one chamber cuts them significantly. A less obvious area of conflict is between the substantive committee and the appropriations committee. In some instances, the agency can be the innocent victim of such disputes.

Spenders' Strategies

There are game strategies that an agency can apply in seeking to get its budget requests approved. This section explains the various strategies which are commonly used, but does not attempt to comment in depth upon how, when, and in what way the strategies should be applied to maximize their effectiveness. Such matters require judgment based upon each separate budget situation.

There are some fairly common safety strategies which are employed. Budget requests are often padded because the agency wishes to be able to meet unanticipated contingencies and the fact that reviewers often almost automatically cut a request. Obvious or nondefensible "padding" can lead to an important loss of confidence, but "extras" can normally be easily defended. A related strategy is to always ask for more. This demonstrates an aggressive agency which has a strong belief in its mission. The increase may not be merited, but the reviewers are forced to address the increase and may forget to argue the possibility of a program level decrease. In connection with strategy, the agency is careful to spend or obligate all the current year funds. The fear is that the reviewer will argue the agency cannot spend what is provided them, so how can the reviewer provide them additional money. Another safe strategy is to alter the written or oral budget presentations as much as possible to highlight the best aspects of the agency's program and minimize the worst aspects.

Budgeting is a complex activity. "Sleight-of-hand" tricks do exist and they can be part of a budget strategy. For example, numbers in budgets are rounded often to the nearest hundred thousand or even million. For some small but politically important budget items, the practice of rounding can be an advantage. Another "trick" is to recast the budget into different categories than those used in the previous year. The redone categories can be utilized to focus attention upon or away from programs depending upon the budget strategic purposes. Also, redone categories inhibit longitudinal analysis and this may be an advantage to the agency. In addition, there are a variety of back-door spending devices; one of them is no-year funds. One sleight-of-hand technique is to use unobligated appropriations or disobligated (i.e., funds previously obligated but for which obligation was subsequently withdrawn, often because of nonuse by grantees) appropriations to finance projects beyond the apparent level of budget year appropriations. For example, let us say that an agency has $15 million left over from last year's budget and also has disobligated $20 million from previous years. This $35 million technically should be deducted from the budget request, but the subtraction is normally not cited or is poorly cited by the agency.

Another sleight-of-hand trick is the fund transfer. An agency can often transfer money from one account to another. By using several transfers among several funds, illusions can be created about the money that was obligated. This unprofessional trick can be used also to defraud the government or mislead reviewing groups such as prospective bond buyers. Careful accounting can uncover such abuses, but such work is detailed and time consuming.

Most spender strategies are direct and simple. The agency merely points out that the tasks it performs have expanded and more money is needed to fund the program. Another argument is to point out the backlog of requests or tasks. The argument is then made that an increase is needed to eliminate the backlog and that a cut would increase the size of the backlog. A third strategy or argument is to appeal to a national standard by showing that the agency can meet the standard with a given level of budget support. This strategy is used often by highly professional groups (e.g., medical and educational).

Sometimes the strategy is to argue with economic concepts. The activity may involve a fee such as entrance fee or license. The agency argues that a given budget level would attract more people to the activity, thus increasing the revenue from the activity. The increased revenue might be larger than the expenses in the budget. A more complex argument is that an increased budget for a program like a subsidy would increase the operation and payroll size. The argument is made that because of the multiplier effect of the subsidy, the government would recover more in additional taxes (e.g., income tax) than paid out for the subsidy. Another argument is that an increased budget would permit greater productivity due to a better per unit cost average or the use of the extra money to purchase labor-saving devices.

Other arguments are predicated more on emotion. The agency argues that the revenue of the government has grown and that the agency should receive a fair share of the growth. A bolder strategy is to argue that a high level commitment exists on the project and that there is no option but to fund the program. A less bold but equally emotional strategy is to plead that the program is "squeezed to the wall" and a certain funding level is essential for meaningful program operation.

In many situations, the agency wishes to start a new program but the newness must be masked. Once funded, a "foot-in-the-door wedge" or "camel's nose under the tent" has been established. This precedent greatly helps the agency convince reviewers because the standard for new programs tends to be harsher than for existing programs. The agency will often argue that the money does not represent a new initiative but rather a continuation of old programs. This may be quite true literally, but the new dimension may constitute an entire new major emphasis which logically should be considered a new program. However, such treatment would bias the reviewers against the effort.

Spenders' strategies can constitute a high political risk for the agency and agency officials. One strategy is to react to a request for cuts by suggesting cuts be taken first on projects which enjoy strong political support. By cutting the "sacred cow" or popular programs, the cutter is placed in a politically difficult position and may withdraw the request to cut the program. The risk for the agency head is that the chief executive may be offended by the use of this strategy and fire the political appointee. A second strategy is to shift the blame. The agency points out that if the full requested amount is not funded, then certain specific activities will not be undertaken. The agency makes it clear to the reviewer that the responsibility for not funding the activites will be placed on the reviewer. In some situations, reviewers are sobered by such responsibility and the related political implications, thus they act favorably on the budget request. A third strategy is to argue that a cut is irresponsible and that the project must be funded at the requested level or not funded at all. This is a sound argument for many projects because there is a lower limit at which the project cannot be sustained as viable. The risk in such an argument is that the reviewer may indeed decide to cut the whole project.

Another high risk strategy is to spend fast to be short. The agency deliberately spends the money at a fast rate and then goes back to the reviewers for supplemental appropriations. This strategy is employed infrequently but does occur especially when the agency is asked to absorb large cuts. This is an extremely high risk strategy because of the likelihood that the top agency officials will be considered to be irresponsible and poor managers. Firing of top officials is often a result of the use of such strategies.

Cutters' Strategies

Just as there are game strategies for an agency, there are strategies for the reviewing groups. Some strategies are safe and are fairly standard. Other strategies are essentially counterstrategies to be used against spenders' arguments and ploys. The discussion here, like the previous spenders' section, is addressed to explaining the strategies and not to an in-depth treatment of their application in a variety of contingency situations.

The safe approaches include reducing increases, questioning hidden "revenues," cutting less visible items, and employing delay. The political support for existing programs can be quite strong and the pressure for increases may be strong also. However, the exact size of the increase is almost always open to discussion and cuts in the increases are easier to sustain. Another safe approach is to investigate and try to isolate "hidden" revenue such as the use of the previous fiscal year's appropriations or the use of existing government property rather than purchasing new property. Normally, some savings can be found with this approach and few can fault the results. A third approach is to cut the less visible or less politically supported items. This approach should be employed with some discretion because such "saving" may be false economy. For example, the replacement program for a city water pipe system can be deferred but the wiser policy is probably a yearly systematic program. Delay is a particularly easily applied strategy. Whenever another study is conducted or delays are caused for other reasons, the result is that the item is not included in the budget. This is one of the most successful cutter's strategies because all that need be done is to raise a question and a delaying study can be justified.

Several fairly standard arguments and ploys exist. One is to always cut something. If no cuts are made, the credible power of the reviewer is questioned. Also, the reviewers are aware that the spenders have a natural tendency to include items that they could do without. Thus cuts will eliminate those "frills." A second approach is to argue that initial allocations are unnecessary. If nothing starts, then budget expansion is diminished. A third approach is to defer or record projects on the grounds that initial dollars cannot be spent correctly by the end of the fiscal year. New programs normally experience difficulty in staffing themselves, thus they rarely can do a decent job in the first year. By arguing that they will not do a decent job in the first year, the cutter can each year prevent the program from coming into existence. A fourth approach is to never allow a precedent to be established. Precedents lead to continued budget requests. An effective ploy is to argue that there is only so much money and that some is available for program increases. The question is then asked: Whose turn is it? This focuses the debate away from the amount and gets the various units to argue against each other. A sophisticated ploy to be used in a few circumstances is to eliminate interagency competition which tends to be more expensive due to the expansive nature of competition itself in the public sector.

The cutter need not accept or live with strategies employed by the spender. Counterstrategies do exist. If the agency says the increase is "so small," the counter is to argue that no item is too small to eliminate or to suggest that such small items can be absorbed without a budget increase. If the agency argues that they should have a fair share of the growth, the cutter can ask what is "fair" and never accept any definition. Another counterstrategy is to challenge work load data. Often such data are collected poorly and can be easily challenged on methodological grounds. The cutter can normally argue that productivity increases—for a number of reasons such as becoming more experienced at a new job (i.e., learning curve)—should mean that increases or even decreases are appropriate in a given program.

One spender's strategy is to place the blame on the cutter for the cuts, but that blame need not be accepted. The cutter can force the agency to say what they believe should be cut first. If the spender is likely to put forth political "sacred cows" for cutting, the cutter can anticipate and neutralize the strategy by insisting that the agency must suggest items to be cut but stipulate which items cannot be considered as candidates for cutting.

Cutters normally have the advantage because they need only question and the spender has the burden of proof. The strongest asset the spender has is expertise and care must be taken to maintain the expert's credibility. Spenders can employ strategies but most of them must be executed with an aura of expertise.

New Programs

The previous strategies are for normal day-to-day budget situations. New programs require extraordinary efforts on the part of the spenders. Often new programs are established in reaction to a crisis or what some consider to be a crisis. Such crises rarely are manufactured, but groups do take advantage of crises to establish new programs or radically increase existing programs. The political climate in a crisis is such that political forces concur that the need is obvious and the debate centers on the "solutions." But even that debate is different in that the political climate calls for a solution, and delay is an unacceptable condition. Standards are lowered and the key is effectiveness. Efficiency becomes a less significant topic. In such an environment, agencies with viable ideas have a much greater opportunity to be accepted and new or radical increases in programs do occur.

Agency or clientele advertising and salesmanship can sometimes result in the creation of new programs. Dramatic names or labels such as *Mission 66* or *Headstart* can be significant in capturing enough popular attention. Good presentations are necessary. A well-organized effort can start new programs, but the presence of anticlientele groups (even small groups) can be fatal to such efforts. Rarely are advertising and salesmanship adequate by themselves. Normally they must be linked to a cause of the day (e.g., environment, pollution, national defense, inflation, unemployment). Ironically, overselling sometimes can be dysfunctional because the new program can become so popular that the agency's other programs suffer. Advertising and salesmanship should not be underrated, but the times and place are more significant in the beginning of most new programs.

Cautions

Unlike a parlor game, the budget game has serious consequences. Spenders' and cutters' strategies are used and sometimes one side or the other plays the game poorly. This is unfortunate because the budget process is usually best served when both sides play the game well. One particularly serious game fault is when the agency leadership forgets that the agency is a *public* agency designed to serve all the people. True, the clientele is only part of the public and most of the agency's dealings need only concern the clientele, but circumstances do exist where the public nature of an agency prohibits continuous harmonious relations with the clientele group (e.g., a coal company dealing with the Interior Department on a strip mining question). Public agencies can be captured by their clientele.

The mood of the times often is much more important than given strategies of spenders or cutters. Such moods change and they create a significant climate which favors, disfavors, or is neutral to specific programs. Government officials are sensitive to current events and recognize that those events are much like the weather for the farmer. The weather is very important and the farmer can do some things to mitigate the bad effects of weather, but it is still a largely uncontrolled governing force. Some political storms must be accepted as either a favorable or unfavorable reality by government officials.

One last caution is noted. If the mood of the times becomes favorable to a program and the reviewers become converts to the mission of an agency, the agency will discover that its new role expectation according to the reviewers is to think and act very big. The meaning of "big" depends on the size of the government and the dimensions of the problem. If the agency doesn't think in expansive terms, then criticisms such as being overly concerned for "petty economies" are likely to occur. Such role expectations are sometimes difficult to comprehend given the normal budget process, but the agency must accommodate to the role expectation or be subject to remarkably unpleasant political pressure.

REVIEW QUESTIONS

1. What political influence patterns exist in the federal government in terms of budgeting? Why are they important to understand?
2. Why is it important for an agency to cultivate a clientele? How is that done? What problems and cautions are important to understand?
3. What are the typical duties of an agency budget office: What views and behaviors should be anticipated?
4. What is the agency budget officer's perspective? Contrasts that to the executive and legislative perspective.
5. Why are confidence, results, and hearings important? Explain how confidence can be enhanced. How can one prepare for hearings?
6. What strategies can be used by advocates of spending and reviewers critical of spending?

REFERENCES

ANTHONY, ROBERT. "Closing the Loop Between Planning and Performance," *Public Administration Review* (May/June 1971).

ANTON, THOMAS J. *The Politics of State Expenditure in Illinois.* Urbana: University of Illinois Press, 1966.

AXELROD, DONALD. "Post-Burkhead: The State of the Art or Science of Budgeting," *Public Administration Review* (November/December 1973).

BAHL, ROY. *Metropolitan City Expenditures.* Lexington: University of Kentucky Press, 1968.

BARBER, DAVID. *Power in Committees: Experiment in the Governmental Process.* Chicago: Rand McNally, 1966.

BAUER, RAYMOND A. and KENNETH J. GEIGON. *The Study of Policy Formation.* New York: Free Press, 1968.

BERMAN, JULES. "The Budget Process: New Rules for an Old Game," *Public Welfare, 33,* 4 (Fall 1975), 24–29.

BICKNER, ROBERT E. "I Don't Know PPB At All," *Policy Science, 2,* 1 (March, 1971), 301–4.

BLACK, GERRY. *The Application of Systems Analysis to Government Operations.* New York: Praeger, 1968.

BORUT, DONALD J. "Implementing PPBS: A Practitioner's Viewpoint," in John P. Crocrine (ed.), *Financing the Metropolis: Public Policy in Urban Economics.* Beverly Hills: Sage Publications, 1970.

BRANDT, J. E. "Education Program Analysis at HEW," in R. H. Haveman and J. Margolis (eds.) *Public Expenditures and Policy Analysis.* Chicago: Markham Publishing Co., 1972.

BROWNING, RUFUS P. "Innovative and Non-Innovative Decision Making in Governmental Budgeting," in Ira Sharkansky (ed.), *Policy Analysis in Political Science.* Chicago: Markham Books, 1970.

BURKHEAD, JESSE and PAUL BRINGEWATT. *Municipal Budgeting: A Primer for the Elected Official.* Syracuse, N.Y.: Syracuse University Press, April 1974.

BURKHEAD, JESSE and JERRY MINER. *Public Expenditure.* Chicago: Aldine-Atherton, 1971.

DENZAU, ARTHUR and ROBERT J. MACKEY. "Bureaucratic Discretion and Public Sector Budgets," *Arizona Review, 25,* 5 (May 1976), 1–9.

FENNO, RICHARD F. "The Impact of PPBS on the Congressional Appropriation Process," in T. R. Chartrand, J. Kenneth and Michael Hugo (eds.), *Information Support Program Budgeting and The Congress.* New York: Spartal, 1968.

FENNO, RICHARD JR. *The Power of the Purse: Appropriations in Congress.* Boston: Little, Brown, 1966.

LYNCH, THOMAS D. *Policy Analysis in Public Policymaking.* Lexington, Mass.: D. C. Heath, 1976.

MOAK, LENNOX L. and KATHRYN W. KILLIAN. *Operating Budget Manual.* Chicago: Municipal Finance Officers Association, 1963.

Municipal Performance Report, 1, 4 (August 1974).

WILDAVSKY, AARON. *The Politics of the Budgetary Process.* Boston: Little, Brown, 1964.

SIX

Program Analysis
and
Budget Reviews

In public budgeting during the policy formulation phase, people are advocating and judging positions of others. Too often, developed material or inquiries are not relevant to the decisions being made. Why? The answer is normally that the budget reviewers do not ask the correct questions and the advocates do not anticipate the questions they should be prepared to answer. This chapter tells what questions should be the focus of good budget preparation and indicates the proper approach to program analysis. This chapter will explain:

1. the set of questions and information of essential importance for a budget analyst to understand;
2. the approach essential for useful program analysis.

Budget Reviews

Budget Analysis

Reviewers are not limited to the agency budget submission in forming their analysis and conclusions. Information can be obtained from the budget submissions, hearings, reports which may be available, other information such as newspaper stories, and answers to specific questions prior to and after budget hearings. The most important information source is normally the agency budget request because it directly addresses the information needs of the budget reviewer. Hearings are also a valuable information source as they can be used to focus upon specific inquiries. Hearings permit direct oral interchange between the agency and the reviewers. Reviewers should also make use of any available reports such as special analytical studies and program evaluation reports. This type of information often is not organized well for budget analysis purposes, but studies and reports do provide useful insight and suggest areas of fruitful inquiry. Other information sources such as national media reports and books can also be extremely helpful in framing inquiries.

Specific questions by reviewers and answers by agency officials are valuable to budget reviewers. These questions and answers can occur before and after hearings. They can be oral or written depending upon the reviewers' request. The major limiting factor is time. Rarely are questions asked prior to budget submissions because the submissions may contain the answers. If there is a short time interval between the submission and the hearing, then written questions and answers may be impossible—normally at least five working days are needed to develop answers, have them approved by top agency personnel, and have them typed and transmitted. If there is an equally short time interval between the hearing and the central budget office decision on the budget, then again written questions may not be possible. Time pressures dictate that the answers must not require new analysis but use existing information.

The key to an outstanding budget review is for the reviewer to gain the necessary program information and insight. No one source of information is adequate and many inquiries can be tailored for the situation. The advocate wishes to anticipate inquiries so that confidence in the agency budget personnel can be enhanced. Both the examiner and analysts preparing the submission have in common a set of information. One wishes to know the information and the other should be ready to supply the information. What can a good budget examiner look for and what should a good analyst be able to provide?

1. what services are to be performed by the agency for society;
2. detailed explanations of the program inputs and outputs;
3. planned program emphases and changes in emphases;
4. crosswalks;
5. program and financial plans.

Services Performed

Results or services performed are important. The budget examiner determines services or types of services which are anticipated from the planned budget. Historical information can be used to illustrate the type of service likely to be provided as well as to establish the credibility of the agency to perform as planned. The budget submission often indicates objectives and states likely products of the agency. The examiner looks beyond specific outputs and tries to ascertain the likely impacts on society and individuals directly and indirectly due to the program. Also, unanticipated good and bad effects are considered. It is helpful if the information is available in the budget request. If not, the information may be available in speeches or program evaluation reports.

The agency normally has an excellent explanation of its likely outputs. Any budget is a plan requiring forecasting so every budget must be qualified that there is no guarantee the events will evolve as planned. This is accepted; if something else were said, the budget examiner would question the realism of the agency. The character of explanation of output and projected benefits depends upon the program's being demand responsive or directed. Demand responsive programs are reacting to individuals and groups which meet the agency's general criteria of need and seek assistance. In contrast, directed programs are established to fulfill a specific need and are managed directly by government. Demand responsive programs are grants-in-aid and direct benefit (e.g., food stamps) programs. In demand responsive programs, the government cannot control the rate or type of demand; thus it is conditioned by outside factors. In directed programs, the government has a high degree of control over exactly what it will do.

Budget examiners can probe direct programs for the management plan of the agency. The agency normally has a detailed plan of how it will use the resources to achieve specific outputs. It should have a definite fix on the likely benefits and spillover effects of the program. The examiner's role is first to make sure such a plan exists, and secondly to see that the plan has a reasonable chance of being successful. The plan and management should be flexible enough to meet likely contingency situations.

Budget examiners handle demand response programs differently. Budget examiners probe these programs in terms of anticipated demands and likely outputs and benefits. Agency management should have excellent forecasts of likely demand. The agency should have prepared an analysis of various likely funding scenarios and estimated the likely outputs and benefits of each scenario. To the extent that the agency can control the meeting of the program demand, the agency should be able to explain what they can do and the significance of their action in terms of the scenarios and resulting outputs and benefits. If the agency cannot demonstrate such managerial ability, then the agency's ability to manage the requested funds properly can be strongly questioned.

If the budget examiner ever sees vagueness in the information provided, this can serve as a red flag to the examiner. Vague subjects can be carefully isolated because vagueness indicates possibly serious managerial problems. If agency management does not know how to deal with a situation or there is serious internal conflict, then agency budget officers must be vague about those situations in the budget request because the uncertainty cannot, by definition, be resolved. Good budget officers may be able to minimize the problem but they cannot hide the use of a vague answer.

Budget examiners can carefully probe the exact reason for the vagueness. The explanation may be merely a poor presentation rather than management difficulties. If the vagueness is isolated early enough, questions and hearings can be used to determine the exact nature of the problem. This probing requires skill; but unless the agency budget officer directly lies, the budget examiner can isolate the problem, given enough time. Even in the rare cases where the agency personnel lies, a skillful examiner can normally isolate the problem because logical consistency is difficult for a liar to maintain.

Exhibit 6-1 is a list of program goals and objectives for a directed program

EXHIBIT 6-1

City of Riverside, California
Program Goals and Objectives (1976)

Program: Street Services

Program Goal: To provide for the safe and efficient movement of vehicles and pedestrians through maintenance and repair of all facilities located within street right-of-way, with the exception of traffic signal control devices.

Sub-programs:

	Street maintenance	Drainage facilities	Street cleaning	Administrative and support services
Sub-program Goal:	To conserve the value of city streets, alleys and sidewalks through an effective maintenance program.	To control waste water and storm drainage in order to minimize danger to life and property and provide for optimum utilization of streets.	To assist in maintaining an optimum aesthetic standard on public streets and parking lots.	To provide leadership, direction and general administrative support necessary for an effective and efficient street services program.
Sub-program Objectives:	Maximize the life of streets and alleys through an effective preventive maintenance program.	Maintain an effective water drainage system.	Maintain public streets and parking lots in a good, clean condition through an effective street sweeping and flushing program.	Develop and coordinate policies and procedures to improve the street services program.
	Provide regular surface maintenance for all streets and alleys in accordance with city policy.			Provide for manpower and equipment resources sufficient to meet the overall goal of the street services program.

Program:
Sub-program:

Street Maintenance

Activities:

	Street and alley maintenance	Concrete repairs	Street painting	Signing
Work Elements:	Chip sealing	Sidewalk repairs	Centerline painting	Regulatory signs
	Crack sealing	Curb and gutter repairs	Stencil painting	Warning signs
	Shoulder maintenance	Cross gutter repairs	Crosswalk painting	Guide signs
	Unimproved street maintenance	Blockwall repairs	Curb painting	Street name signs
	Alley maintenance	Root pruning		Sign shop
	Street and permit patching			
	Asphalt repairs			
	Bridge repairs			
	Weed control			
	Mosquito and rat control			
	Palm frond removal			
Operational Objectives:	Resurface a total of 620 miles of streets on an average of once every 6 years or 103 miles annually	Maintain and repair curbs, gutters, sidewalks damaged by city tree roots.	Refurbish all street painting annually.	Install all traffic signs and street name signs requested by traffic engineering
*Current Service Levels	*Currently resurfacing only 79 miles annually as follows: Overlaying—26 miles; Slurry sealing—40 miles; Chip sealing—13 miles. (77%)	*Currently only maintaining and repairing 25% of locations. (25%)	*Currently refurbishing on an average of once every 2 years. (50%)	*Currently meeting objective. (100%)
			Complete all traffic engineering requests for street painting within 2 months.	Repair and replace all traffic signs and street name signs as required.
			*Currently meeting objective. (100%)	*Currently meeting objective; approximately 2,800 signs replaced during 1973 calendar year. (100%)

Program:
Subprogram:

Street Services
Street Maintenance

Activities:	Street and alley maintenance	Concrete repairs	Street painting	Signing
Operational Objectives, Continued:	Fog seal all Class A streets every 5 years.			Convert all warning and regulatory signs to new national standards utilizing international symbols by federal target date of January 1, 1975.
*Current Service Levels	*Currently no program. (0%)			*Currently converting 2,000 signs annually beginning in January 1973. At present rate all 10,000 signs will not be changed until January 1, 1978.
	Seal all cracks in pavement as needed.			
	*Currently no program since termination of P. E. P. program. (0%)			Produce a variety of miscellaneous signs and plaques for departmental offices, award and ceremonial purposes, etc.
	Clean and maintain 11 miles of alleys annually.			*Currently meeting objective. (100%)
	*Currently meeting objective. (100%)			
	Grade and maintain all unimproved street shoulders annually.			
	*Currently meeting objective. (100%)			

Program:

Subprogram:

Street Services

Street Maintenance

Activities:	Street and alley maintenance	Concrete repairs	Street painting	Signing
Operational Objectives, Continued:	Grade and maintain 35 miles of Class D streets semi-annually.			
*Current Service Levels	*Currently grading and maintaining on an annual basis. (50%)			
	Repair all chuck holes on major and collector streets within 24 hours of notification.			
	*Currently meeting objective. (100%)			
	Complete all permit patching within 24 hours of notification.			
	*Currently completing patching within 48 hours. (50%)			
	Spray all drainage facilities for weed control on a quarterly basis.			

Program: *Street Services*

Subprogram: *Street Maintenance*

Activities: *Street and alley maintenance* | *Concrete repairs* | *Street painting* | *Signing*

Operational Objectives, Continued:

*Currently accomplishing on a semi-annual basis. (50%)

Current Service Levels

Abate all mosquito breeding sources.

*Currently abating all known sources. (100%)

Investigate and survey home-owners' requests with regard to rat problems.

*Currently meeting objective. (100%)

124

(street services) for the city of Riverside, California. It illustrates how an agency can demonstrate its management plan for budgetary purposes.

Program Inputs and Outputs

The budget examiner should determine key input, process and output measures. These concepts are explained in more depth in chapter 12. Briefly, there are measures which tend to be more indicative than other measures. These indicators show the resources going into the program, what activities are taking place, and the results attributable to the program. These measures are used for comparative and trend analytical purposes. By performing elementary analysis, the budget examiner can determine questionable program budget requests, poor management practices, and identify important changes in the program's environment which are not correctly reflected in the budget request.

Exhibit 6-2 is a checklist used by the city of Los Angeles to review performance reports. Notice how the budget examiner is sensitive to the interrelationship of input, process, and outputs. The examiner maintains a questioning, arm's length relationship with the agency.

The budget examiner can also check the accuracy of tables and data supplied by the agency. Exhaustive checks are not necessary, but any uncommon results, important statistics, and common places where errors occur can always be checked. Tables can be checked by observing if there is proper internal consistency among tables. Often totals of summary columns can be checked against other summary columns for internal consistency. Simple arithmetic errors do occur even on the most important budget requests. Commonly errors occur by not using the correct pay rate scale or by placing personnel into the wrong classification.

EXHIBIT 6-2

Checklist for Review of Performance Reports

General

1. Check total gross man-hours for department with the combined total standard hours plus paid overtime hours as shown for each pay period on the IBM Personnel Audit Reports of the Controller (on file in Budget Administration Division).

Personnel

2. Have any new activities or sub-activities been added over those shown in original work program?
3. If so, how many positions are being used? Cost estimate?
4. Are any previous activities or sub-activities eliminated or curtailed?
5. If so, how many positions which were included in last year's work program have been eliminated? Cost estimate?

Source: Los Angeles, California, City Administrator's Office.

6. Net increase or decrease in cost as result of additions and deletions?
7. Are there any special projects on which work was performed on a one-time basis only?
8. If so, what sub-activities were affected and how many man-hours were devoted to such special projects?
9. How does the actual number of personnel utilized compare with the number of authorized positions?

Man-Hours

10. Where both net man-hours and gross man-hours are reported, what is the percentage of net total to gross total? Are there any sub-activities which have lower percentages than the overall average percentage? Which are they and how much variation from average is there? What are the causes? (Vacations, sick leave, other absences?)
11. How does actual work performed compare with the estimate for each sub-activity?
12. Has there been an increase or decrease in the number of personnel actually utilized over last month's figures?

Man-Hours Per Unit

13. How does the gross man-hours per unit for each sub-activity compare with last month's figures?
14. How does the net man-hours per unit for each sub-activity compare with last month's figures?
15. What is the reason for any increase or decrease?
16. In sub-activities where work performed and work unit are comparable, what is the variation between gross man-hours per unit for such sub-activities?
17. What is the variation between net man-hours per unit for such sub-activities?

Overall Appraisal

18. Based on the above analysis, could any employees have been transferred temporarily during slack periods?
19. If so, how many and in what classes of positions?
20. Based on the above analysis, were any additional employees required to handle peak loads?
21. If so, how many and in what classes of positions?
22. Were there any backlogs of work resulting from lack of sufficient personnel?
23. If so, how much?
24. What class of personnel and how many employees would be required to eliminate backlogs?
25. Are backlogs the result of seasonal variations? Of improper scheduling of vacations? Of greater than normal absences due to sickness? Of unfilled positions? If the latter, what is the recruitment situation?
26. At the end of each quarter, determine what percentage of last year's annual program has been completed for each sub-activity.
27. Will the remaining portion of the annual program be completed by the end of the current fiscal year if that rate of progress is maintained?
28. Will more or less personnel be required in each sub-activity to complete annual program?
29. If so, how many and in what classes of positions?

Budget examiners can carefully review the money requested and be sensitive to hidden revenue sources or "sleight-of-hand" tricks. This is a conventional spender's strategy and the diligent reviewer can determine when such strategy is being used. The examiner must be well versed in backdoor spending techniques and must know if any of them can be used by the agency. The examiner can profit from the use of accounting reports. Use of fund transfer, lag time among administrative reservations, obligations, expenditures, and closing of accounts can be significant in determining hidden revenue. Other types of hidden revenue or improper expenditure estimates require considerable knowledge of the programs, but examiners can sometimes find such savings. For example, possibly the program can use existing government facilities rather than rent or lease new property. Another possibility is interagency or intergovernmental cooperative management agreements which allow savings due to economy of scale.

For the budget examiner, detailed tables from agencies isolate personnel by grade, type, unit, and status (permanent, temporary, part- or full-time). A critical resource is always personnel. Does the agency have too many or too few personnel for the assigned task? Maybe the agency has enough people, but they are of the wrong grade or type, or are poorly distributed among the units. Two common problems are for the agency to overexpand its highest ranks and not to reallocate its personnel once a major task has been accomplished. Examiners cannot address such questions without detailed information on personnel. Another problem is that the personnel hired are not properly trained to do the upgraded and more complex work requirements. Judgments in this area must be predicated on a knowledge of the personnel as well as the type of new challenges facing the agency.

Budget examiners can often profit by comparing the agency's overhead and direct costs. A common mistake in bureaucracies is to allow overhead (i.e., those people and costs who serve to make the agency operate) to grow at the expense of direct costs (i.e., those people and costs who perform the activities directly associated with the agency's mission). Examples of overhead are personnel, legal, housekeeping, and budget activities. The proper size of overhead and even the definition of overhead are topics subject to debate. Ideally, overhead would be large enough to facilitate agency effectiveness and efficiency. In some situations, the overhead activities can grow to a point where agency effectiveness and efficiency are actually decreased. The budget examiner can examine the facts and determine if overhead is becoming excessive.

Some budget items are particularly sensitive and can be watched very closely. Those expense items are often (but not necessarily always) travel, household moving, and training. They are sensitive because abuses can easily occur. Politicians often will ask questions on these topics, and they are often among the most controllable of expense items, thus they are often reduced during the current year. Budget examiners should be aware of these items and insure they are defensible. Deep cuts in these budget items are usually unwise. They provide essential management flexibility, enable managers to develop their people, and provide useful "rewards" for the best personnel. Requests must be defensible, but deep cuts are to be resisted until necessity forces such action in the current year.

The data can be used to identify relationships between program demands and work load. For example, there tends to be a positive identifiable relationship between the population under 25 in an area and the number of parole officers needed. If such relationships can be verified, then the examiner is in a much better position to judge the budget request.

Trends on program inputs and outputs are valuable information for the budget examiner. For example, if resources have been increasing and outputs decreasing, then serious questions must be raised concerning the efficiency and possibly even effectiveness of the program. What are the causes underlying trends and deviation of the apparent natural trend? Does there appear to be any positive or negative relationship between and among trends? For example, does the use of salt or sand in snow conditions tend to be more effective? This information can lead to suggestions resulting in the use of cheaper substances while maintaining the same level of service to the public.

Comparative data on program inputs and outputs are also valuable information. What do other comparable cities spend for the same type services? What levels of output do they achieve? What explains the differences? Can those positive advantages be achieved in the budget examiner's city?

3 Emphasis and Change

Whether the budget request is presented in incremental or zero-base format, the budget examiner needs information on yearly budget emphases and changes in emphases from prior years. Decision makers wish to know how much stress is being placed on a given program relative to other program efforts. Balance is a political consideration, thus it is useful information for decision makers. They also wish to know if the agency is shifting its policy from previous years. This can best be determined by comparing the budget request with previous budget requests and actual obligation/expenditure patterns.

Budgets can be categorized into various logical subdivisions. A single categorization is probably inadequate for the variety of analytical needs of the budget examiner. One categorization should reflect the major agency tasks, projects, and continuing activities. Another categorization may be necessary to relate the inputs (e.g., dollars requested) to agency goals and intended benefits. However, often one categorization may be sufficient for both purposes if the agency is not handicapped by multiple inconsistent objectives. Exhibit 6-1 illustrates one of those less complex agency situations. A categorization using line item information is normally not useful because various purposes can lie behind the use of the same objects of expenditure.

Categorizations can provide comparative information over several fiscal years. Dollars requested, possible specific inputs and outputs can be presented in terms of the prior year, actual current year estimates, budget year estimates, and possibly budget year plus five estimates. Such a display of data permits comparative analyses by fiscal year. Thus program increases and decreases over time can be isolated.

Complex programs, involving contracts extending beyond the budget year, can be misleading in terms of increases and decreases. Obligations can be made for continuing, expanding, or starting new programs. The decrease or increase in a given fiscal year only gives useful information on the rate of obligation, and says nothing about the use of the money. The categorization in such programs should indicate the changes in the funding level of programs divided into sub-categories of continuing and expanded programs. Also any new programs can be identified as such. As noted in the previous chapter, the spender's strategy calls for the use of flexible definitions by the spender. The budget examiner can understand the nature of each program so that definitions and categorizations can be challenged.

The previous categorizations and related work are all designed to help the budget examiner identify emphases and shifts. What programs, projects, activities, or tasks are receiving greatest stress? This is judged in the context of the available resource, the maximum effort which could be given, and the relative emphases among the programs. Each is important in judging "emphasis." What programs, projects, activities, or tasks are receiving increased or decreased support? To answer that question fully, the budget examiner discovers whether changes are addressed to existing or new programs. Also, the examiner relates the change to program outputs including anticipated benefits or harm to society and individuals. This analysis helps answer the followup question: Is the change worth it? Budget examiners seek *hard data* and get *written responses* to this type of inquiry in order to avoid later misunderstandings between the examiner and agency officials.

Crosswalks

One of the most useful analytical tools for the budget examiner is the crosswalk. It is a simple matrix table relating different categories. It serves as a conceptual bridge between two organizational means to describe and control agency activities. By constructing several bridges, the examiner can explore various organizational perspectives on what should be done and what is done as well as check important interrelations. Some of the more common categories which can be crosswalked are:

1. programs, projects, activities, tasks;
2. uniform object classifications;
3. appropriation structure;
4. major organizational units;
5. objectives used in connection with management-by-objectives or program evaluations;
6. funds (including grants-in-aid) used in government accounting.

A few simple examples can illustrate the use of the crosswalk. A common crosswalk is between the so-called program structure (e.g., a given set of mutually exclusive programs, projects, activities, and tasks) and the appropriation structure. The program structure is used by the executive to make major decisions on program direction. The appropriation structure is the langauge used by the legislature to make its decisions. Both decision makers are significant so the agency and the budget examiners must be able to translate from one language to the other—the crosswalk is the device which permits translation.

Another common crosswalk is between the program structure or appropriation structure and the major organizational units in the agency. This permits the examiner to pin down who is responsible and judge management capability to carry out the budget. Without such a crosswalk, lower level management responsibility and judgments about capability cannot be made by the examiner.

Two other useful crosswalks for accountants and budget examiners are (1) appropriation structure—uniform object classification, and (2) funds—uniform item object classification. The budget examiner uses these crosswalks when a line-item budget is used to control the government. Also these crosswalks are useful to achieve a better understanding of exactly what does take place under various labels. Exhibit 6-3 illustrates an activity to appropriation crosswalk where the appropriation is by major object of expenditure.

An unused but potentially significant crosswalk is between the MBO objectives and the program structure or appropriation structure. MBO can be an extremely useful public management technique, but often it is applied without reference to the budget. This is foolish because how can one reasonably expect objectives to be met without also establishing that necessary resources are available to conduct the program? The two should not be treated in isolation, but they are by many agencies. If they are treated separately this strongly indicates a lack of coordination of management direction within the agency because both MBO and the budget are tools to achieve management direction.

If the agency has activities which fulfill more than one objective at a time, then a program evaluation objective-program structure crosswalk is treated somewhat differently from the other crosswalks. Normally, each matrix square states dollar amounts representing mutually exclusive activities. This permits the crosswalk to be validated for internal consistency by merely checking if the horizontal and vertical summary columns are equal. In the case of evaluation objectives, dollar amounts can be counted more than once if they fulfill more than one purpose. For example, a given activity may increase safety and reduce energy consumption (e.g., enforcing the 55 mile per hour speed limit). Thus, the crosswalk matrix squares would show the dollar amount (maybe even the name of the activity) under two different vertical categories. This type of double counting can also exist with a crosswalk using MBO objectives.

The budget examiner can ask to see various crosswalks for the reasons suggested above. Essentially, crosswalks help the examiner determine if the

EXHIBIT 6-3

Summary of Appropriations to Activities
Classified by the Major Objects of Expenditure
(000 Omitted)

Name of activity	Total	Personal services	Contractual services	Materials, supplies	Equipment	Capital outlay	Debt service	Contributions, indemnities	Interfund transfers
Public Safety									
Police	$6,712	$5,903	$9	$425	$172	$175	$7	$20	$1
Animal Regulation	99	79	—	16	4	—	—	—	7
Fire	4,551	3,945	13	246	77	225	9	29	—
Inspection	833	763	—	67	3	—	—	—	—
Social Service	14	13	—	1	—	—	—	—	—
Civil Defense	73	—	—	73	—	—	—	—	—
Lifeguard Service	310	260	—	28	22	—	—	—	—
Radio Maintenance	254	159	27	40	28	—	—	—	—
TOTAL PUBLIC SAFETY	12,846	11,122	49	896	296	400	16	49	8

Source: Operating Budget Manual, Lennox Moak and Kathryn Killian, MFOA, Chicago, 1963, p. 229.

agency has internally consistent management direction and control capability to insure the integrity of that direction. If the agency does not act with one management direction, the crosswalks expose that problem. If the agency cannot provide crosswalks, this suggests poor management. It is possible for the agency to manage its affairs well without using crosswalks, but they should be able to construct them if there is a consistent management direction. If crosswalks cannot be constructed or if the ones provided show inconsistent management policy, then the budget examiner can probe further to isolate the exact nature and reasons for the internal management inconsistency.

Crosswalks can also be used to check for external consistency of management direction with past publicly announced positions, and orders of higher authorities. A set of crosswalks are among the best evidence of the exact management policies of an agency. Those policies may not be consistent with the agency's past policies or positions articulated to the public or policy directives from higher authorities. If the budget examiner happens to have the crosswalks from past budgets, then they can be compared with the most recent crosswalks. In this manner, policy shifts can be isolated. Budget examiners can also determine if the policy direction from the crosswalks matches public positions and policy established by higher authorities. If there is inconsistency, then further probing may be warranted to determine the reason for the inconsistency.

Program and Financial Plan

Program and financial plans (PFP) are required periodically (quarterly or semi-annually). They are summary tables of the budget categorized by major programs and activities. In the federal government, the PFP includes both obligations and disbursements; but obligations are normally sufficient for state and local government purposes. The information covers the past year, current year, budget, and budget year plus five.

The PFP should be analyzed by the examiner for patterns reflecting policy and consistency with previously established management policy. The PFP should reflect any changes in policy and it is particularly useful prior to the budget call to forecast possible agency requests. Quick comparisons against past PFP's can be made to see if an evolution in policy is occurring. If changes are not occurring, the agency should be questioned, because agency policy is rarely constant and no change reflects a neglect to update the PFP. The PFP is an advance warning and the examiner can encourage the agency to use the PFP in that manner.

Program Analysis

There is an important difference between budget review and program analysis. In budget review, the focus is upon understanding existing or planned management policy as reflected in the budget. Secondary questions of efficiency are considered, but the primary thrust is to examine the planned management operation. In program analysis, the focus is upon considering the new policy directions which can be reflected in the budget. Both budget reviews and policy analyses are necessary for proper consideration of a budget.

An often-heard complaint of high level executive officials is that they really could not get the necessary information from the agencies to judge budget requests. Often this is more an admission of professional incompetency than a commentary on the budget process. If a reasonable effort as explained here went into budget examining by competent professionals, then the central review staff would be in a position to judge the management policy reflected in the request and alternative policy directions. Almost all questionable items and management problems would be isolated. Sensitive policy considerations would be understood. Decisions may still be difficult to make because the choices are unpleasant; but nothing more could be asked, given the limitations of analysis.

This section focuses upon program analysis. This approach to examining policy issues relative to the budget was popularized in the 1960s with planning-programming-budgeting.

Selecting Issues

Selection of potential issues can proceed systematically. What are the unsettled influential issues which determine program direction and emphasis? What issues are being raised by key influential people in the legislature, executive, clientele, media, and judicial settings? What are the apparent policy dilemmas facing the agency? The analysts can use these questions to develop a reasonable list of potential issues for analysis. Normally program issues are abundant. The usual problem is not to find issues but to select the best issues for program review purposes. The Urban Institute has developed the following criteria for selecting issues for analysis.

Importance of an issue

1. Is there a decision to be made by the government? Can the analysis significantly influence the adoption of various alternatives?
2. Does the issue involve large costs or major consequences for services?
3. Is there substantial room for improving program performance?

Feasibility of analysis

4. Can the problem be handled by program analysis?
5. Is there time for the analysis to be done before the key decisions must be made?
6. Are personnel and funds available to do the analysis?
7. Do sufficient data exist to undertake the analysis, and can needed data be gathered within the time available?

The first consideration is the importance of the issue. As suggested by the above criteria, the potential significance of an analysis of the issue, the consequence, and potential for improvement should be considered. If no one will use an analysis of an issue, then proceeding with the analysis is certainly foolish. Given the lack of time to perform analysis, the analyst is normally wise to concentrate on the big issue especially if notable improvements are possible.

The next consideration is the feasibility of analysis. Many problems do not lend themselves to program analysis or the time constraint is so brief that useful analysis cannot be conducted prior to the time the key decisions are made. Possibly personnel, funds, or data limitation may exist which preclude analysis. Each of these factors must honestly be assessed before work on program analysis begins or the effort may be worthless.

Exhibit 6-4 presents some illustrations of the issues which might be subject to program analysis.

EXHIBIT 6-4

Illustrative Issues for Program Analysis

Law Enforcement

1. What is the most effective way of distributing limited police forces—by time of day, day of week, and geographical location?
2. What types of police units (foot patrolmen, one- or two-man police cars, special task forces, canine corps units, or others) should be used and in what mix?
3. What types of equipment (considering both current and new technologies) should be used for weaponry, for communications, and for transportation?
4. How can the judicial process be improved to provide more expeditious service, keep potentially dangerous persons from running loose, and at the same time protect the rights of the innocent?
5. How can criminal detection institutions be improved to maximize the probability of rehabilitation, while remaining a deterrent to further crime?

Fire Protection

1. Where should fire stations be located, and how many are needed?
2. How should firefighting units be deployed, and how large should units be?
3. What types of equipment should be used for communications, transportation, and firefighting?
4. Are there fire prevention activities, such as inspection of potential fire hazards or school educational programs, that can be used effectively?

Health and Social Services

1. What mix of treatment programs should do the most to meet the needs of the expected mix of clients?
2. What prevention programs are desirable for the groups that seem most likely to suffer particular ailments?

Housing

1. To what extent can housing code enforcement programs be used to decrease the number of families living in substandard housing? Will such programs have an adverse effect on the overall supply of low-income housing in the community?
2. What is the appropriate mix of code enforcement with other housing programs to make housing in the community adequate?
3. What is the best mix of housing rehabilitation, housing maintenance, and new construction to improve the quantity and quality of housing?

Employment

1. What relative support should be given to training and employment programs which serve different client groups?
2. What should be the mix among outreach programs, training programs, job-finding and matching programs, antidiscrimination programs, and post-employment follow-up programs?

Waste

1. How should waste be collected and disposed of, given alternative visual, air, water, and pollution standards?
2. What specific equipment and routings should be used?

Recreation and Leisure

1. What type, location, and size of recreation facilities should be provided for those desiring them?
2. How should recreation facilities be divided among summer and winter, daytime and nighttime, and indoor and outdoor activities?
3. What, and how many, special summer programs should be made available for out-of-school youths?
4. What charges, if any, should be made to users, considering such factors as differential usage and ability to pay?

Issue Assessment

Once the issues have been defined, then a preliminary assessment can be made before an in-depth analysis is conducted. In most situations, an agency suggests an issue and the central budget office decides which issue to investigate. That issue or issues may or may not be the ones suggested by the agency. The involvement of the central budget office is wise as it helps to insure the significance of the report once it is written, but the lack of a preliminary assessment of the issue is not wise. In far too many analytical situations, reports have been commissioned without a proper appreciation of what was requested. The instructions requesting the study may have been too vague or misleading. Another possibility is that on more thought the study may not have been requested at all thus saving thousands or even millions of dollars in conducting an analysis. Preliminary assessments are extremely useful.

The issue assessment is a written presentation which identifies and describes the major features of a significant issue facing the government. The assessment is only a few pages long, but it clearly sets out the ingredients which would be considered in a major issue study. According to Harry P. Hatry of the Urban Institute, the outline or major subjects in an issue assessment are:

The Problem

1. What is the problem and its causes? Identify specific groups (e.g., the poor) affected. How are they affected? Identify characteristics of the group. How large and significant is the problem now? What are the likely future dimensions of the problem?

Objectives and Evaluation Criteria

2. Define the fundamental purposes and benefits of the program. Identify the means to judge—evaluation criteria—the accomplishment or progress toward the program objectives.

Current Activities and Agencies Involved

3. Identify all relevant groups involved in attempting to deal with the problem. Identify what each group is doing including costs and impacts. Activities, cost and benefits should be projected into the future.

Other Significant Factors

4. Cite the other major factors including political realities that affect the problem. Identify unusual resources, timing limitations, or other factors of significance.

Alternatives

5. Describe the alternative programs to meet the problem and the major characteristics of each.

Recommendations for Follow-up

6. Choices among alternatives is an inappropriate subject because, by definition, this work is only an assessment. Recommendations can be made on the next administrative step (e.g., full-scale analysis). What is the best timing and scope of the needed follow-up analysis? Should the analysis be a quick response or an in-depth study? Frank descriptions of analytical difficulties should be cited. What major data problems exist? How should they be dealt with under the circumstances?

The assessment serves as the basis to decide to request a special analytical study and to frame instructions for the study.

Commentary on Analysis

The conduct of analysis largely depends upon the subject to be analyzed, the context of the study, and the techniques used. Each of these subjects is outside the scope of this chapter and can properly be studied under the heading of microeconomics, operations research, systems analysis, and statistics. Chapter 11 discusses some elementary analytical concepts useful in budgeting as well as in explaining benefit-cost analysis.

There are ten factors—five technical and five bureaucratic—which particularly influence the results of analysis. Those factors are:

1. study size;
2. study timing;
3. methodological adequacy;
4. consideration of implementation;
5. nature of problem studied;
6. decision maker interest;
7. implementor's participation;
8. single-agency issue;
9. proposed changes in funding;
10. immediate decision needed.

There are five factors which appear to be more significant. The three most significant "technical" factors are study timing (i.e., studies were well timed so that study findings were available at key decision points); consideration of implementation (i.e., studies included an explicit consideration of political and administrative issues which might affect the implementation of study findings); and nature of problem studied (i.e., studies focused on well-defined problems rather than on broad or open-ended ones). The two most significant "bureaucratic" factors are immediate decision needed (i.e., issues which could not be deferred by policy makers); and decision maker interest (i.e., issues in which decision makers had shown clear interest).

In program analysis, care must be taken to avoid four common mistakes which occur due to an unrealistic desire to analyze for the sake of analysis. One mistake can be labeled "search under the lamp." A well-known story tells of the man who was searching at night for his lost watch under a street light. A friend comes by and offers to aid in the search. The friend asks where the man lost the watch and the man replies that the watch was lost half a block up the street. The friend then asks why the man is searching next to the street lamp. The man answers that the light is much better under the street light. In policy analysis situations, analysts often will concentrate their investigation on those aspects which are easy to measure and downplay the aspects difficult to measure. Thus they are looking under the street lamp instead of "up the street" where the watch was lost.

Another common mistake is becoming fascinated by technique. An intellectual challenge for an analyst is to use and develop more sophisticated analytical—often mathematical—techniques. The normal desire is to select issues which require complex techniques or use more complex techniques when simpler ones would be adequate. Analysts should address the analytical problems and not techniques, otherwise there is means-ends confusion.

A third mistake is to delay reports and even policy decisions so that analyses can be performed for their own sake. Analysts can be consumed with interest in the analytical question much like some people are consumed by crossword puzzles, mysteries, and good books. This consuming interest can overwhelm the original reason for the analysis. As was pointed out earlier, report timeliness is critical and sometimes analytical purity is sacrificed for timeliness.

The fourth mistake is to overanalyze. In some situations, a good analyst quietly thinking for a few hours may produce results equal to or better than an army of survey researchers. We automatically tend to use certain well-known approaches to analysis without appreciating their limitations and the tolerance for error implicit in the issue being studied. The advantage of the issue assessment mentioned earlier is to avoid such a mistake.

A final commentary on analysis is that there may be only "poor" solutions to problems. This commentary may seem obvious, but this realization is often difficult for decision makers to accept. If a program analysis is conducted and only poor "solutions" are cited, the decision maker can conclude either the "solutions" are indeed poor or the analysis was bad. Thus, the analyst can be placed in an awkward position. The only professionally acceptable course of action is to be sure there are no desirable answers and to explain this fact properly in the analyst's report.

Presentations of Results: Some Prescriptions

A common failure of program analysis is providing a poor presentation of study results. The work may be excellent, but the presentation is inadequate.

The first advice on presenting results is to review them carefully before they are distributed. The pressures of meeting a deadline and the distasteful chore of proofing combine to discourage proper review of papers before they are distributed. These final checks are essential if embarrassing mistakes or insensitive political statements are to be avoided.

Report findings should be in writing. Oral reports are useful but they should supplement or summarize written reports. Written reports provide the essential record which is often useful even years after a report was prepared.

Care must be taken to prepare compact, clear summaries. The summary is normally the first important portion of the report that is read—the other material may never be read. Long, vague summaries are dysfunctional as they discourage use of the report.

In most program analysis reports, two or three options are discussed. If only one option were discussed, then the credibility of the report would be questioned. Many options only tend to confuse matters. Two or three options are adequate normally to illustrate the varieties of solutions. If the range of solutions is broad, the presentation of only two or three options is done to illustrate the types of solutions.

Studies must set out limitations and assumptions. Professional standards alone require such candor. On a more practical level, professional reputation and confidence are enhanced by frank, honest reports. A decision maker may not like the qualifications, but if something goes wrong the analyst is protected by that candor. Also, the decision makers are appraised fully of the risks inherent in their decisions.

Studies should discuss potential windfalls and pitfalls related to the issue. Windfalls are collateral benefits resulting from actions and decisions. Pitfalls are collateral hazards or disadvantages. Both can be easily overlooked in the analyses and by decision makers. The potential for oversight is the reason why this material should be in the report.

The studies should contain simple graphics where possible to communicate major findings and conclusions. Most readers will benefit from both written and graphic explanations. Graphics should not stand alone—reference should be made to them in the text. Complete graphics should be avoided because readers may not be able to understand them.

Clarity requires that jargon be avoided. If a special vocabulary is well known and used, then such jargon (e.g., piggyback containers, subsystem) can be used. Jargon is the shorthand means of communication. However, most program analysis reports are meant for managers and other decision makers unschooled in the jargon, thus it only makes the report difficult to read.

Reports and studies should be written for the decision makers. Authors of reports and studies should know who are the intended and likely users of their work. What are the backgrounds, knowledge, and biases of the report and study users? If the users have extensive technical knowledge, then authors should use that fact in preparing the report. If the user has strong biases and the report finding runs counter to those findings, then greater care should be taken to explain and fully document the findings.

From the public budgeting perspective, one of the most obvious failures in the presentation of program analysis results is the omission of how the recommendations should be translated to operational management direction. People working in budgeting are interested in policy debates and analysis, but their lives involve operational decisions. Study findings and recommendations must be translated to the operational before they can be treated as something more than a possibility. Exactly in what ways should the current program be changed? What specifically are the present and future budget implications? These questions should be addressed in the program analysis reports and studies if they are to be meaningful to the budget process.

Role of the Chief Executive

The product of program analysis is meant for decision makers, especially chief executives. If there is support from the chief executive and that person uses the products of program analysis, then there is a reasonable chance that program analysis will be significant in the government decision-making process. On the other hand, without top level support and use, program analysis as an activity is worthless. Detailed top level involvement is not needed but the following types of involvement are essential. According to the Urban Institute, officials should:

1. participate actively in the selection of program and policy issues for analysis;
2. assign responsibility for the analysis to a unit of the organization which can conduct the study objectively;
3. ensure that participation and cooperation are obtained from relevent agencies:
4. provide adequate staff to meet a timely reporting schedule;
5. insist that the objectives, evaluation criteria, client groups, and program alternatives considered in the analysis include those of prime importance;
6. have a work schedule prepared and periodically monitored;
7. review results, and if findings seem valid, see that they are used.[1]

Conclusions

Both budget reviews and program analyses are significant budget activities. Budget reviews are the inquiries essential to determining what the agencies are doing. This knowledge permits decision makers to assess the weak spots in the budget request and judge the management capability of the group requesting budget support. Understanding what constitutes a thorough budget review permits the agency budget official to anticipate inquiries and establish that highly important confidence level discussed in chapter 5. Program analyses are designed to consider new policy direction. Ideally, they provide the budget process with fresh, well-considered policies which can be reflected in future budgets. Together budget reviews and program analyses provide the analytical means to apply greater intelligence to the difficult task of preparing and deciding upon budgets.

This chapter provided some guidance on how one goes about budget reviews and program analyses. However, there is no recipe for the use of that guidance. These activities require highly intelligent diligent thinkers who can work under pressure. A blending of analytical expertise and bureaucratic sense is required. The analyst must consider each challenge separately and adapt the guidance presented in this chapter in terms of contextual situation. Unfortunately, a contingency theory for budget reviews or program analysis has not yet been developed. Therefore, each professional must apply his best judgment without the benefit of a rigorous, systematically tested contingency theory.

A great deal of stress is placed upon the correct budget format whereas the more significant budget reviews and program analyses are not emphasized. Format reforms like line-item, performance, program, zero-base are means to foster control and analysis. Each format is only important in the larger, more significant

---

[1]Harry Hatry, Louis Blair, Donald Fisk, and Wayne Kimmel, *Program Analysis for State and Local Government* (Washington, D.C.: The Urban Institute, 1976), p. 11.

context of budget reviews and program analyses. Political rhetoric and other factors lead us to discuss format rather than to seek an upgrading of budget reviews and program analyses tailored to specific contexts. Better budgeting will result from better budget reviews and program analyses. Those will occur when better talent is hired, a great deal more training is provided in budgeting, and data and format requests are designed for the budget situation.

REVIEW QUESTIONS

1. What should be asked in a typical analysis of a budget request?
2. Explain the significance of a crosswalk. What would be crosswalked and why?
3. In what ways is program (policy) analysis different from budget reviews?
4. Explain how one goes about developing a list of major program issues and selecting from that list.
5. Why should an issue assessment be made prior to a full-scale analysis? What should be considered in such an assessment and why?
6. What factors influence an analysis? Why is the chief executive particularly significant? What type of chief executive support is important?
7. Explain some of the common mistakes in analysis and presentation of analytical results.

REFERENCES

BIERMAN, HAROLD, JR. and SEYMOUR SMIDT. *The Capital Budgeting Decision*. New York: Macmillan, 1966.

COOK, THOMAS J. and FRANK SCIOLI, JR. "Resources for Public Policy Analysis," *Policy Studies Journal*, 1, 2 (Winter 1972).

DYE, THOMAS R. *Understanding Public Policy*. Englewood Cliffs, N.J.: Prentice-Hall, 1972.

GOODNOW, FRANK J. "The Limits of Budgetary Control," *Proceedings of the American Political Science Association*, Baltimore 1913.

HATRY, HARRY P. "Overview of Modern Program Analysis Characteristics and Techniques: Modern Program Analysis—Hero or Villain?" Washington, D.C.: Urban Institute, 1969.

———, LOUIS BLAIR, DONALD FISK, and WAYNE KIMMEL. *Program Analysis for State and Local Government*, Washington, D.C.: Urban Institute, 1976.

HOFFMAN, D. ROBERT et al. "Federal Financial Management: Accounting and Auditing Practices." American Institute of CPA, 1976.

JACOBS, FARWELL and NEAVE JACOBS. *Financial Institutions*. Homewood, Ill.: Richard D. Irwin, 1972.

LINDBLOM, CHARLES E. *The Policy Making Process*. Englewood Cliffs, N.J.: Prentice-Hall, 1968.

MCCAFFERY, JERRY. "MBO and the Federal Budgetary Process," *Public Administration Review*, 36, 1 (January/February 1976), 33–39.

MILLER, ERNEST G. "Implementing PPBS: Problems and Prospects," *Public Administration Review* 23, 5 (September/October 1969).

MOAK, LENNOX L. and KATHRYN W. KILLIAN. *Operating Budget Manual*. Chicago: Municipal Finance Officers Association, 1963.

SCHWARTZ, ELI. "The Cost of Capital and Investment Criteria in the Public Sector," *Journal of Finance*, 25 (March 1970), 135–42.

SCOTT, CLAUDIA DEVITA. *Forecasting Local Government Spending*. Washington, D.C.: The Urban Institute, 1972.

WILDAVSKY, AARON. *The Politics of the Budgetary Process*. Boston: Little, Brown, 1964.

SEVEN

Operating Budgets and Cash Management

The actual execution of the budget and fund management are not as politically and behaviorally oriented as the budget formulation phase, but they are complex and important. Control is the most significant emphasis in budget execution because both the executive and legislative officials demand that the agency follow the established policy set down in the budget. A significant concern is the correct use of idle cash due to the lag between collecting taxes and spending money. Idle cash can be invested thus earning extra revenue for the government. This chapter will explain control of budget execution, important budget concepts and reports associated with operating budgets, and cash management and government security investments. Other topics in this chapter include:

1. how responsibilities can be fixed on key officials and why that designation is helpful in ensuring proper control;
2. budget execution suggestions which reflect an appreciation of common management problems;
3. factors and pitfalls which should be weighed in developing the operating budget;
4. current year adjustment and policy reinterpretations;
5. administrative reservations, allotments, and other budget concepts;
6. expenditure controls;
7. cash internal control;
8. management information systems;
9. significance and procedures for cash management;
10. techniques used to determine proper cash and security positions;
11. basics of investment in marketable securities.

Designing Control

Fixing Responsibility

If control is to be established, careful consideration must go into designing procedures and fixing responsibility. One of the most effective ways to achieve control is to associate a specific program or programs with an office. Only the person holding that office has the power to obligate or control expenditures. Care is taken to avoid having more than one person authorizing obligations for the program; thus errors or fraud can be traced to the responsible person. If responsibility is split, then mistakes are more difficult to correct and legal actions are more difficult to pursue.

The Federal Anti-Deficiency Act is designed to focus responsibility. The director of the Office of Management and Budget must apportion appropriated money and other funds into specific amounts available for portions of the fiscal year for particular legally sanctioned projects or activities. The appropriation and funds are apportioned to the agencies. Two officers are given special responsibilities. The agency head is responsible for obligations and the integrity of the budget control system. The agency budget officer is responsible for insuring the money is not over obligated. The Anti-Deficiency Act states that a person knowingly and willfully violating the apportionments can be fined and imprisoned. If the person violates the apportionments without knowledge, then that mistake subjects the person to administrative discipline such as a reprimand, suspension from duty without pay, or removal from office. This Act fixes responsibility quite clearly and it has been an effective device.

Budget Execution

Budget execution depends on top level support. Top management must recognize the importance of proper budget execution and support the budget office. No procedures can work unless top management uses them. If the agency head is willing to overspend the budget or refuses to insist that useful budget forms be followed, then budget execution will be chaotic and lack control. The agency head need not develop the procedures or take an active role, but that agency head must support the budget officer who does develop the procedures. Ideally, the agency head would understand public budgeting sufficiently to demand proper budget execution, but that is not essential to the budget officer who is highly competent. If the agency head supports the budget officer, then budget execution can work effectively. The operating managers in the organization must also support the budget system. They must understand the system in terms of how it affects them and what they must do in support of the system. Ideally, they should understand the larger context of the system and public budgeting in general so that problems and requests can be anticipated. If operating managers do not support the system, then reports and other needs are not timely or are incorrect, thus embarrassing and possibly even causing administrative hardships.

Budget execution also depends on a qualified budget staff and a positive attitude toward the concept of public trust. If the budget staff is unaware of the needs of budget execution, then serious management problems are likely to occur. If there are insufficient people on the staff, then they will be overwhelmed, thus forcing them to concentrate on major problems and allowing some routine matters to become major problems. Many employees, especially top management and budget office employees, have a sense of public trust. If they view their job as a means to further private interests, then the possibility of corruption is increased. In addition, employees should be concerned with economy and efficiency. The first concern should be program effectiveness, but economy and efficiency are important if the government is to get maximum use for its tax dollar. Also budget behavior tends to foster a maximum spending approach, and an economy-efficiency ethic is necessary to overcome this natural tendency in budgeting.

A budget execution system should be established which gives direction to agency activities and permits continuous and current reviews to determine if planned objectives are being met. One approach is to link an operating budget with management-by-objectives (MBO). If this is done, each agency unit is asked to develop objectives and progress reports. A crosswalk (explained in chapter 6) is used to link MBO and the operating budget. The operating budget should be keyed to the major line units in the organization so that programs, objectives, and dollar amounts are related to line organizational units.

In order to work smoothly as an organization and to avoid intercommunication difficulties, established procedures are needed to change work plans, schedules, and use of funds. Those procedures should be designed to insure all factors are considered and all key people in and outside the organization are notified of the decision in a timely manner. Circumstances do arise where procedures must be short-circuited; but if the procedures are designed properly, short-circuiting of procedures will be infrequent. The design of procedures is always a difficult task and care must be taken to make them as simple and effective as possible.

To fix responsibility, formal authorization is given each official who will order the spending of money. The authorization is reviewed to be sure such delegations of authority are permissible under law. The authorization is written carefully so that any later confusion and misunderstandings on the authorization are eliminated. Allotments and operating budgets can be coordinated with the formal authorizations so that officials know how much money they must deal with as well as any other guidance necessarily associated with the dollar amounts.

The accounting and related record systems can be designed to serve prescribed budgetary needs. Accounting is described in more depth in the following chapter. Briefly, the budget execution activity is carried out in a larger context than accounting, but the actual recording of transactions should be done so that analysis can compare actual practice with planned practice as defined in the budget. This comparison is essential if the analyst is to know if the policy was carried out.

Another concern in budget execution is to develop a system which monitors considerations such as legality, propriety, and economy. In some governments, the legality and economy issues are monitored by means of preaudits. The advantages of catching these errors must be considered against the complex expensive procedures added to government operation. In many grant-in-aid programs, an elaborate procedure to check legality, propriety, economy, equal opportunity, and environmental quality is probably justifiable. If the program is a routine daily operation such as street maintenance, then an elaborate clearance procedure would be foolish. In those circumstances, management judgment would be needed to seek special advice on matters like environmental issues when unusual conditions warranted such advice. The use of special clearance procedures can be institutionalized if the issue becomes common; thus overall time and effort can be saved by checking the matter before obligations are made.

Once the budget execution system has been designed, there are three helpful operational considerations. First, if possible, performance standards—maybe in connection with management-by-objectives—can be established in connection with the operating budget. This would greatly aid in productivity studies and performance budgeting. Second, the nature of the unit's activity often does not lend itself to performance standards; but if it does, advanced planning linking performance estimates with available funding levels is also a useful management method. Third, regardless of the type of government activity, financial obligations can be scheduled in advance to achieve a desired rate of expenditure and avoid a final month deficit.

In developing and using a budget execution system, several factors are weighed carefully. Must the operating budget be prepared under unusual legislative appropriation conditions, or is a revision (e.g., supplemental appropriation) likely? Is a continuing resolution in effect? What size and structure is the organization (e.g., field, regions, area offices)? What type of financial concepts (these are explored later in this chapter) are appropriate to use in the context of the organization? What are the sources of funds and how is that important to the budget execution system? What financial, quantified work unit data, personnel, and manpower measures should be collected, and how? How should personnel ceilings and personnel restrictions be enforced or reflected in the budget execution system? What should be the frequency, level, and coordination means for budget execution reporting? Each of these questions must be considered and answered in the context of the work environment. Each answer can help budget officials better design and operate the budget execution system. Followup is essential. Frequent and regular reports are needed to check on work progress, objectives yet unaccomplished, and the status of the various funds (funds are explained in the next chapter on accounting). If a problem or question arises from the reports, then prompt, regular and careful followup is needed or the problems and questions tend to be forgotten until they become major problems. An organized system of audits and inspections must be established to verify and supplement the reporting system. If audits and inspections do not exist then fraud, cheating, or merely poor operational practices are more difficult to isolate before they become a widespread problem.

Pitfalls to avoid

An operating budget can:

1. become unmanageable to top, middle, and first line managers if it is not carefully designed for each level of management;
2. be too complex and detailed for management and thus become cumbersome or useless;
3. be too late or too inaccurate for decision-making purposes;
4. be out-of-synchronization with the accounting system;
5. be out of touch with the rest of the budget process;
6. be ignored by top management, thus guaranteeing its ultimate failure.

Some of these major pitfalls were discussed in the previous section, but they should be stressed again. Designing an operating budget requires careful attention. For example, the budget and accounting offices involve various people who are trained differently. Each group views its needs separately and often the operating budget system is developed or becomes nonsynchronized with the accounting system. Care must be taken to avoid this natural tendency.

An operating budget must serve all levels of budgeting. A tendency is to be too demanding of the first line managers and thus make their tasks even more complex. Care can be taken to understand the needs and burdens placed on each level of management. However, the operating budget must provide information in a timely manner especially to top management, and it should provide essential information for other phases in the budget cycle.

If the operating budget is ignored by top management, then the whole process is likely to be a failure. The key person in the agency is the head, and that person has the power to make exceptions to the operating budget. This power is essential in order to provide managerial flexibility to adapt to unusual circumstances which can and do arise. If that power is abused by frequent needless exceptions, then the discipline of the operating budget breaks down and advantages of the procedures are lost. An equally serious matter is when the agency head does not even create a budget execution system or does not update the system. The agency cannot be protected from bad management when it occurs at the highest levels.

Current Year Adjustments

Regardless of how well a budget is planned, adjustments are made in the current year. Sometimes the adjustments involve transferring funds from one fund or appropriation to another. Sometimes the adjustment involves new appropriations and the legislature must pass supplemental appropriations. The reasons for changes vary from poor management to unanticipated events (e.g., heavy snow falls) to political strategies (e.g., legislative approval is more likely in a supplemental request). In many state and local governments, the law requires almost all changes must be approved by the legislature. In some local governments, the executive has greater latitude and does make changes unilaterally to such an extent that the changed operating budget is significantly different from the legislatively approved budget.

Normally, changes are small and appropriations are written broadly enough so that legislative approval is not needed. If significant changes do occur and new legislation is not needed, the agency is still wise to inform the legislature of the change. Otherwise, a poor relationship can develop between the agency and its appropriation committees.

Often transfer of appropriations occurs when functions are transferred to other agencies. The sums are not changing, but who has control of the funds is changing. This often occurs in government reorganizations.

Requests for budget adjustments are rigorously reviewed with the exception of when functions are transferred. Budget adjustments should be rare or both the executive and the legislature will spend most of their time reconsidering most of their decisions. Emergencies do exist, but the request should involve an emergency. Also supplementals are not consistent with uniform budget considerations which weigh all budget demands at the same time. Exhibit 7-1 illustrates a request form for budget adjustments. Information needed includes:

1. Was the item in the orginal budget request?
2. Is the money for a recurring or nonrecurring expenditure?
3. What type of adjustment is requested?
4. What is the account number, title and amount of adjustment?
5. Certificate of unencumbered balance (explained in the next chapter).
6. Reason for the request.

Budget Concepts and Reports

Allotments and Budget Concepts

After the money has been appropriated by the legislature and apportioned by the central budget office to the agency, then the agency has control over the funds and agency budget controls are used. The primary control is the allotment. It provides authority from the agency head to the operating officials to incur obligations within prescribed amounts for a specific period of time. The allotments must be consistent with appropriations and apportionments. Allotments and operating budgets can be melded because the operating budget fulfills the function of an allotment and more. Allotments can be made using organizational units, activities, geography, or object classification as the categories depending upon management needs. Allotments are made normally at the highest practical operating level in order to focus managerial responsibility. The level depends on the amount of authority delegated in the particular organization.

Allotments can be designed to complement the management structure of the agency and the problems faced by the agency. Normally, allotments are quite specific on highly sensitive controllable object classifications such as travel. Often the agency must cut current year funds severely and the controllable items receive the burden of such decisions. Thus the controllable items must be "controlled" through the use of specific allotments. Also allotments often are subdivided in terms of "targets," "allowances," "work plans," "financial plans," or other categories depending upon the management devices used by the agency. The categories and names of categories are not significant as long as management control and delegation of responsibility are facilitated. Exhibit 7-2 is an example of an initial allocation and allotment schedule used in a city government.

The use of budget terminology is not uniform; but regardless of the terms used, the concepts are important to understand. Thus far authorization, appropriation, apportionment, and allotment have been explained and those terms are used uniformly. Each represents a different hurdle which must be passed before money is actually spent. Other useful concepts (labels based on common usage) along the way to spending the funds are administrative reservations, obligations, accrued expenditure, and outlay or disbursement. To this list should be added inventory and cost even though they occur after money has been spent.

Administrative reservations are setting aside some funds for a specific purpose. This technique is commonly used by agencies which grant money, but it can be used by other groups which have a lag between deciding who should receive the money and drafting the legal obligating documents. Some certitude is needed as to the likely availability of funds and the administrative reservation provides that assurance. In a few instances, the legal obligating documents cannot be written. Thus, the possibility exists that funds will not be forthcoming in spite of the administrative reservation. The lag between reservation and obligation can be only a matter of minutes or it can be several weeks, depending on administrative circumstances and requirements.

Expenditure Controls

Expenditure controls are techniques which help to ensure that expenditures are made only in the amounts and for the purposes specified in the appropriation act. There are two types of expenditure controls: budget and administrative. Budget controls are geared to the appropriations and apportionments. Administrative controls are applied generically to specific operations of the agency, to insure

EXHIBIT 7-1

DEPARTMENT: CODE #: _____ NAME: _____
SUB-ORGANIZATION UNIT: CODE #: _____ NAME: _____
ACTIVITY: CODE #: _____ NAME: _____

1. Item was ____ was not ____
   included in the department's
   original budget request

2. Type of Expenditure
   Recurring ____
   Non-recurring ____

3. Type of Adjustment
   ____ Inter-Classif. Transfer
   ____ Inter-Divisional Transfer
   ____ An Allocated Reserve Transfer
   ____ Supplemental Appropriation

The Budget Adjustment Requested will Require the Following Revisions:
4. From: 5. For Accounting Dept. Use Only

Account No.	Account Title	Amount	Unencumbered Bal. Before Adjustment	Unencumbered Bal. After Adjustment
	CROSS TOTALS			

6. To:

TOTAL TO BE ADJUSTED TO ABOVE

7. Reasons for Adjustment Request: (Set forth reasons the adjustment is required, the factors involved in arriving at costs, and the status of the account from which transfer is made.)

Approval Requested by: _____ Date: _____
Approved as to Availability of Funds by the Central Accounting Office:

Approved by Budget Officer: _____ Date: _____
Approved by Chief Executive: _____ Date: _____
Approved by President of Council: _____ Date: _____

Source: Operating Budget Manual, Lennox L. Moak and Kathryn W. Killian, MFOA, Chicago, 1963, p. 311.

EXHIBIT 7-2

Schedule of Initial Allocations and Allotments
1963 General Fund Appropriations
(000 Omitted)

Appropriation Title Account Code	Personal Services 100 Class		Purchase of Services 200 Class		Materials and Supplies 300 Class		Equipment 400 Class		Other Classes		Total Allocation
	Allocation	Allotment Reserve	Class	Amount	Class	Amount	Class	Amount	Class	Amount	
Streets											
Administration	$ 394	$ 313	200	$ 7	300	$ 6	400	$ 2			$ 409
Highways	2,265	1,932	200	28	300	55	400	9	500	$ 6	2,872
			261.61	46	305.05	69	405.05	24			
					307.07	74	411.11	31			
					314.14	36	428.28	100			
					315.15	96					
					328.28	33					
Sanitation	12,462	9,877	200	7	300	59	400	39			15,807
			205.05	1,000	305.05	82	428.28	1,080			
			211.11	31	310.10	29					
			260.60	111	311.11	66					
					314.14	33					
					315.15	519					
					316.16	41					
					318.18	43					
					323.23	38					
					328.28	168					
Survey and Design	1,308	1,043	200	13	300	28	400	20			1,429
			250.50	60							
Traffic Engineering	984	770	200	8	300	37	400	8			1,549
					305.05	189	410.10	108			
					310.10	139	428.28	46			
					316.16	30					

Appropriation Title Account Code	Personal Services 100 Class		Purchase of Services 200 Class		Materials and Supplies 300 Class		Equipment 400 Class		Other Classes		Total Allocation
	Allocation	Allotment Reserve	Class	Amount	Class	Amount	Class	Amount	Class	Amount	
Streets (continued)											
Street Lighting	$ 349	$ 277	200	$ 1	300	$ 12	400	$ 13			$ 3,859
			220.20	2,653	305.05	26	428.28	21			
			260.60	688	310.10	97					
TOTAL	$17,762	$14,232		$4,652		$2,005		$1,501		$ 6	$25,926
Public Welfare											
Administration & Social Services	$ 690	$ 534	200	$ 13	300	$ 8	400	$ 2	505.05	$ 495	$ 9,402
			290.90	8,194							
Surplus Foods Distribution Program	171	132	200	11	300	10					540
			210.10	38							
			285.85	310							
Children's Reception Center	131	101	200	1	300	23	400	1			155
Child Welfare Center	413	320	200	13	300	32	400	3			498
					313.13	36					
Youth Conservation Services	421	329	200	26	300	10	400	3	505.05	120	734
			250.50	143	313.13	12					
						1					
Total	$ 1,826	$ 1,416		$ 8,748		$ 131		$ 9		$ 615	$11,329

Source: Philadelphia, Pennsylvania, Budget Bureau.

funds are spent correctly. Administrative controls are to prevent the waste or misuse of public funds at the operating level.

There are two types of budget controls: allotments and reports. Allotments were explained earlier in this chapter. They are a device to regulate the timing of obligations and expenditures during the year. Reports are used to show what expenditures have been made and how this compares with what should have been made. A set of reports, which could be used in many different governments, is published by the Municipal Finance Officers Association.

There are a variety of reports commonly used: daily financial reports, monthly financial reports, quarterly financial reports, monthly performance reports, revenue reports, and annual reports. Daily financial reports are listings showing all transactions by department account. Monthly financial reports are cumulative daily reports which summarize (1) personnel costs by full-time, part-time, temporary, overtime, and other, and (2) costs by major object of expenditure. Quarterly financial reports point out variances between the current and prior year's expenditures. The monthly performance reports contain code numbers, descriptions, selected key work units, number of persons engaged in producing units, and explanations of significant variances. Common data elements include budgeted work units for the year, units programmed for the current month, amount during the first prior year and current year, percent already completed, and percent variance from that programmed to date.

There are two common types of administrative controls: encumbrances accounting system and competitive bids. An encumbrance is a claim on money; thus encumbered money is not available for new commitments. The administrative reservation defined earlier is an encumbrance. The advantages of encumbrances are (1) they keep officials in government from overspending, and (2) the use of the concept enables officials to be certain of how much money is available for new commitments. Competitive bids involve requiring offers for the purchase of goods or services from potential vendors or contractors. The advantages normally of competitive bidding are (1) the procedure tends to avoid careless and possibly costly awarding of contracts, and (2) the procedure reduces dangers of favoritism in return for kickbacks or political favors.

Expenditure controls and other administrative practices such as preaudits should be carefully considered. The common reasons for detailed expenditure controls are to minimize fraud and insure that higher level policy is carried out. Detailed expenditure controls can also be called "red tape." The use of these controls means time and money must be used to write and review the reports. Also the controls tend to inhibit operating departments and their officials from taking initiatives and being creative because so much paper work must be done.

A fraud red tape dilemma exists. Does the government wish to risk fraud (or cries of nonresponsiveness to political leaders) or add more red tape? Neither is pleasant, but the lesser evil is red tape. In the case of fraud, analysis can be used to determine the optimal point of costly control. Expensive administrative controls should be added up to the point that the cost of fraud is equal to the cost of the controls. Such an analysis would be difficult to accomplish given the uncertainties; but even if it were possible, the political wisdom to minimize fraud would tend to force administrators to opt for more controls—red tape. Politically, no politician wishes to be placed in the situation where any fraud was said to be condoned.

Cash Internal Control

The budget officer must be sure that proper cash internal control exists. Fraud and misuse of funds cannot be prevented completely, but they can be discouraged to the point where only rare cases occur. Twelve simple practices can make a significant difference.

1. All disbursements, except for petty cash, should be made by check. Cash invites theft and fraud because it is much more difficult to trace and associate with specific persons. Also cancelled checks provide a receipt. Petty cash is an exception in that detailed controls for small items can cost more than the items.
2. The signing of checks in advance should be prohibited. Signed checks are similar to cash. By waiting to sign checks, the time they are negotiable is shortened and it is easily ensured that the checks do correspond to the purchase.
3. Checks should not be drawn to "cash." The checks should be used to create a trail; so that if there is fraud, investigators can isolate the illegal transaction. Also, a check drawn on "cash" is more difficult to associate with a specific voucher and invoice, thus confusion is not lessened but compounded.
4. Bank accounts should be reconciled independently. If that is done, errors can be detected more easily because a second independent person is not likely to be biased in making the error in the same manner. More importantly, the likelihood of fraud is lessened because two people instead of one would have to be involved in the crime.
5. Checks should be reconciled with the statement using sequenced (numbered) checks. This permits tighter control of the checks and helps spot omissions much more easily. Also, if the checks are not numbered, theft of checks is much more difficult to detect.
6. Checks should be issued only on written authority. Checks should be traceable to invoices, purchase orders, and encumbrances. This is best done with a written record. More significantly, confusion on issuing of money should be minimized and written authority is the best way to avoid misunderstandings. The protection of the disbursing agent is enhanced if that agent *can prove* all disbursements were proper and that can best be done with a written record.
7. An inventory control should exist over blank and voided checks. Without such control, fraud and theft is made easier and a good criminal investigator would question the person who did not maintain such control for possible criminal involvement.
8. Separate bank accounts should be maintained for every fund. As explained in the next chapter, each fund must be maintained separately and this is done through separate bank accounts. This prevents a mingling of money and facilitates separate accounting and auditing.
9. Surprise counts should be made of the petty cash. Elaborate controls are by definition not desirable, but some means is necessary to encourage honesty on the part of those

responsible for the fund. No one should be placed in the position where he is above or beyond suspicion. Surprise counts of petty cash is a sufficient inexpensive control. Care should be taken to stress that the surprise count is a standard operating procedure which should not be taken as a personal questioning of honesty.

10. Checks should be matched with vouchers. If one cannot trace a check to an invoice to a purchase order, then confusion exists which can lead to paying bills twice, not paying some bills, and other confusions.

11. Vouchers and supporting documents should be marked once a check has been issued. This prevents mistaken or fraudulent multiple use of the same justifying documents.

12. Cash receipts and deposits should be recorded daily. The logging in of cash receipts provides an essential proof that money has been received and when. Depositing of the receipts in the bank discourages large losses through theft. Also, once in the bank, the idle cash can be invested, thus earning extra revenue for the government. Even a day's interest on large sums is an extremely significant revenue source for a government.

Management Information Systems

Budget information can be part of a management information system (MIS) or it can be a separate system. An MIS uses sophisticated computerized procedures and routines. The advantage of a computerized system is that it offers speed and reliability in dealing with massive volumes of information. However an MIS is only a tool which must be programmed correctly and given valid information. Ideally, a budget information system fosters the following:

1. *Control:* ensure operations take place in conformance with the budget and that funds are not expended in excess of available revenues.

2. *Planning and analysis:* evaluate with accurate, reliable, relevant information, alternative allocations of resources and the efficiency of government operations.

3. *Accountability:* ensure public monies are collected and disbursed properly and that an auditable record is kept of all transactions.

The parts of a budget information system depend on the complexity of the government. A few possible subsystems are budget preparation, budget status, legislative tracking, and treasury. A budget preparation subsystem would permit quick access to critical data. A budget status subsystem would provide current data on appropriations, administrative reservations, outlays, and so on. A legislative tracking subsystem would permit a quick comprehensive monitoring of legislative actions. A treasury subsystem would prepare the data and reports required on disbursements and outlays. If the data involved is not overwhelming, the agency or government may be wise to process such information manually. If speed or processing of large amounts of information is needed, then a computerized system should be implemented.

Pitfalls do exist. A good budget information system is complex and quite difficult to design as every detail must be decided in order to program the computer properly. The budget process demands timely information so system failures and breakdowns cannot be tolerated. Also computer errors often can be most embarrassing as they tend to affect groups (such as giving each member of a group too much money because a decimal place is misprogrammed). Computerized information systems can provide greater productivity to routine operations, but they require programmers who understand the complexities of budgeting and valid information when they are operating.

In a few governments, integrated financial management systems (IFMS) are being used. The exact design varies, but Exhibit 7-3 is a good illustration of an IFMS. It was designed for New York City partly in reaction to that government's mid-1970 fiscal problems. Like other information systems, it accumulates, organizes, stores, and makes information available when needed. It contains a number of subsystems which are linked in the sense that information is shared among the subsystems.

The structure of the New York City IFMS is based upon integrating elements and a group of subsystems. The integrating elements are a chart of ac-

EXHIBIT 7-3

IFMS Integrated Data Base

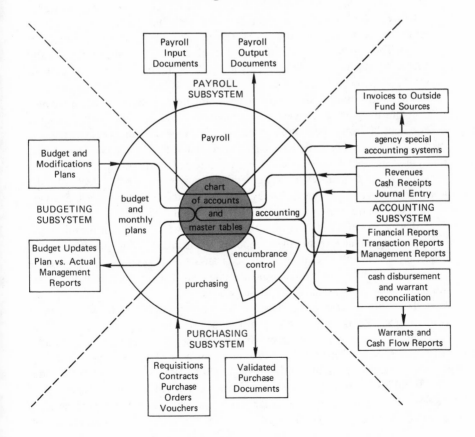

counts, standardized formats for transactions, and master tables. The chart of accounts is the basic dictionary for characterizing transactions throughout the system. The standardized formats for transactions permit the system to track and monitor its own activities. The master tables permit the cross-referencing of data. The group of subsystems is composed of budget and monthly plans, accounting, payroll, and purchasing. The first two subsystems are most important as they provide guidance to the other systems. The make-up of the subsystem is suggested in Exhibit 7-3 and the subsystem ingredients can best be understood by reflecting on the contents of this, the next and the last chapters.

Cash Management and Investments

Cash Management

The government does not collect and disburse money at the same time. There is a time lag and it is sometimes referred to as *cash flow*. A *cash flow problem* is when the amount which should be paid exceeds available cash even though there are enough government assets. Normally, those assets are in the form of obligations or taxes owed to the government which have not yet been paid or collected. The opposite of a cash flow problem is idle cash. Governments usually do not have cash flow problems unless they are highly dependent upon transfer payments (e.g., grants from other governments).

The more common situation is determining the best cash position so money is available for payrolls as well as for payment of debts, and "extra" cash is invested until it is needed in the current year. For this to occur, forecasts must be made of the monthly cash balance needed to meet obligations. Government revenue does not come in evenly and is collected from several sources. For example, at the federal level, 25 percent of the revenue is not collected by the treasury. When and how much money is collected must both be forecasted as well as the expenditure rate by month for the government.

The cash position is determined by either of two factors. One is the minimum compensating balance requirement imposed by the commercial bank used by the government. The other is the self-imposed transaction balance developed considering risks and current interest rates on that idle cash. The desirable cash position is the larger amount determined by those two factors.

There are several approaches for determining the best balance. The most common practice is to hold a certain number of days' expenditure as a cash balance. The exact number of days will depend upon the judgment of the budget officer or treasurer. This practice is useful for most small governments. A second approach is called Economic Ordering Quality (EOQ). In this mathematical model (see Exhibits 7-4 and 7-5), carrying costs represented by the forgone earned interest are weighed against the total cost of the transactions. The government has an opportunity cost for holding rather than investing the cash. Also each bank

EXHIBIT 7-4

Economic Ordering Quality Formula

$$P = b\left(\frac{T}{c}\right) + vT + i\left(\frac{c}{2}\right)$$
where

P = total cost of cash management

b = fixed cost per transaction of transferring funds from marketable securities to cash or vice versa

T = total amount of cash payments or expenditures over the period involved

c = size of transfer, which is the maximum amount of cash

v = variable cost per dollar of funds transferred

i = interest rate on marketable securities

The formula used to solve for the optimal transfer size and initial cash balance is

$$C^* = \sqrt{\frac{2bT}{i}}$$

The average cash balance is computed by dividing C^* by 2.

EXHIBIT 7-5

EOQ Illustration*

A city has total cash payments of $6 million for a six-month period. During this period, the payment (T) will be made at a steady rate, the cost per transaction (b) is $50, the interest rate (i) is 3 percent, and the cost per dollar of funds transferred (v) is 0.05 percent. Therefore:

$$c = \sqrt{\frac{2bT}{i}} = \sqrt{\frac{2(50)\ (6,000,000)}{.03}} = \$141,421$$

The optimal initial cash balance and transfer size is $141,421 and the average cash balance is $141,421 divided by 2 or $70,710. By dividing 6,000,000 by 141,421, the number of transfers (42) can be calculated. The total cost of cash management for the six month period is:

$$P = \$50\frac{(\$6,000,000)}{\$141,421} + \frac{.0005\ (\$6,000,000)}{} + \frac{.03\ (\$141,421)}{2} = \$7,242$$

*Exhibit 7-5 is an illustration of the EOQ formula used by J. Richard Aronson and Eli Schwartz in *Management Policies in Local Government Finance*.

transaction (e.g., transferring from securities to cash) involves an administrative cost to the government. If the number of transactions drive up the cost, then more money can be saved by having a higher cash amount available. A formula helps determine the optimum size cash balance.

A third approach is called Miller-Orr Model. The same basic concepts are involved except the focus is placed upon the upper dollar limit needed for cash purposes. When the cash balance touches the upper boundary then a pre-determined amount of securities is automatically purchased. When the cash balance touches zero or an amount slightly above zero, then a predetermined amount of securities is sold, thus increasing the cash balance. The upper and lower boundaries are determined with transaction cost and lost earned interest in mind. The greater the likely cash fluctuations, the greater the control limits. The Miller-Orr Model is best applied when cash balances fluctuate randomly.

Commercial Bank Services

Which bank should a government use? There is a difference in earned interest and extra bank services which can lower government administrative cost. Also there is the fact that local banks are likely investors in local or state government securities. Political factors must be weighed. Local banks do provide local jobs. Also bank officials are often heavy political contributors. Often all those factors are weighed when decisions are made on which bank a local government should use. Because a government uses many accounts, one possibility is to spread the business among all the local banks.

An unusual service provided government is the warrant. It is mentioned in Exhibit 7-3. A warrant is a draft payable through a bank and it is used to slow disbursements. When a warrant is presented for payment, the bank will not pay until the warrant is accepted by the government. This device can be used in cash management to help regulate the amount of cash available. The disadvantage is the higher bank service charge and government cost to manage the use of warrants.

A past practice, which is becoming obsolete, is "playing the float." A float is the difference between the total amount of checks drawn on a bank account and the amount shown on the bank's books. If the size of the float can be determined accurately, then the bank balance can be lower and the idle cash can be invested. For small governments this is not significant, but for large governments the amount of money can be large and the earned interest on only a few days' investment is significant and worth the effort.

The practice of playing the float is becoming obsolete with the greater use of electronic fund transfer systems which tend to eliminate the float. The Federal Electronic Funds Transfer System illustrates the new practice. It was implemented by the Treasury Department and Federal Reserve System in 1976. A computer link is established between the Treasury Department and the New York Federal Reserve Bank. The system provides the capability for automatic receipt of fund transfers as well as computer assisted generation of fund transfers among Treasury, Federal Reserve Banks, member banks, and others using the Federal Reserve

Communication Systems. Thus processing of checks can be done instantly instead of taking several days.

Controlling Payables

Paying bills can mean saving money. Given the fact that idle cash is earning interest, bills should not be paid until they are due unless the discount for early payment is higher than the earned interest. In order to maximize earned interest, governments often make grants using a letter of credit. This enables the government to draw interest instead of the grantee.

Care should be taken to ensure knowledgeable people are paying the bills. Normally, the management and control of payables is centralized to provide that expertise. In larger governments, another method used is to use field units with headquarters establishing spending and disbursement levels. The following general guidelines[1] are useful in tailoring agency or government disbursement and collectibles policies and procedures:

1. Each agency should have a carefully developed disbursement plan as a part of its forecast of outlays. The plan should be consistent with the agency's objectives, strategies, program plans, and budget.
2. A payment schedule and control system should be established.
3. Procedures should be established for evaluating economic factors, including the time value of money, in establishing payment schedules. Unless there are significant programmatic or policy factors, payments should generally be made at the time they are due.
4. Except for very large purchases where special analyses might be warranted, cash discounts are usually desirable.
5. Procedures should be reviewed to assure that payments to small vendors and for occasional purchases are not delayed beyond the due dates.
6. Fuller use should be made of letters of credit and other established procedures for managing the timing of payments for government programs.
7. Procedures should be established for regular comparison of actual and planned disbursements.
8. The causes and impact of significant variances from disbursement plans should be evaluated and plans adjusted when necessary.
9. Agencies with significant amounts of receipts should have a collections plan which is a part of the overall forecasts and consistent with the agency's objectives, strategies, program plans, and budget.
10. Collection schedules and control systems for billing and cash processing should be established.
11. Economic factors, including the time value of money, should be considered in development of billing cycles and collection procedures. The importance of prompt collection and deposit of cash should be recognized.
12. Procedures should be established for regular comparison of actual with planned collections.
13. The causes and impact of significant variances from planned collections should be evaluated and plans adjusted when necessary.

---

[1] The guidelines were prepared by the U.S. Joint Financial Improvement Committee.

Investment in Marketable Securities

Once the cash and security position has been determined, then the government is ready to invest the money for the desired short period of time. Often as much as 70 percent of the total liquid assets can be invested in securities. State law often limits the choice of securities to "safe" investment such as U.S. Treasury securities, U.S. agency securities, obligations of other municipalities within a state, and bank certificates of deposit. Permissible investments do not include common stock. The safeness of some government securities (e.g., New York City bonds in 1975) is more questionable today. Investing in such securities may be permitted under law, but such investments are unlikely until the risk of default on the securities is nearly eliminated.

Not all securities will earn the investor the same return on investment. That return is called "market yield" and it is determined by a combination of:

1. length of maturity;
2. default risk;
3. marketability;
4. call provision;
5. tax status.

If a government is to invest, then the security market must be watched to determine what is a reasonable market yield and that yield should be sought. Long-term securities tend to receive higher yields, but yields 15 to 30 years are not significantly higher. The key influence is the expectation of what will happen to the interest rate. Generally, when interest rates are expected to rise, the yield also rises. In poor market conditions, investors may be offered a risk premium to induce them to invest in long-term securities. Only when interest rates are expected to fall significantly in the future do long-term securities—currently yielding less than short-term securities—become attractive.

Default risk is the possibility that the borrower will fail to pay the principal or interest. All other factors constant, the greater the possibility the borrower will fail to meet the obligation, the greater the premium or market yield on the security. U.S. Treasury and U.S. government agency issues are considered default free so they establish the lower limit for securities. The credit worthiness of other issues is judged by the major security rating firms such as Moody's Investor's Service and Standard and Poor's. Sometimes investors demand a risk premium before investing in issues other than default-free securities.

Marketability involves the ability of the security owners to convert the security to cash. This is particularly important when idle cash is used to purchase the security, because the government may wish to convert the security quickly back into cash. Marketability concerns both the price realized and the amount of time required to sell the asset. The more marketable a security, the greater will be the ability of its owner to execute a large security transaction. Less marketable securities require higher yields.

A call provision on a security allows the issuer to buy the security back at a stated price before maturity. The call provision is to the borrower's benefit because the borrower can refund the issue if interest rates move significantly lower. The investor is disadvantaged because the security is called in a period of low interest rates and the investor's funds must then be placed in lower yield returning securities. Not surprisingly, investors demand a yield inducement and maybe a premium as well to invest in callable securities. Callable government securities are becoming more popular but are unusual in federal government securities.

Tax status has two effects on market yields. In the first place, governments do not have to pay taxes on investment income, thus this is not an expense to them. Secondly, state and local government securities are tax havens for many private investors, thus this affects the government security market by driving the yield down. Generally speaking, the fact that local governments do not pay federal income tax means that they should invest in higher yield federal securities rather than state and local government securities. Another difference in investment strategy involves deep discount bonds and the tax rates on ordinary and capital gains. This distinction is significant to the individual who is a taxpayer but is not significant to the investing government. Thus a government should not take advantage of the "bargain" yields on high coupon bonds selling at par or above. In general, governments should simply invest in securities showing the highest pretax return.

Types of Marketable Securities

There are four types of securities commonly used by state and local governments. They are U.S. Treasury obligations, federal agency securities, repurchase agreements (REPO), and negotiable certificates of deposit. Each has its special advantages.

There are two major types of U.S. Treasury obligations: treasury notes and treasury bills. Treasury bills pay about 6 percent interest, are auctioned weekly for 91 to 182 day maturities. One-year bills are sold separately. Treasury bills carry no coupon but are sold at discount. These securities are extremely popular as short-term investments. The secondary market is excellent and transaction costs are low. Treasury notes hold one- to seven-year maturity but they are used in the secondary market for short-term investments. In general these two types of securities are the safest, most marketable, and yield the lowest return on investment.

There are other types of securities issued by the federal government carrying the same assurances as U.S. Treasury obligations but having slightly better yields. Principal agencies issuing securities are the federal land banks, federal home loan banks, federal intermediate credit banks, the Federal National Mortgage Association (called "Fannie Mae"), the Government National Mortgage Association ("Ginnie Mae"), and the banks for cooperatives. Maturities range from a month to 15 years, but about two-thirds of the issues are for less than a year.

The repurchase agreement (REPO) is an innovation of government security dealers who recognize the selling potential of securities tailored to specific short time periods. With REPOs, dealers agree to repurchase the security at a specific future date thus increasing the number of transactions and the resulting total fees from those transactions. Government investors benefit because they can get securities for the specific time periods they need, thus gaining the desired earned interest. There is little marketability but that is unimportant because REPOs are normally only for a few days. There is no default risk because the securities are almost always U.S. Treasury securities.

Another commonly used short-term investment is the negotiable certificates of deposit (CD). A CD is the deposit of funds at a commercial bank for a specified period of time at a specified rate of interest. This investment device was originated in 1961 and it normally provides a yield better than treasury bills with maturity in 30 to 360 days. A sizable secondary market exists but marketability is usually nonexistent for small bank CDs. The default risk is related to the possibility of bank failure which is normally a low risk for most banks. Commonly local governments use CDs from local banks to support the region economically.

Portfolio

A portfolio is merely the collection of securities one holds. Government investors, as noted before, are limited to the legally sanctioned list of securities. The key consideration for a government's portfolio is to have the cash available when needed for the operations of the state, city, county, and so on. Default risk is minimum and a call risk is unusual. Taxability is not a direct factor therefore computations are simplified to the return on investment. Government investors should concentrate on maturity and marketability.

For the short term, needs are best satisfied by treasury bills, REPOs, and CDs. A significant portion of the emergency liquidity needs should be met with treasury bills and REPOs.

Intermediate and long-term needs are handled differently. Treasury notes and bonds as well as U.S. securities are used for intermediate purposes. Again, the key is to insure cash is available when needed, so maturities must be timed correctly or marketability must be excellent if the timing is not correct. U.S. agency securities provide better yields but this advantage must be weighed against their marketability. In some cases, long-term investments are used especially for larger potential emergencies or when funds are accumulated over years for a given purpose. In such cases, long-term treasury and agency securities are normally used. The most important consideration for long-term investments must be the future course of interest rates. The highest yield is not as important as the date of maturity or possible marketability. Often governments take the more conservative approach of confining their investments to short-term securities.

In summary, investments of idle cash should be made, but an expertise is needed to do it correctly. This section gives the reader some of the basics, but much more knowledge and experience are needed to deal properly in government securities. This chapter and chapter 11 are complementary. In chapter 11, the government is not the investor but the borrower. A better knowledge of both chapters will be obtained by reflection on the complementary character of the two.

REVIEW QUESTIONS

1. Compare and contrast apportionment, allotment, and administrative reservations.
2. Explain the significance of the Anti-Deficiency Act.
3. Explain how the budget execution process can support management of the organization.
4. What are the common pitfalls one can anticipate and how can budget execution system design assist in minimizing those pitfalls?
5. Explain a procedure for current year adjustments of appropriations and justify that procedure.
6. Compare and contrast budget and administrative controls.
7. Explain the fraud-red tape dilemma.
8. Explain how the normative concepts associated with budget execution relate to the following management concepts: management-by-objectives, public trust, performance measures, planning, progress reporting, financial reporting and record keeping, and management information systems.
9. Explain the importance of and how to achieve cash internal control.
10. Explain the importance of cash management.
11. Why are guidelines for disbursement and collections significant and what are the administrative implications of those guidelines?
12. Investing idle cash is a complex undertaking. What knowledge is particularly useful to undertaking that task?

REFERENCES

ARONSON, J. RICHARD and ELI SCHWARTZ. *Management Policies in Local Government Finance*. Washington, D.C.: International City Management Association and Municipal Officers Association, 1975.
MOAK, LENNOX L. and KATHRYN W. KILLIAN. *Operating Budget Manual*. Chicago: Municipal Finance Officers Association, 1963.
TURNBULL, AUGUSTUS. *Governmental Budgeting and PPBS: A Programmed Introduction*. Reading, Mass.: Addison-Wesley, 1970.
U.S. Civil Service Commission, Bureau of Training, The Management Science Training Center. *Budget Formulation*. Washington, D.C.: 1976.

U.S. Joint Financial Management Improvement Program. *Money Management*. Washington, D.C.: January 1976.

U.S. Joint Financial Movement Program. *Operating Budgets*. Washington, D.C.: November 1975.

Urban Academy. *An Introduction to IFMS*. New York: New York City Urban Academy, December 1976.

EIGHT

Accounting and Auditing

This chapter discusses the fundamentals of government accounting and auditing. Stress is placed on explaining those accounting and auditing concepts which are particularly useful to public budgeting. A large section of this chapter is devoted to describing an elementary set of accounting reports which greatly aid the public budget process. Finally, a brief explanation of auditing is provided. At the completion of this chapter, the reader should know:

1. the fundamental definitions, beliefs, and norms of government accounting;
2. the fundamental concepts upon which government accounting is developed including fund accounting, accounting systems design, and internal control systems;
3. financial reports which are particularly useful for public budgeting;
4. computerization of accounting systems;
5. the various types of auditing.

Accounting Fundamentals

Accounting consists of *recording transactions* of an agency in financial terms including the classification of those transactions, summarizing, reporting, interpreting and analyzing for the user of the data. The key words are "recording transactions." Transactions are financial decisions such as obligating money, deciding to disburse, and setting aside funds for a purpose. Accounting is merely keeping track of and analyzing those transactions by using summaries and classifications. Accounting provides management with a means to evaluate management performance, to plan for future operations, and, lastly, to achieve financial control.

Appendix 8-A (at the end of the chapter) presents the approved Principles of Governmental Accounting and Reporting. The 13 principles are deceptively simple. They stress that accounting should complement legal requirements and budgets. Fund accounting is used. Under the principles, government assets are not to be depreciated as in private sector accounting and a modified accrual method of accounting is recommended. Standard classification, terminology, and reports are suggested. Financial reports are to show current conditions and yearly reports should be prepared and published.

Government accounting is predicated upon disclosure and integration with other management activities. Full disclosure of the financial results of government is essential or abuse can go undetected. Accounting produces financial information for management purposes which permits effective control over and insures the accountability of all funds, property, and other assets. Reliable accounting serves as the basis for preparing and supporting budget requests, for controlling the execution of the budgets, and for providing needed financial information for reviewing groups. Government accounting, which is integrated and consistent with all accounting operations throughout the government, permits comparative analyses, thus strengthening the analytical ability of management.

Accounting Norms and Budgeting

Certain norms are accepted in government accounting. The control accounts or fiscal accounts—which record receipts, obligations, and disbursements—must embrace the detail that supports the budget. If that is not the case, then the budget and accounting information cannot be related. Decisions on the forms of accounting records should be centralized, but the routine decentralized. Standard definitions and classification cannot be achieved without centrally controlled decisions on such matters, but the actual routine of accounting should be handled in the field where the action is taking place. Accounting must accompany a pattern of internal audit and control. Unless some inspections occur which verify the required accounting practices are being used, the organization will not take the requirements seriously. Actual costs and measures should reflect management success and failure. Accounting is merely a reflection of performance and the reflection must show the good and bad news in order to help managers understand their true situation. Flexibility in accounting is desirable but in the context of overall uniformity. If useful summary information is to be compiled, then accounting uniformity is essential. On the other hand, accounting requirements can inhibit the organization from responding to its environment. This dilemma is always the challenge of top government accountants who must design the accounting systems.

A key step in accounting is obligation. If an item is being bought, then the agency normally issues a purchase order or a more formal contract. The purchase order is a valid offer. The vendor will send the goods requested and the bill to the agency based upon a valid purchase order or contract. In the case of personnel, a contract or a mere agreement to work for certain remunerations constitutes the obligation. The agency must pay for services rendered and tenure protections commonly exist for government employees. Once an order is placed and accepted by the vendor, then the government is obligated to pay—given that the contract is fulfilled by the vendor. At this stage, the agency records the order as an *accounts payable* item when the purchase order is sent. Normally, not all the money obligated must be paid because some orders are deficient in some manner and the government is not obligated to pay in such circumstances.

Once the goods have been received and placed in inventory, then an accrued expenditure exists until such time as the check is issued. This concept is useful if there is a large purchasing function because the demand on cash and government liability would be monitored more closely. In many other types of government functions, this concept is not needed. In this chapter the reports cited do not use "accrued expenditure" because the concept normally is not needed.

Expenditures is another step. This is when the invoice has been received from the vendor, and money—in the form of a check—is actually issued by the government. Today, expenditures are controlled closely. In the federal government, the rate of disbursement, especially on grants, is monitored and controlled for fiscal policy reasons. In all levels of government, but to a lesser extent in the federal government, the rate of disbursement is monitored and controlled in order to avoid shortages of cash and to take advantage of short-term idle cash investments.

Two additional budget and accounting concepts can also be applied. Once the goods are in hand but not being used, they are considered *inventory*. This concept is useful because inventory can be converted to cash if necessary; thus separate treatment helps the decision maker have a better understanding of agency convertible assets. Another concept is *cost*. Once the goods are taken from inventory, they are considered used and are a cost. At this point, the item is no longer an asset.

Government accounting is keyed to the operating budget. Accounting is especially useful in tracking the obligations and expenditures against the budget. In government accounting, the term *encumbrance* is used. It is a claim on money. As soon as an obligation is made, the money needed to pay the obligation is set aside and no longer included in the balance of money available for new commitments. In budgeting for personnel costs, encumbrances are sometimes not essential because the cost is highly routine and regular in its flow. However in budgeting for purchases of equipment, materials, supplies, other contracts, and grants, encumbrances are quite important and the accounting system should provide data on those encumbrances as well as later related expenditures. This point shall be made again in the discussion concerning Exhibits 8-2 and 8-3.

In state and local government, a large share of the funds used comes from grants from the federal government. Federal requirements normally stipulate that each grant should be treated like a fund with separate records maintained on all receipts and expenditures. The permitted cost and required supporting documents are spelled out in federal guidelines. Generally, the requirements are similar to those for normal government accounts. The appropriate local share of the grant is a unique feature of the federal guidelines. Normally, the local government can use cash, gifts, as well as value of goods and services for the local share. Also federal regulations include provisions for auditing of financial records plus acceptable internal control procedures such as those discussed later in this chapter.

Financial Administration

The key to good financial administration is good account records. All financial transactions must be recorded. They must then be summarized and classified. Also all such transactions must be related to the appropriate fiscal year.

Government accounting uses the accrual rather than the cash method of accounting. In the cash method, income is recorded when it is received and expenditures are recorded when they are paid. In other words, transactions are recorded as of the date the cash changes hands. The advantages of the cash method are that it is easy to administer and the cash balance is easily determined. The critical disadvantage is that expenses and revenues cannot be related to the budget and its fiscal year. Thus accountability is impossible.

In the accrual method of accounting, revenues are recorded when they are earned or billed and expenditures are recorded when they are obligated. The accrual method does permit accountability but it also distorts the revenue and cash position of the government. The cash position must be calculated separately as described earlier in chapter 7. Governments use a modified accrual method primarily because there are fundamental differences between a private enterprise operation and a government undertaking. This difference will become apparent when the various financial reports are discussed.

Accounting is built upon three operational tools: vouchers, journals, and ledgers. A *voucher* is a document which confirms the fact that a financial transaction has taken place. For example, payroll checks, purchase orders, receipts for rent payment, and even appropriation laws are vouchers. The *journal* is the first record book (now sometimes a computer printout) of the transactions. It is a chronological listing of the transactions and shows the date of the transaction's occurrence, the dollars, and a brief explanation of the transaction. A *ledger* is a group of accounts which pertain to the same subject, that is, a subject matter listing of information. These tools are important because together they provide the means to record usefully, summarize, and classify the transactions.

Government accounting uses the fund concept. A fund is a sum of money set aside for a particular purpose and accounted for separately from the other monies of the government. The purpose behind fund accounting is to control the handling of money to insure that it will be spent only for the purposes intended such as highway construction. The concept is extensively used but it does reduce management flexibility thus making public management more difficult.

There are several types and groups of funds. A listing of them illustrates the variety of funds which do exist. The types of funds are general, dedicated revenue source (e.g., highway trust fund), debt service, capital project, enterprise (e.g., arsenal), trust or agency, intergovernmental service fund, and special assessment. The groups of funds are current government operations, capital spending, commercial type, and custodial type.

Accounting System Design

There are several factors to consider when designing an accounting system. Information should be timely, accurate, and objective. Obviously, this is an ideal and trade-off must be made especially between timeliness and accuracy. The system should be consistent with all legally established minimum requirements. Particular attention should be given to the collection and recording of information because this is the place where most errors occur. Care must be taken to design cross- and double-checks to isolate and correct such errors. Another concern is classification, summarization, and storage. Proper design here rests upon an excellent grasp of how the information can best be used. Thought also goes into evaluating the use of electronic data processing. The advantage is speed and enhanced analytical capability. The risks to consider are computer assisted fraud and the possibility of massive, extremely embarrassing mistakes.

The final factor to weigh in designing an accounting system is internal control. The system should fix responsibility on specific individuals. Policies and procedures should be written to avoid misunderstandings. Only designated personnel should be authorized to perform certain key functions such as disbursement. Forms should be carefully considered so that they reduce the likelihood of error and fraud. All reporting should be regularly and carefully analyzed or else the reports should be eliminated. Care must be taken to establish built-in cross- and double-checks of forms, people, and units in order to isolate errors and prevent fraud. For example, independent record keepers can be used to act as cross checks on each other. A further safeguard is to use independent auditors. One final but key point to internal control is to get, train, and keep good people in the accounting unit.

Reports and Analysis

Accounting is one of those subjects that can best be understood by example. The previous portions of this chapter explain accounting and financial administration fundamentals. This portion explains specific reports which illustrate some of the fundamentals and demonstrate the usefulness of accounting. The reports or analyses are drawn from chapter 15 of Aronson and Schwartz, *Management Policies in Local Government Finance*. The following five financial reports are discussed:

1. statement of revenue: estimated and actual;
2. appropriation and expenditure ledger account;
3. statement of encumbrances, and authorization;
4. fund balance change;
5. balance sheet.

Statement of Revenue

Exhibit 8-1 concerns comparing estimated with actual government revenue. This accounting report provides highly useful information to help analysts judge the accuracy of forecasting techniques. This report should be keyed to funds, tax source, and fiscal year. As the reader may recall, separate estimates must be made for each tax source and separate accounting forces us to examine the estimates by funds and fiscal year. The recorded estimate should be the official one used by the government in computing its budget. Again the reader may recall, the government should pass a resolution indicating what is the assumed (projected) revenue. The actual revenue should be that amount actually collected.

By examining Exhibit 8-1, the reader will notice where estimation errors were made. The important errors are those which result in significantly less revenue for the government. These errors are particularly harmful and result in using tax anticipation notes. If the revenue source is small, then large errors can be tolerated. If the revenue source is large, then even small optimistic errors cannot be

EXHIBIT 8-1

Milesville General Fund
Statement of Revenue—Estimated and Actual
Fiscal Year Ended June 30, 1977

Revenue Source	Estimated Revenue	Actual Revenue	Actual over- or (under) estimated
Taxes	$240,000	$290,000	$50,000
Licenses and permits	30,000	36,000	6,000
Intergovernmental revenue	120,000	90,000	30,000
Charges for services	40,000	45,000	5,000
Fines and forfeitures	6,000	9,000	3,000
Miscellaneous	4,000	10,000	6,000
Total	$440,000	$480,000	$40,000

tolerated. In Exhibit 8-1, the intergovernmental revenue (e.g., state payment, revenue sharing, or grant-in-aid) was significantly in error. Fortunately, the conservative estimates on the other revenue sources more than offset the mistake so that the entire estimate was off about nine percent. Exhibit 8-1 tells the analyst that more effort must go into correctly forecasting revenue.

The subsequent exhibits (8-2, 8-3, 8-4, 8-5) are complementary. Each tells the analyst a part of a story, but together they tell a reasonably comprehensive story about the whole government. For example, each is concerned with encumbrance and expenditures. If a question is raised on encumbrances in the balance sheet (Exhibit 8-5), the ultimate answer may be found in the appropriation and expenditure ledger account (Exhibit 8-2) or the statement of expenditures and encumbrances (Exhibit 8-3). The analyst must be able to read all the financial reports and understand their interrelationship.

Appropriation and Expense Ledger

Exhibit 8-2 is a subsidiary or partial appropriation and expenditure ledger account. As defined earlier, a ledger concerns a subject and in this case the subject is a specific account (or fund) including information on encumbrances, expenditure, and essential voucher information. This report uses regularly and routinely collecter voucher information.

Exhibit 8-2 tells us a story. On July 1, 1976, the fiscal year began with $125,000 being appropriated to the supplies account of the general fund. This meant that $125,000 was available to be obligated and spent. On July 10, 1976, some laboratory equipment was ordered which cost $25,000 thus reducing the amount to be obligated to the total of $100,000. Details of the order can be found on purchase order number 104 and this order constitutes a voucher. On October 15, 1976, an automobile or parts for automobiles were ordered costing $10,000. This increased the encumbered balance to $35,000 and reduced the unemcumbered balance to $90,000. On November 3, 1976, the ordered laboratory equipment finally arrived and was paid for. However, either some of the merchandise was damaged or a discount was given because the actual expenditure was $24,500. This meant that the total encumbrance was reduced by $25,000 to $10,000. The difference of $500 between the encumbrance and expenditure required a $500 upward adjustment in the unencumbered balance because that money was again available for obligation.

This type of financial report is quite useful. The analyst knows how much money is always available in each account for obligation, how much has already been spent, and how much is obligated but not yet actually spent. At any time in the current year, the operating budget may have to be revised. A summary appropriation and expenditure ledger account is essential for an intelligently done revision. Also the account tells managers how much they can plan on using and how much can be (or should be) spent before the end of the year.

EXHIBIT 8-2

**Milesville General Fund—Supplies Account
Appropriation and Expenditure Ledger Account
Starting July 1, 1976**

Date	Explanation	Encumbrances			Expenditures		Appropriations	
		Increase	Decrease	Balance	Amount	Total	Amount	Unencumbered Balance
Jul. 1	Budget						$125,000	$125,000
Jul. 10	Lab. equip.—P.O. #104	$25,000		$25,000				100,000
Oct. 15	Autos—P.O. #410	10,000		35,000				90,000
Nov. 3	Lab. equip.—P.O. #104		$25,000	10,000	$24,500	$24,500		90,500

Statement of Expenditure, Encumbrances, and Authorization

Exhibit 8-3 is an elaborate summary statement of appropriations and expenditure. It is done for each separate fund, and compares appropriations with expenditures and encumbrances involving a two-year period. This statement assumes that the fund balance is closed at the end of two years thus providing sufficient time to pay obligations from the previous year. A two-year period is a reasonable time, but a short or longer time period can be selected. The reader may notice that the $800 close to fund balance and other information appears in exhibit 8-4. The reader may also note that the information can be further subdivided into activities and objects.

Exhibit 8-3 is extremely informative. Out of $425,000 appropriated there was left unobligated only $11,200 or about 2 percent of the total. However, most of the money was in the welfare category and the expenditure forecast error in that category was 16 percent. This error coupled with a zero encumbrance would raise a question for a budget analyst. The low 1977 encumbrances total is a pleasing sign that last of the year spending was low and proper pacing of obligation probably took place. The prior year was even lower so the manager might watch a possible developing laxness in this area, but there certainly is no cause for alarm.

An analysis of the "close to fund balance" is particularly interesting. The sanitation function had a negative "close to fund balance" so that more money was spent than encumbered. This is a very serious matter and a violation of antideficiency laws. Someone should be reprimanded or fired for this action. Other interesting occurrences were the large $300 and $265 amounts in two categories. They represent 75 percent of one category and 48 percent of the other. Both percentages are high but the amounts are low. Possibly further investigation is warranted, but such an investigation is not strongly recommended. The total percentage of encumbrances to the "close to fund balance" is high at 16 percent but the amount is low so nothing extremely serious appears to be wrong beyond the antideficiency error.

Fund Balance Change

Exhibit 8-4 focuses attention on available assets and the fundamental changes which occurred during a fiscal year. It is done for each separate fund and highlights the key additions and subtractions associated with the fund change during the year. The excess of revenue over expenditure is added after it is adjusted upward for the prior year reserve for encumbrances. Deductions are made for the reserve for encumbrances and increase in reserve inventory and supplies. The revenue in the computation is cited in Exhibit 8-1 and the expenditure cited in Exhibit 8-3. Also the reserve for encumbrances for both years and the expenditures charged to prior year reserve for encumbrances can be found in Exhibit 8-3. The

EXHIBIT 8-3

Milesville General Fund
Statement of Expenditures and Encumbrances
Compared with Authorizations
Fiscal Year Ended June 30, 1977

	Prior year reserve for encumbrances	Expenditures chargeable to prior year reserve for encumbrances	Close to fund balance	1977 Appropriations	1977 Expenditures	1977 Encumbrances	1977 Unencumbered balance
General government	$1,500	$1,500		$ 45,000	$ 41,000	$2,000	$ 2,000
Public safety	750	750		100,000	98,000	500	1,500
Highways and streets	450	400	$ 50	60,000	60,000		
Sanitation	250	275	(25)	40,000	39,000		1,000
Health	150	140	10	20,000	18,000	1,300	700
Welfare	1,000	800	200	30,000	25,000		5,000
Culture-recreation	400	100	300	16,000	13,200	2,000	800
Education	500	235	265	14,000	12,600	1,200	200
Transfer of funds				100,000	100,000		
Service fund	$5,000	$4,200	$800	$425,000	$406,800	$7,000	$11,200

*The NCGA would prefer breaking down expenditures by activity and object as well. This has been omitted for the sake of brevity.
†If there has been material revision of appropriations since the adoption of the original budget this should be indicated here with columns showing the original budget and revisions.

EXHIBIT 8-4

Milesville General Fund
Analysis of Changes in Fund Balance
Fiscal Year Ended June 30, 1977

Fund balance, July 1, 1976		$ 84,500
Add:		
Excess of revenues over expenditures, 1977		
Revenues	$480,000	
Expenditures	406,800	
		73,200
Reserve for encumbrances, June 30, 1976	$ 5,000	
Less: Expenditures charged to prior year reserve for encumbrances	4,200	
		800
		$158,500
Deduct:		
Reserve for encumbrances, June 30, 1977	$ 7,000	
Increase in reserve inventory and supplies	2,000	
		9,000
FUND BALANCE, JUNE 30, 1977		$149,500

increase in reserve inventory and supplies is reflected in Exhibit 8-5 and will be discussed more later.

The fund balance tells us how much money can be spent without fear of overspending. It also explains the component parts of that figure. The revenue less expenditure tells us there is a 15 percent surplus which is certainly unusual in most governments. The fund increased $65,000 which constitutes a 177 percent yearly increase. Some questions about this increase should be raised by a budget examiner as either taxes can be cut or expenditures can be increased. Certainly, the fund is in a healthy position starting the next year unless some unusual expenditure increase is forecasted.

Balance Sheet

The balance sheet is illustrated in Exhibit 8-5. The government balance sheet is similar to a private business balance sheet, and is based on the simple formula: total assets equals total liabilities, reserves, and the fund balance. Assets include cash, short-term investments, property tax receivables, amounts due from other funds, and inventory. Liabilities include accounts payable and payroll taxes payable. Reserves include reserves for encumbrances and inventory of supplies. The balance sheet is designed to emphasize available assets. especially quickly available assets. A balance sheet must be prepared for each fund and each fiscal year.

The interesting feature of the government balance sheet is the items not found in it. The balance sheet does not include depreciation, profit, or stocks. As noted in Appendix 8-A, government accounting normally does not include depreciation. Capital items are reflected in the capital budget and debt administration. Government can have a surplus but not a profit. If money is returned to the taxpayer, it is called a rebate but it is unusual. Government programs provide a service and normally are not also designed to make a profit. The initial capital or designated paper representing ownership in a private business is called stock. By definition, a government is owned and controlled by the people through the political process, therefore the notion of private ownership is logically impossible. Instead, the fund balance is used to indicate available resources in the fund.

The balance sheet is informative especially if it is presented in a comparative format. In Exhibit 8-5, the fund has grown significantly with little growth in total liabilities. Not a great deal of money is held in cash and idle cash is invested in short-term investment. The reader will note that the investment is cited at cost rather than the higher market value. This is to provide the safest conservative estimate, but both cost and market value should always be shown. This information shows the loss or profit anticipated from the investment. The amount of property tax receivables and allowances for uncollectable taxes has declined. This is a good sign because it indicates a sound tax base and good collection practices. The inventory of supplies and its mirror reserve have not grown radically, so unnecessary purchases probably did not take place. The significant increase was in the fund balance. An analyst would question this increase and wish to examine the fund balance in more detail.

In a balance sheet, the "due from other funds" is a significant item. In this particular balance sheet (Exhibit 8-5) there is no apparent problem, but problems can exist. The use of many funds means that some interfund transfers are necessary. It is possible to abuse these transfers for the purpose of confusing or hiding the real condition of the various funds. Fraud, poor management, or deliberate attempts to present a better picture of financial conditions are some of the reasons for an abuse of transfer. An analyst can be aware of this potential and can make an inquiry if the "due from other funds" distorts the total assets in the balance sheet. The inquiry would involve the legality and motivation behind any unusually high assets due to the transfer.

The financial reports are an important use of the accounting system. They provide information useful in budget preparation, operating budgets, and auditing. Knowledge of the complexities of public budgeting and government are essential if the financial reports are to be interpreted correctly. Each financial report is read in the context of the other reports and knowledge of the budget process.

EXHIBIT 8-5

Milesville General Fund
Balance Sheet
June 30, 1976 and 1977

ASSETS		1977		1976
Cash		$ 15,000		$ 8,000
Short-term investment—				
at cost		120,000		50,000
(market value $123,000)				
Property taxes				
receivable	$35,000		$45,000	
Less				
Allowance for				
uncollectable				
taxes	3,000	32,000	4,000	41,000
Due from other				
funds		1,500		2,200
Inventory of				
supplies		10,000		8,000
Total Assets		$178,500		$109,200

LIABILITIES, RESERVES, AND FUND BALANCE	1977	1976
Accounts Payable	$ 10,000	$ 9,200
Payroll Taxes payable	2,000	2,500
Total Liabilities	12,000	11,700
Reserve for encumbrances	7,000	5,000
Reserve for Inventory of supplies	10,000	8,000
Fund Balance	149,500	84,500
Total Liabilities, reserve and fund balance	$178,500	$109,200

Computerized Accounting Systems

This section of the chapter explains the fundamental decisions to be made in computerizing an accounting system. Many small governments can save a significant amount of operating expenses and greatly improve their management capabilities by shifting from a hand-posted accounting system to computerized operation. Often small governments may have only bank statements or small bookkeeping activities which are difficult to maintain due to high personnel turnover. A standard computer software package can be designed for small government in each state. Such a system could be used by most cities in a state, require a minimum amount of effort to operate, and provide adequate financial data to local public managers. Such a system was developed in 1976 in Tennessee. Their computerized "General Ledger and Budgeting Accounting Program" cost $600 to $2500 to operate depending on the number of transactions. It serves as an example of what can be done.

A fundamental ingredient of the Tennessee system is a codification of the accounting fields based on the state uniform standardized chart of accounts. The use of the code does assume correct coding of the transactions. A qualified person is needed to analyze the reports, correct coding mistakes, and isolate problems in coding. The codification in Tennessee was as follows:

XX—XXX—XXXXX—XXX—XXX—XX

City code: to identify the city on the computer file;

Fund code: to identify groups and specific fund;

Basic account or purpose account: to identify accounts such as assets, liabilities, revenue, expenditures, reserves, etc.;

Object account: to identify primary and secondary objects of expenditures;

Optional code: for project cost accounting;

Second optional code: to identify responsibility centers.

Input and Output

The input for the Tennessee system is vouchers. A copy of the checks plus entry information (e.g., fund, function, object, debit, credit, description) go to the computer center. Cash reports on deposits, budget, and a general journal form (for corrections, adjustments, recordings of accounts payable, and encumbrances) are also sent to the computer center with the appropriate entry information. Data is batch processed and the sending unit is responsible for the accuracy of the input. The computer center does run an input edit on the cards to (1) insure each transaction is entered dually according to accounting practice, (2) each expenditure and encumbrance has an object code, and (3) no code number has been used that is not in the chart of accounts. The edit is only for easily caught errors. More significant errors must be caught with an inspection procedure and an examination of the reports produced with this data.

The computer can generate an amazing number of useful reports based on the previously described input. These include:

1. the balance sheet;
2. trial balance;
3. general journal entry register;
4. budget entry register;
5. cash receipts journal;
6. cash disbursement journal;
7. deposit register;
8. analysis of change in cash on hand;
9. statement of estimated, realized, and unrealized revenue by specific source;
10. statement of expenditures compared by appropriation (function and object);
11. statement of object expenditures by account number;
12. detailed general ledger analysis (helps trace transactions for each account).

Much more complex computerized accounting systems than the Tennessee example exist. By examining a simple system however, the relationship of the computer to fundamental accounting concepts and financial reports can be understood more easily. Also the usefulness of computers becomes more apparent. The task of preparing reports on each fund is time consuming. A computer can take much of the dull routine out of accounting work and do it much more accurately.

Auditing

Purpose of Auditing

Auditing is a vital activity. It checks on the correct operation of the accounting system including validating inventories and existing equipment; proper legal authority to perform the activity; adequacy of internal control; fraud, waste, and mismanagement; and the effectiveness of the program. Two common varieties of audit are the pre- and post-audits. Pre-audits are done before obligations are made. In many states, an elected auditor performs essentially pre-audit functions. Pre-audits focus upon determining legality and examining vouchers. The depth and detail of a pre-audit vary, but the importance of independence is always present. The disadvantages associated with pre-audit are that they:

1. reduce the level of responsibility;
2. lead to red tape;
3. foster interagency friction;
4. are costly.

The post-audit is the more common form of auditing. It also should be done by an independent group. It can focus upon verification of documents, checking transactions and procedures, or examining administrative effectiveness and efficiency. Post-auditing is not closing of accounts as discussed earlier in terms of Exhibit 8-2. However, sometimes accounts cannot be closed without an audit.

Audits can be conducted within an agency. If that is done, the audit should be independent and focus upon evaluating legality of actions and effectiveness of administrative controls. Such audits commonly:

1. review compliance with and appraise performance under policies, plans, and procedures established by management for carrying out its responsibilities;
2. examine financial transactions;
3. test the reliability and usefulness of accounting and other financial and program data produced in the agency;
4. review the effectiveness with which the agency's resources are utilized;
5. examine the effectiveness of safeguards provided over agency assets to prevent or minimize waste or loss.

Internal Versus External Audits

Internal audits can be distinguished from internal inspections. The latter are designed to confirm that policy, procedures, and reporting are being carried out correctly. They are addressed to employees who are responsible for carrying out particular operations such as meat inspection, food stamp applicant screening, and unemployment insurance interviews. Internal auditing addresses broader concerns of legality, effectiveness, and efficiency.

External audits are similar to internal audits, but they are done by independent agencies. A typical external audit examines accounts, checks on the accuracy of recorded transactions and inventories, does on-site review of stocks, verifies physical existence of equipment, and reviews operating procedures and regulations. The congressional audit agency for the U.S. federal government is the General Accounting Office (GAO). This agency reports directly and is responsible to the Congress. By law, an agency must respond to GAO reports thus forcing an agency to comment on the problems raised by GAO and encouraging a statement on how the agency will resolve the problems. GAO investigates fraud, waste, and mismanagement. Their audits often focus upon delegation of responsibility, policy direction including program evaluation, budget and accounting practices, and the adequacy of internal controls including internal auditing. Legislative audits are commonly post-audits, thus the group appropriating the money often makes the final check on its expenditures.

Appendix 8-B is a GAO prepared self-evaluation guide for government audit organizations. It is based on the standards for audit of governmental organizations, programs, activities, and functions. A review of that appendix will help the reader understand what audit units and auditors should do.

REVIEW QUESTIONS

1. Explain the fundamental accounting principles and concepts of government accounting. Explain how they guide accounting practices.
2. The accounting dilemma of flexibility and uniformity is a serious management challenge. Why?
3. Cite specific examples of how accounting supports budgeting. Why is this significant?
4. Why is the key to good financial administration good account records? Why is accrual accounting necessary but also confusing?
5. Explain how one can go about an analysis of a city's financial situation by using a few key financial reports.
6. How can one isolate likely input errors by examining output financial reports? Cite some illustrations.
7. Contrast pre- and post-audit procedures. Which is likely to develop "red tape"? Why?
8. Distinguish and explain external audit, internal audit, inspection, and program evaluation.
9. Compare and contrast the audit self-evaluation guide and budget and program analysis (see chapter 6).
10. Compare and contrast administrative reservations, obligations, accrued expenditures, outlays, and cost.

Appendix 8-A

PRINCIPLES OF GOVERNMENTAL
ACCOUNTING AND REPORTING

THE NATIONAL COMMITTEE ON GOVERNMENTAL ACCOUNTING
1313 EAST 60TH STREET, CHICAGO, ILLINOIS (1968)

Legal Compliance and Financial Operations

1. A governmental accounting system must make it possible: (a) to show that all applicable legal provisions have been complied with: and (b) to determine fairly and with full disclosure the financial position and results of financial operations of the constituent funds and self-balancing account groups of the governmental unit.

Conflicts Between Accounting Principles and Legal Provisions

2. If there is a conflict between legal provisions and generally accepted accounting principles applicable to governmental units, legal provisions must take precedence. Insofar as possible, however, the governmental accounting system should make possible the full disclosure and fair presentation of financial position and operating results in accordance with generally accepted principles of accounting applicable to governmental units.

The Budget and Budgetary Accounting

3. An annual budget should be adopted by every governmental unit, whether required by law or not, and the accounting system should provide budgetary control over general governmental revenues and expenditures.

Fund Accounting

4. Governmental accounting systems should be organized and operated on a fund basis. A fund is defined as an independent fiscal and accounting entity with a self-balancing set of accounts recording cash and/or other resources together with all related liabilities, obligations, reserves, and equities which are segregated for the purpose of carrying on specific activities or attaining certain objectives in accordance with special regulations, restrictions or limitations.

184

Types of Funds

5. The following types of funds are recognized and should be used in accounting for governmental financial operations as indicated.

1. The General Fund to account for all financial transactions not properly accounted for in another fund;
2. Special Revenue Funds to account for the proceeds of specific revenue sources (other than special assessments) or to finance specified activities as required by law or administrative regulation;
3. Debt Service Funds to account for the payment of interest and principal on long-term debt other than special assessment and revenue bonds.
4. Capital Projects Funds to account for the receipt and disbursement of moneys used for the acquisition of capital facilities other than those financed by special assessment and enterprise funds;
5. Enterprise Funds to account for the financing of services to the general public where all or most of the costs involved are paid in the form of charges by users of such services;
6. Trust and Agency Funds to account for assets held by a governmental unit as trustee or agent for individuals, private organizations, and other governmental units.
7. Intragovernmental Service Funds to account for the financing of special activities and services performed by a designated organization unit within a governmental jurisdiction for other organization units within the same governmental jurisdiction.
8. Special Assessment Funds to account for special assessments levied to finance public improvements or services deemed to benefit the properties against which the assessments are levied.

Number of Funds

6. Every governmental unit should establish and maintain those funds required by law and sound financial administration. Since numerous funds make for inflexibility, undue complexity, and unnecessary expense in both the accounting system and the over-all financial administration however, only the minimum number of funds consistent with legal and operating requirements should be established.

Fund Accounts

7. A complete self-balancing group of accounts should be established and maintained for each fund. This group should include all general ledger accounts and subsidiary records necessary to reflect compliance with legal provisions and to set forth the financial position and the results of financial operations of the fund. A clear distinction should be made between the accounts relating to current assets and liabilities and those relating to fixed assets and liabilities. With the exception of Intra-governmental Service Funds, Enterprise Funds and certain Trust Funds,

fixed assets should not be accounted for in the same fund with the current assets, but should be set up in a separate, self-balancing group of accounts called the General Fixed Asset Group of Accounts. Similarly, except in Special Assessment, Enterprise, and certain Trust Funds, long-term liabilities should not be carried with the current liabilities of any fund, but should be set up in a separate, self-balancing group of accounts known as the General Long-term Debt Group of Accounts.

Valuation of Fixed Assets

8. The fixed asset accounts should be maintained on the basis of original cost, or the estimated cost if the original cost is not available, or, in the case of gifts, the appraised value at the time received.

Depreciation

9. Depreciation on general fixed assets should not be recorded in the general accounting records. Depreciation charges on such assets may be computed for unit cost purposes, provided such charges are recorded only in memorandum form and do not appear in the fund accounts.

Basis of Accounting

10. The accrual basis of accounting is recommended for Enterprise, Trust, Capital Projects, Special Assessment, and Intragovernmental Service Funds. For the General, Special Revenue, and Debt Service Funds, the modified accrual basis of accounting is defined as that method of accounting in which expenditures other than accrued interest on general long-term debt are recorded at the time liabilities are incurred and revenues are recorded when received in cash, except for material or available revenues which should be accrued to reflect properly the taxes levied and the revenues earned.

Classification of Accounts

11. Governmental revenues should be classified by fund and source. Expenditures should be classified by fund, function, organization unit, activity, character, and principal classes of objects in accordance with standard recognized classification.

Common Terminology and Classification

12. A common terminology and classification should be used consistently throughout the budget, the accounts, and the financial reports.

Financial Reporting

13. Financial statements and reports showing the current condition of budgetary and proprietary accounts should be prepared periodically to control financial operations. At the close of each fiscal year, a comprehensive annual financial report covering all funds and financial operations of the governmental unit should be prepared and published.

Appendix 8-B

part one
QUESTIONS ON THE
GENERAL STANDARDS

I. AUDIT SCOPE

A. Statutory Provisions

1. Does the audit organization have authority to examine financial transactions, accounts, and reports, as well as to determine compliance with applicable laws and regulations?

_____

2. Does the audit organization have authority to review economy and efficiency in the use of resources?

_____

3. Does the audit organization have authority to review whether the desired results of programs or activities are achieved?

_____

B. Fulfillment of Responsibilities

1. Does the audit organization usually do financial and compliance audits?

_____

2. Does the audit organization usually do economy and efficiency audits?

_____

3. Does the audit organization usually do program results audits?

_____

C. Audit Planning

1. In determining audit scope, does the audit organization consider the information needs of those who will use the report?

_____

II. STAFF QUALIFICATIONS

A. Education

1. Has the organization established specific educational level qualifications for its staff?

2. Are new professional staff required to hold 4-year degrees from accredited colleges and universities?

3. Do the majority of the audit staff hold at least a Bachelor's degree from an accredited college or university?

4. Does the audit organization actively encourage and provide financial support to its staff for continuing formal education?

5. Is the audit organization authorized to hire staff with degrees in disciplines other than finance and accounting?

6. Does the audit staff include members with degrees in management related disciplines other than finance and accounting?

B. Professional Achievements

1. Are staff members encouraged to obtain professional recognition, such as becoming a certified public accountant?

2. Are staff members encouraged to participate in professional organizations?

3. Does the audit organization encourage and help pay for staff efforts to attain professional achievements? (e.g., pay for CPA exam coaching course)?

C. Training Program

1. Does the audit organization have a formal career development and training program?

2. Does the program, excluding on-the-job training, include training in:

   a. Auditing theory and procedures?

   b. Government organization and operation?

   c. Management controls and techniques?

d. Program evaluation techniques?

e. Computer systems and EDP auditing techniques?

f. Evidence gathering including interviewing techniques?

g. Elements of audit findings?

h. Oral communication and report writing?

3. Does the audit organization periodically measure the effectiveness of the career development and training program?

D. Staff Appraisal System

1. Does the audit organization formally appraise the performance of staff members on a consistent, periodic basis?

2. Is the system for staff appraisal formalized in writing and communicated to all staff members?

3. Are staff members periodically advised of their promotion potential?

4. Does the appraisal system provide adequate staff data to assure that the qualifications of the staff assigned to the audits are commensurate with the scope and complexities of the assignment?

E. Use of Consultants

1. Does the audit organization have authority to hire consultants and experts?

2. Does the audit organization have funds available to hire consultants and experts when needed?

3. Are consultants and experts used when needed?

III. INDEPENDENCE

A. Head of the Audit Organization

1. If the head of the audit organization is appointed, is legislative confirmation required?

2. Does the head of the audit organization (either appointed or elected) completely disassociate himself from partisan politics?

3. Is the head auditor's term of office a specified number of years? _____

4. For an elected auditor, has the term of office been established so it does not coincide with that of other chief public officials? _____

5. Is the auditor protected from being removed from office without a hearing? _____

B. Organizational Independence

1. Is the audit organization free from restrictions on its funds or activities by the organizations it audits? _____

2. Is the audit organization located where it reports to the highest practicable level of government? _____

3. Does the staff of the audit organization come under a merit or civil service system? _____

C. Audit Freedom

1. Is the audit organization free to:

   a. Determine the scope and character of its audits?

   b. Choose and apply its own audit procedures?

   c. Select the activities to be examined?

   d. Examine all necessary books, records, and other supporting documentation?

   e. Select and assign audit staff?

   f. Report results of audits? _____

2. Does the audit organization have adequate means for obtaining records and documents? _____

D. Availability of Audit Reports

1. Are reports available to others on request? _____

2. When other governmental audit organizations are known to have an interest in particular subject areas, are they notified of reports issued pertaining to those areas?

E. Conflicts of Interest

1. Does the organization have a system whereby staff members of the audit organization must report instances where they may not be personally independent of the audited entity because of:

 a. Official, professional, or personal relationships?

 b. Preconceived ideas or personal likes or dislikes concerning an organization, program, or individuals?

 c. Previous management involvement with the entity audited?

 d. Financial interest?

F. Selection of External Auditors

1. If public accountants or other professionals are engaged to perform audits or parts of audits, is there assurance that these individuals have had no former association with the entity under audit which might affect their independence?

2. If reports prepared by public accountants or other professionals are to be issued by the audit organization under its own cover letter, does the organization have written instructions for review of such reports?

IV. DUE PROFESSIONAL CARE

A. Organization and Responsibility

1. Does the audit organization have clearly defined lines of responsibility and authority?

2. Does the audit organization have a formal functional statement for each segment of the organization?

B. Policies

1. Are there adequate written policies for:

    a. Preparing audit workpapers? _____

    b. Reviewing audit workpapers? _____

    c. Retaining audit workpapers? _____

2. Are there adequate written policies for:

    a. Preparing audit reports? _____

    b. Reviewing audit reports? _____

    c. Distributing audit reports? _____

3. Are policies communicated to the staff? _____

C. Planning System

1. Does the organization have a formal system for planning, scheduling and controlling audit assignments? _____

2. Does the current planning schedule show:

    a. Audits to be performed? _____

    b. Estimated time required to do the audits? _____

    c. Approximate dates of the audits? _____

3. Does the audit organization periodically compare available staff time with estimated audit requirements and set work priorities accordingly? _____

D. Quality Control System

1. Are periodic progress reports prepared by supervisors at the audit sites and sent to the audit managers? _____

2. Are supervisory reviews conducted and documented for each audit? _____

3. Are objective reviews of audit reports made to insure that factual matter is reported accurately, completely, and fairly and that findings and conclusions are supported by enough evidence in the audit workpapers to demonstrate the correctness and reasonableness of the matters reported? _____

part two
QUESTIONS ON THE EXAMINATION
AND EVALUATION STANDARDS

I. AUDIT PLANNING

A. Preliminary Planning

1. Before the detailed audit was conducted was a survey made to identify where problems existed and where work needed to be done?

2. If an economy and efficiency audit or program results audit was done, was the survey sufficient to determine what specific points should be addressed?

3. In some instances audits of the same organizations, programs, activities, or functions may be required by Federal, State and/or local laws, regulations or ordinances. Did the audit staff contact other governmental audit organizations at the same or different levels of govern-ment and inquire about their audit requirements with the objective of making one audit serve the needs of all interested governmental levels?

4. Did the audit staff obtain legal assistance in identifying laws and regulations affecting the audited entity and include them in the audit program?

5. Was the size of the audit staff adequate in relation to the scope of the audit and the time in which it was to be completed?

6. Were the qualifications of auditors assigned to the audit commensurate with the needs of the audit?

7. Did the audit staff have a mutual understanding of audit scope and objectives with those authorizing the audit?

8. Was an entrance conference held with top management officials of the audited entity to explain the objectives and scope of the audit and to arrange for necessary working space, records, tours, etc?

_____

B. Audit Program

1. Was a written audit program prepared?

_____

2. Did the audit program contain basic background information about the objectives and organizational characteristics of the audited entity?

_____

3. Were the objectives of the audit clearly presented in the audit program?

_____

4. Did the audit program clearly define the intended scope of audit coverage?

_____

5. Did the audit program specify whether the audit was to include financial and compliance, economy and efficiency, and/or program results aspects?

_____

6. Did the audit program require reviewing the system of internal management control as it related to the subject area audited?

_____

7. If an economy and efficiency audit was conducted, did the audit program specify criteria for determining whether management was performing its operations in an efficient and economical manner?

_____

8. If a program results audit was conducted did the audit program clearly specify the criteria to be used for evaluating the effectiveness of the program?

_____

9. Did the audit program contain procedures for the auditor to follow to achieve the audit objectives?

_____

10. Did the audit program set forth the general format to be followed in audit reports and a general discussion of the type of information desired in them?

_____

II. STAFF SUPERVISION

A. Clearly Defined Responsibilities

1. Was one individual assigned supervisory responsibility for the work at each audit site?

2. If audit work was performed by staffs at different audit sites, was one individual responsible for the work at all sites?

B. Supervisory Review

1. Were supervisors available during the audit to discuss scope, objectives, procedures, reporting, and problems with the audit staff?

2. Were supervisory reviews conducted regularly and in proportion to the qualifications and experience of the audit staff?

3. Do workpapers show evidence that supervisory reviews were conducted?

4. Were supervisory reviews conducted to insure:

a. conformance with standards?

b. the audit program was followed?

c. audit objectives were accomplished?

d. workpapers supported findings and conclusions?

e. workpapers provided sufficient data to prepare a meaningful report?

5. Was a time budget prepared for the audit?

6. Was a record kept of actual staff time spent on the audit?

III. COMPLIANCE WITH STATUTORY AND REGULATORY REQUIREMENTS

1. Did the audit staff sufficiently examine transactions and operations to determine whether the entity acted in compliance with applicable laws and regulations?

IV. EVIDENCE AND AUDITING
PROCEDURES

1. Do audit workpapers show that the audit staff obtained an understanding of the audited entity before determining specific audit tests and procedures?

2. Do audit workpapers show that audit staff followed up on findings from previous audits to determine whether appropriate corrective measures had been taken?

3. Do audit workpapers show that the following were considered in determining audit tests and procedures:

   a. Results of internal control evaluations?

   b. What was necessary to achieve the audit objectives?

   c. Were only those matters related to the audit objectives considered for audit?

4. If statistical sampling procedures were employed, do workpapers contain:

   a. Writeups on the basis for sample selection?

   b. Writeups of conclusions reached from the samples?

5. Were there any areas of audit where it appeared statistical sampling procedures might have been used but were not?

6. Were all procedures called for in the audit program completed or reasons given for not completing them?

V. EVALUATION OF INTERNAL
CONTROL

1. Do audit workpapers show that the audit staff studied the organization of the entity well enough to conclude:

   a. Whether responsibility for financial and operational activities was fixed?

b. Whether authority for financial and operational activities was clear?

c. Whether authorizing, approving, recording, and reviewing financial and custodial activities were done by persons other than those who performed the activities?

d. Whether individuals understood their responsibilities?

2. Do the workpapers show that the audit staff studied the entity's financial and program operations policies well enough to determine:

a. Whether policies were stated clearly in writing?

b. Whether policies were communicated throughout the organization?

3. Do the workpapers show that the audit staff tested the entity's financial and operational procedures will enough to conclude:

a. Whether accounting records maintained for resources and operations were adequate and maintained on a current basis?

b. Whether the accounting system produced information needed to conduct operations?

c. Whether the accounting system produced information for determining future financial, property, and personnel needs?

d. Whether adequate procedures existed to provide controls over acquisition of goods and services?

e. Whether controls existed to keep errors and irregularities in operational and financial data to a minimum?

f. Whether completed transactions were reviewed internally to insure they were appropriate and correct?

g. internally reviewed for appraisal of results and for compliance with prescribed policies and procedures?

h. Whether procedures existed for taking action on internal review findings and recommendations?

4. Did the audit staff review the work of employees in the financial and operational departments well enough to conclude whether they discharged their duties satisfactorily?

5. Was physical protection given to resources and records to keep the risk of loss by destruction, theft, or damage to a minimum?

VI. FINANCIAL AND COMPLIANCE AUDITS—GENERAL

1. If weaknesses in financial operations were identified during the review of internal control or suspected for any other reason, were they followed up to determine the importance and the causes of such matters?

2. ...were appropriate procedures followed and sufficient tests made to see that financial operations were properly conducted?

3. Did the audit staff determine whether the audited entity was accounting for resources, liabilities, and operations in accordance with generally accepted accounting principles or with other specified accounting principles applicable to the organization, program, function or activity audited?

4. Were financial reports audited to insure that:

    a. The information they contained was presented fairly and accurately?

    b. They were prepared in accordance with generally accepted accounting principles or with other specified accounting principles applicable to the organization, program, function or activity audited, and applied consistently from one period to the next?

5. Did the audit staff conduct sufficient tests to determine whether the entity was complying with the requirements of applicable laws and regulations?

6. Were representation letters obtained from management on key issues relating to financial and other statements?

VII. AUDITS OF ECONOMY AND EFFICIENCY MATTERS

1. If any weaknesses affecting efficient and economical operations were identified during the evaluation of internal control, were they followed up sufficiently to determine the importance and the cause of such matters?

2. Was audit work performed to determine whether the entity was managing its resources (personnel, property, space, etc.) in an economical and efficient manner?

3. Where uneconomical or inefficient practices were found to exist, were the importance and causes of these matters examined?

4. If the audit staff developed its own criteria for evaluating economy and efficiency, was the reasonableness of the criteria discussed with officials of the auditee and their views considered before criteria was finalized?

VIII. AUDITS OF PROGRAM RESULTS

1. If any weaknesses affecting program effectiveness were identified during the evaluation of internal control, were they followed up sufficiently to determine the importance and the causes of such matters?

2. In reviewing the results of programs or activities, did the audit staff consider:

   a. The existence, relevance and validity of criteria

the entity used to measure its effectiveness?

b. The appropriateness of methods the entity used to evaluate results?

c. The accuracy of data the entity used to measure program effectiveness?

d. The reliability of results the entity obtained?

e. Whether legislation or other expressions of intent provided the entity adequate guidance on the objectives of programs and how programs were to be implemented?

f. Whether the entity was accomplishing the results intended by legislation as described in the legislative history?

g. Whether the intended results were accomplished within the cost anticipated at the time the legislation was enacted?

h. Whether the entity's officials had the information they needed to supervise and control?

i. Whether the entity's officials had adequate internal review resources to monitor program operations and identify shortfalls?

3. Where the audit staff was required to identify performance criteria, was the reasonableness of the criteria discussed with officials of the auditee and their views considered in developing the final criteria?

4. If the audit work required using special expertise, did the audit staff include persons having the appropriate skills?

IX. WORKPAPERS

1. Does each audit workpaper show:

a. The name and location of the audited entity?

b. Identification of the specific audit assignment?

c. The subject matter of the workpaper?

d. Date or period applicable to the subject matter?

e. Identification of the auditor who prepared the workpaper?

f. The date the workpaper was prepared?

g. Source(s) of information appearing on the workpaper?

h. A legend for all marks or symbols used?

i. A systematic indexing system?

j. Necessary cross-references to other related workpapers?

2. Are workpapers legible and neat?

3. Do workpapers contain a clear statement of purpose that is related to audit objectives and reporting?

4. Are workpapers clear and understandable without supplementary explanation?

5. Were workpaper summaries prepared for audit segments and findings?

6. Do workpaper summaries show:

a. The objective of the audit segment?

b. Audit work done, including justification for reducing normal scope?

c. Results achieved?

d. Auditor's conclusions?

e. Auditor's recommendations?

7. Was the audit program cross-referenced to the audit workpapers?

8. Does the audit organization have a policy to retain work-

papers for a period of time to satisfy legal and administrative requirements?

9. Are workpapers retained in accordance with the policy?

X. EXIT CONFERENCE

1. Was an exit conference held with management officials of the entity audited to explain audit findings, conclusions, and recommendations?

2. Do the workpapers contain a written record of the exit conference?

3. Was consideration given to officials' responses to findings, and appropriate follow-up made with respect to additional facts or data obtained?

part three
QUESTIONS ON THE REPORTING STANDARDS

I. FORM AND DISTRIBUTION

A. Form

1. Was a written report prepared on audit results?

2. Were the prescribed format and procedures followed in preparing the report?

B. Distribution

1. Were copies of the audit report distributed to appropriate officials of the organization or governmental body requiring or arranging for the audit?

2. Were copies of the audit report distributed to officials of the audited entity responsible for taking action on audit findings and recommendations?

II. TIMELINESS

    1. If an audit report was required by a certain date, was this requirement met?

    2. Was the audit report timely enough for legislative and management officials of the audited entity to take action on the audit results?

    3. Were significant audit findings discussed with officials during the audit so early corrective action could be taken?

III. CONTENT

    A. Clarity, and Conciseness

        1. Is the audit report as concise as possible yet clear and complete enough to be understood?

        2. Is the language of the report as clear and simple as the subject matter permits?

    B. Objectivity and Constructive Tone

        1. Are audit findings and conclusions presented objectively?

        2. Are opinions and conclusions in reports clearly identified as such?

        3. Does the audit report place primary emphasis on improvement rather than on criticism of the past?

        4. Are critical comments presented in balanced perspective, recognizing unusual difficulties or circumstances faced by the operating officials concerned?

        5. Were the views of the auditee considered and presented in the final audit report?

        6. Were significant management accomplishments included in the audit report? (e.g., Particularly those which may be beneficial to other program managers.)

C. Scope

1. Does the audit report include a summary statement of the audit objectives?

2. Is the activity, its location, and the time period covered by the audit stated in the report?

3. Does the audit report clearly indicate which elements of audits examination—financial and compliance, efficiency and economy, and program effectiveness—were made and the extent of each element?

D. Adequacy of Support and Convincingness

1. Was report material factual and fairly presented?

2. Does the audit report contain enough detailed supporting information to make a convincing presentation?

3. Does the audit report contain information on underlying causes of problems noted in the audit?

4. Did someone in the audit organization not directly associated with the audit verify the accuracy of the report contents by checking back to the workpapers?

5. Was a copy of the final audit report cross-referenced to the audit workpapers and retained as part of the workpaper file?

6. If significant, pertinent information was omitted from the report because it was deemed privileged or confidential, was the nature of information described, and the law or other basis under which it was withheld stated?

E. Recommendations

1. Does the audit report include recommendations for actions to correct problems reported?

2. If the audit report does not contain recommendations concerning the reported problems, does it state the reasons why corrective measures were not included and additional work needed to formulate recommendations?

3. Does the audit report also identify other issues and questions needing further study and consideration by the auditor or others?

IV. FINANCIAL REPORTS

1. If a disclaimer or adverse opinion on the financial report could not express an opinion on the financial reports, were the reasons stated in the audit report?

2. Were material changes in accounting policies and procedures and their effect on financial reports explained in the audit report?

3. If there were violations of legal or regulatory requirements, including noncompliance, were they explained in the audit report?

4. If a qualification was required because of material inconsistency in financial reporting, does the report explain:

   a. The reasons for the qualification?

   b. The effect on financial reports?

   c. The auditor's opinion on the acceptability of the change?

5. If conformity to special accounting principles (instead of generally accepted accounting principles) was required, were the special accounting principles identified in the opinion?

6. Does the audit report contain supplementary information about the contents of financial reports for full and informative disclosure about the financial position and activities of the entity audited?

7. Does the auditor's opinion accurately state the facts on the basis of workpaper content and other supporting documents?

8. If supplemental data accompanied the basic financial statements, did the audit report explain whether the data had been audited and the extent of any examination made of it?

9. If a qualified opinion was is-

sued, were the phrases that include "except" or "exception" properly used?

10. If earlier period statements used for comparative purposes were unaudited or not examined by the auditor, were appropriate comments made in the financial statements or in the audit report?

11. Did the auditors take steps to report any material events that took place after the date of the financial statements?

12. On the basis of the reviewer's study of the workpapers and evidential matters, does it appear that disclosures in the financial statements are adequate?

part three
COMMENTS

REFERENCES

American Accounting Association. "Report of the Committee on Accounting For Not-For-Profit Organization," *Accounting Review*, Supplement to vol. 46 (1971), pp. 81–163.

APPLEBY, PAUL. "The Role of the Budget Division," *Public Administration Review*, 18, 3 (Summer 1957), 156–59.

ARONSON, J. RICHARD, and ELI SCHWARTZ. *Management Policies in Local Government Finance*. Washington, D.C.: International City Management Association and Municipal Officers Association, 1975.

BARTIZAL, JOHN R. *Budget Principle and Procedure*. Englewood Cliffs, N.J.: Prentice-Hall, 1940, 1942.

BATER, FRANCIS M. *The Question of Government Spending*. New York: Harper & Row, 1960.

BIERMAN, HAROLD, JR., and SEYMOUR SMIDT. *The Capital Budgeting Decision*. New York: Macmillian, 1966.

BLOCKER, JOHN GARY. *Budgeting in Relation to Distribution Cost Accounting*. Laurence, Kansas: School of Business, 1937.

BUCK, ARTHUR EUGENE. *The Budget in Government of Today*. New York: Macmillan, 1934.

BURKHEAD, JESSE. *Government Budgeting*. New York: John Wiley, 1956.

CRECINE, JOHN P. *Governmental Problem Solving: A Computer Simulation of Municipal Budgeting*. Chicago: Rand McNally, 1969.

ERNEST, E. "The Accounting Preconditions of PPB(S)," *Management Account*, 53 (January 1972), 33–37.

FISHER, G. W. *Financing Local Improvement by Special Assessment*. Chicago: Municipal Finance Officers Association, 1974.

FREEMAN, ROBERT J., and EDWARD S. LYNN. *Fund Accounting*. Englewood Cliffs, N.J.: Prentice-Hall, 1974.

HENRY, M. L., et al. "New York State's Performance Budget Experiment," *Public Administration Review* (July/August 1970).

JOINES, W. W. "Computerized General Ledger and Budgeting Accounting Systems," *Government Finance*, 5, 2 (May 1976), 27–32.

National Committee on Government Accounting. *Governmental Accounting, Auditing, and Financial Reporting*. Chicago: Municipal Finance Officers Association, 1968.

RONDINELLI, DENNIS A. "Revenue Sharing and American Cities: Analysis of the Federal Experiment in Local Assistance," *Journal of the American Institute of Planners*, 41, 5 (September 1975), 319–33.

STOIN, A. W. *Local Government Finance*. Lexington, Mass.: Lexington Books, 1975.
———. "Symposium: Performance Budgeting: Has the Theory Worked?" *Public Administration Review* (Spring 1960).

THIERANF, R. J. and RICHARD A. GROSSE. *Decision-Making Through Operations Research*. New York: John Wiley, 1970.

TURNBULL, AUGUSTUS. *Governmental Budgeting and PPBS: A Programmed Introduction*. Reading, Mass.: Addison-Wesley, 1970.

NINE

Capital Budgeting and Debt Administration

This chapter discusses state and local debt, capital budgeting, and issuances. The concept of debt is defined and classifications commonly used are explained. Capital budgeting is contrasted to operating budgeting with emphasis placed on capital facility planning and the capital budget cycle. The practical aspects of state and local bonding are explained including designing an issue, the prospectus, notice of sale, debt records, reporting, and bond ratings. This chapter introduces capital budgeting and debt administration with an emphasis placed on the specific knowledge particularly useful to a person dealing with these challenging subjects. At the completion of this chapter, the readers should understand:

1. the commonly used definition of debt;
2. why debts are incurred;
3. alternatives to debt;
4. types and forms of debt;
5. revenue bonds;
6. commonly used tests and limits on debt;
7. early warning guidelines for municpal financial operations;
8. significance of the New York City financial crisis on debt administration;
9. municipal bankruptcy, financial problems, and remedies;
10. the difference between capital and operating budgets;
11. capital facility planning and its significance;
12. analytical questions useful to probe capital budget requests as well as the role of judgment in making such decisions;
13. the similarity of the capital and operating budget cycles;
14. the essential decisions and expertise critical in designing a municipal bond issue;
15. what is and should be in a bond prospectus and notice of sale;

16. investment syndicates and their significance;
17. the importance of good bond administration and data associated with debt reporting;
18. bond ratings, what influences them, and why they are significant.

State and Local Debt

Definitions

When persons charge items on Master Charge or Visa, they are incurring a debt. They normally receive the items and pledge that they will pay for these items within a certain time period. When they get a bank loan for a car, they have incurred a debt. They have agreed to pay back the loan amount (called principal) plus an extra amount (called interest) for the privilege of borrowing the money over an extended period of time.

Governments also borrow money; thus they incur short- and sometimes long-term obligations to pay back the principal and interest. However, some types of debt (e.g., trade accounts payable and conditional repayment loans) sometimes do not involve interest payments. Debt constitutes an obligation which must be paid under the established legal conditions. The Bureau of Census uses the following definition which stresses interest bearing obligation:

> All long-term credit obligations of the government and its agencies, and all interest bearing short-term (i.e., repayable within 1 year) credit obligations. Includes judgments, mortgages, and "revenue" bonds, as well as general obligation bonds, notes and interest bearing warrants. Excludes non-interest bearing obligations, amounts owed in a trust or agency capacity, advances and contingent loans from other governments, and rights of individuals to benefit from employee-retirement funds.

Governments incur debt for several reasons. In some cases, cash is needed before the actual revenue is collected. Debt is used to harmonize those divergent patterns of current expenditures and revenue. Often, the government wishes to finance a significant capital construction project or even large equipment purchases. Current revenues cannot pay for such large purchases so a loan is negotiated. Sometimes a debt is incurred in order to refinance an existing—e.g., short-term—debt. On occasion, debt is incurred to finance operating deficits. A form of debt, often not appreciated as debt, is a government's pension benefit obligation. Bonds are normally not sold for this purpose but pensions are an increasingly significant government obligation which places severe financial pressure on governments.

Governments do not have to incur debts but the alternatives to debt are difficult to use effectively. One alternative, called a sinking fund, is to accumulate funds over time much like an individual's Christmas savings plan. The funds are invested until such time as the money is needed. Another alternative is to pay-as-you-go thus paying for the equipment or building costs out of operating expenses.

The difficulty with both alternatives is that capital facility needs of governments often do not fit the pace of financing of the funding techniques. A city sometimes cannot wait 10 or 20 years to build a water purification plant needed for a sinking fund or pay-as-you go financing approach. Emergencies and irregular expenditure demands do occur and debt is sometimes the only practical alternative under the circumstances.

Classifications of Debt

Most of the liability items in the state and local government balance sheet are debts of the government. They include bonds, certificates of indebtedness, mortgages, notes, accounts payable, warrants payable, liens, judgments, unfunded pension obligations, and selected contingent liabilities. Excluded are contingent items and reserves for encumbrances.

The largest amount of debt is in the form of bonds. They are a written promise to pay a specified sum of money (called the face value or principal amount) at a specified date or dates (called the maturity dates) together with periodic interest at a specific rate. Serial bonds, which are the most common type of bond, are designed so that a specific number of bonds are retired each year. In contrast, term bonds, which are infrequently used, are normally designed to pay the interest over time but pay the principal when the loan period has applied. Sinking funds are normally used by the borrower to collect the necessary large principal payment at the end of the loan period. Most bonds are payable to the bearer and they have detachable coupons representing the interest payments. Upon presentation of the matured coupon to the bond maker's paying agent, the proper interest represented on the coupon is paid. Bonds can be registered to provide protection to the bond holder as the ownership is registered on the books of the issuing government or paying agent. The disadvantages of registered bonds are that they cost more due to the added administrative charge and they are more difficult to sell to a third party.

The other forms of debt are normally not as significant unless they happen to involve large obligations. Certificates of indebtedness vary from state to state, but they are frequently used in connection with agency resources or assets. A mortgage bond uses property to secure the obligation without transferring title, but most of them still do not give the government's creditor the right to foreclose. Notes are widely used to represent evidence of financial obligation of normally a short-term nature. Accounts payable are government firm liabilities such as wages earned but not yet paid as well as the common unpaid bills. The now uncommon warrant is a government-issued document to the bank upon which payment is made with the approval of the government. A lien is a claim upon property arising from failure of the owner to make timely payment of a claim. A judgment is a court decision that the government has a liability or debt to a person who has sought redress through the courts. An unfunded pension liability is where a government does not place sufficient funds in an appropriate pension fund but that government is still liable for those pensions. A contingent liability is when an agreement stipulates that a liability will occur if a certain condition is met. For example, a city agrees with the area-wide transit board to help finance a transit system once the population density and traffic congestion reaches a given level. Controversies often arise over the condition and the fulfillment of the agreement.

Debts can be classified by pledge of security. One type is the "full-faith-and-credit" debt in which a government's credit, including the implied power of taxation, is unconditionally pledged. For example, a city states it will pledge itself unconditionally to pay a bond obligation. Another type is a moral debt in which the issuer or a guaranteeing government has a moral but not a legal obligation to pay. The financial community would rarely be interested in a moral debt unless a government was responsible for that debt. What commonly occurs is some government body (e.g., a housing authority) pledges its user charges or some other revenue source to pay the debt and another unit of government (e.g., the state) gives its moral backing to the debt. The financial community does normally require a default remedy to be spelled out by the government. The best pledge from the investor's point of view is a full-faith-and-credit obligation plus a specific user charge to pay the indebtedness.

Exhibit 9-1 presents the state and local debt broken down by pledge characteristics. Note that short-term borrowing is also shown in the exhibit. Since the late 1960s, the general obligations have held at about 54 percent and limited liability obligations have stabilized at about 39 percent. In the 1970s, short-term borrowing became a more significant part of the total issues. State governments tended to use limited liability obligations more than local governments. Local governments used short-term borrowing more than state governments.

Short-Term Debt

Short-term borrowing is normally done for the following reasons:

1. The community is short of the necessary revenue to pay for services. For example, the city forecasted the revenue incorrectly and there is not enough money to pay the planned expenditures.
2. A brief loan is needed and will be paid back as soon as taxes are collected. The money owed to the city may not have been collected, but obligations must be paid. A brief loan is needed to bridge this cash flow problem until the debts owed the city are paid.
3. The community has an emergency and necessary funds are not available.
4. The funds are needed to start a capital improvement project, but a long-term bond issue has not yet been approved.

So-called tax anticipation notes (TANs) and revenue anticipation notes (RANs) are common names for short-term borrowing. They should be avoided through careful management in order to avoid the interest costs associated with borrowing. Ideally, the tax payments should be timed so that revenue is available at the beginning of the fiscal year. This eliminates the need for notes and interest charges. Certainly, TANs and RANs should be paid as soon as the taxes are collected. Also, these notes should not be taken out against delinquent taxes for the reason that collectibility is questionable.

Bond anticipation notes (BANs) are also common and are an excellent tool in dealing with the complex bond market. Good strategy may be for a government to use a BAN and wait until the bond market becomes more favorable for long-term government securities. Regardless of the motivation for this form of short-term borrowing, a formal payment calendar should be established so that the debt can be paid off or refinanced without any difficulty.

Developments in the Debt Concept

Innovation can clearly be seen in the use of debt in the past 30 years. The most well-known innovative debt concept is the revenue bond. It was first used in 1897 to support the construction of the Spokane, Washington Water Works. This debt mechanism coupled with a means to raise revenue was not popular until after World War II. Then court decisions held that authorities (e.g., Port of New York and New Jersey and Triborough Bridge Authority) had separate legal status. People in government were seeking new ways to finance public facilities without increasing taxes, and revenue bonds provided an answer. Briefly, the reasons for increased use of revenue bonds are as follows:

1. Although the revenue bond had a higher interest cost than the general obligations bonds, that cost decreased significantly.
2. There was more use of public authorities and an expansion of types of authorities (e.g., airports, public parks, recreation areas and facilities, stadia and public sport facilities, power projects, housing, public markets, college dormitories, port facilities, etc.).
3. Restrictions on general obligations closed this mechanism thus forcing the use of revenue bonds.
4. It was relatively easy to obtain revenue bond approval especially due to the non-referendum requirement.
5. The ability to apply user charges to pay for debt services was appealing.

Another but lesser used version of revenue bonds are lease rental bonds. Let us say a school district cannot get voter approval on a bond issue. One ploy used is to create a nonprofit authority to build and then lease the new school to the school district. A long-term school board lease with the authority provides the necessary security so that revenue bondholders know that debt services will be paid. Thus the school is built and financed by a revenue bond. Because the authority is merely a financing mechanism, some financial groups treat these arrangements as general obligation bonds. Instead of assisting a unit of government, the same type of

EXHIBIT 9-1

State and Local Debt Outstanding by Character, Selected Years, 1952-1975

Year	Total Billions of Dollars	Total Percent of Total	Long-Term General Obligations Billions of Dollars	Long-Term General Obligations Percent of Total	Long-Term Limited Liability Obligations Billions of Dollars	Long-Term Limited Liability Obligations Percent of Total	Short-Term Billions of Dollars	Short-Term Percent of Total
1952	$ 30.1	100%	$ 23.4	78%	$ 5.3	18%	$ 1.4	4%
1957	52.7	100	32.7	62	17.8	34	2.2	4
1962	81.3	100	48.3	59	29.2	36	3.8	5
1967	114.6	100	62.8	55	44.8	39	7.0	6
1968	121.2	100	65.1	54	47.6	39	8.5	7
1969	133.5	100	70.9	53	52.6	39	10.1	8
1970	143.6	100	75.3	52	56.0	39	12.3	9
1971	158.8	100	84.0	53	59.6	38	15.2	9
1972	174.6	100	95.9	55	63.0	36	15.7	9
1973	188.5	100	102.9	55	69.7	37	15.9	8
1974	206.6	100	111.0	54	79.0	38	16.7	8
1975	221.2	100	115.6	53	85.9	39	19.8	9
State Debt Outstanding by Character								
1952	$ 6.9	100%	$ 4.9	71%	$ 1.7	25%	$ .3	4%
1957	13.7	100	6.5	47	7.0	51	.2	2
1962	22.0	100	10.3	47	11.3	51	.4	2
1967	32.5	100	13.6	42	17.6	54	1.3	4
1968	35.7	100	14.7	41	18.9	53	2.1	6
1969	39.6	100	16.2	41	20.7	52	2.7	7
1970	42.0	100	17.7	42	21.1	50	3.2	8

Year	Total	%		%		%		%
1971	47.8	100	21.5	45	22.8	48	3.5	7
1972	54.5	100	25.3	46	25.3	46	3.9	8
1973	59.4	100	28.4	48	27.3	46	3.7	6
1974	65.3	100	30.9	47	30.8	47	3.6	6
1975	72.1	100	33.7	47	33.8	47	4.6	6

Local Debt Outstanding by Character

Year	Total	%		%		%		%
1952	$ 23.2	100%	$18.5	79%	$ 3.6	16%	$ 1.1	5%
1957	39.0	100	26.2	67	10.8	28	2.0	5
1962	59.3	100	38.0	64	17.9	30	3.4	6
1967	82.1	100	49.2	60	27.2	33	5.7	7
1968	85.5	100	50.4	59	28.7	34	6.4	7
1969	94.0	100	54.7	58	31.9	34	7.4	8
1970	101.6	100	57.6	57	34.9	34	9.1	9
1971	111.0	100	62.5	56	36.8	33	11.7	11
1972	120.1	100	70.6	59	37.7	31	11.8	10
1973	129.1	100	74.5	58	42.4	33	12.2	9
1974	141.3	100	80.1	57	48.2	34	13.1	9
1975	149.1	100	81.8	55	52.1	35	15.2	10

Source: Advisory Commission on Intergovernmental Relations, *Understanding the Market for State and Local Debt*, M-104, May 1976 (updated); *Significant Feature of Fiscal Federation 1976–77*, M-110, March 1977.

authorities are sometimes created to help industry in their plant and equipment acquisition. These industrial aid revenue bonds are paid off through a lease which exists between authority and industry.

Industrial aid bonds were started in Mississippi to encourage industrial growth in the state. Most states use such revenue bonds, but Mississippi and a few other states are unusual in that even general obligation borrowing authority can be used to assist industry. The bonds are retired through revenue generated from leases between the government and industry.

Tests and Limits

At the local and state levels, questions are raised when increasing the local or state public debt is contemplated. Some argue that no debt is best. Others say that if the services can be greatly increased by substituting capital for current expenditures such as labor costs, then such investments are wise. Others argue that capital expenditures benefit tomorrow's taxpayer and paying a debt appropriately shifts the cost for the project to tomorrow's taxpayers. Others use a more pragmatic test: If (1) the government can service the debt (i.e., meet the payments as well as meet other normal expenses of government), and (2) can refinance its debt through the market, then the debt is acceptable.[1] Servicing a debt can be a tremendous burden on a community. A commonly used danger sign is when the debt service approaches 20 to 25 percent of the total budget. In some communities this limit is exceeded, but nationally the aggregate debt figures for state and local governments are less than 10 percent of the total budgets.

A more serious problem is refinancing the debt. Exhibit 9-2 presents some significant facts. The short-term (less than one year) borrowing has been larger than the long-term borrowing amount in the 1970s. Often the reason reverts to the high interest rate and the difficulty of getting voter approval for long-term debts. Regardless of the reason, the requirment placed on state and local governments is to retire the debt or to refinance the short-term debt each year. This places pressure on the market, and the weaker government borrowers find it very difficult to find investors. These weaker government borrowers are not in a position to pay off the bonds, so default becomes a very real possibility in spite of the fact that they normally can meet the interest payments.

Governments normally having the most difficulty are those experiencing weak economic growth. If an area is growing, then there is demand for borrowing, but there is an improving tax base to pay that debt. If the tax base is shrinking but the cost of government is increasing, then the government is more likely to be classified as weak and not able to attract investors when refinancing is sought.

---

[1]Some argue even this test is not appropriate given the changing municipal market demands and conditions. There is no uniform acceptance of any single simple test.

EXHIBIT 9-2

Annual Dollar Volume of State and Local Borrowing, 1950-1975 (in millions)

Year	Long-Term Amount	Percent of Long-Term of Total Amount	Short-Term Amount
1950	$3,693.6	(69.6)	$1,611.1
1951	3,278.1	(66.6)	1,636.8
1952	4,401.3	(68.2)	2,049.2
1953	5,557.9	(73.0)	2,756.6
1954	6,968.6	(67.5)	3,350.2
1955	5,976.5	(69.7)	2,592.9
1956	5,446.4	(66.8)	2,706.3
1957	6,958.2	(63.0)	3,273.5
1958	7,448.8	(65.5)	3,910.5
1959	7,681.0	(64.7)	4,178.6
1960	7,229.5	(64.3)	4,006.2
1961	8,359.5	(64.9)	4,514.2
1962	8,558.2	(64.2)	4,763.5
1963	10,106.7	(64.8)	5,480.8
1964	10,544.1	(66.0)	5,423.3
1965	11,084.2	(62.9)	6,537.4
1966	11,088.9	(62.9)	6,523.5
1967	14,287.9	(64.0)	8,025.3
1968	16,374.3	(65.4)	8,658.6
1969	11,460.2	(49.3)	11,783.1
1970	17,761.6	(49.8)	17,879.9
1971	24,369.5	(49.0)	26,281.5
1972	22,940.8	(47.6)	25,221.8
1973	22,952.6	(48.1)	24,667.4
1974	22,824.0	(44.0)	29,040.7
1975	29,224.3	(50.2)	28,972.8

Source: Advisory Commission Intergovernmental Relations, *Understanding the Market for State and Local Debt,* M-104, May 1976.

Investors' views are significant. They wish to buy safe bonds or notes which will earn them some money. There are no ideal indicators; however, investors do use the following indicators in making decisions:

1. Does the ratio of debt to full value exceed 10 percent?
2. What is the ratio of debt to market value of the real property? How does that compare with other governments?
3. What is the debt per capita? How does this compare with other governments?
4. What is the ratio of debt to personal income (per capita income)?
5. What is the debt service to total budget ratio?

Standard and Poor's (a major bond rating firm) has developed a series of early warning guidelines which municipalities would be wise to monitor carefully in considering their own financial operations:

1. current year operating deficit;
2. two consecutive years of operating fund deficit;
3. current year operating deficit that is larger than the previous year's deficit;
4. a general fund deficit in the current year—balance sheet—current position;
5. a current general fund deficit (two or more years in the last five)
6. short-term debt outstanding (other than BAN) at the end of the fiscal year, greater than 5 percent of main operating fund revenues;
7. a two-year trend of increasing short-term debt outstanding at fiscal year end;
8. short-term interest and current year debt service greater than 20 percent of total revenues;
9. property taxes greater than 90 percent of the tax limit;
10. net debt outstanding greater than 90 percent of the tax limit;
11. total property tax collections less than 92 percent of total levy;
12. a trend of decreasing tax collections—two consecutive years on a three-year trend;
13. declining market valuations—two consecutive years—three-year trend;
14. overall net debt ratio 20 percent higher than previous year;
15. overall net debt ratio 50 percent higher than four years ago.

State constitutions and laws do establish artificial limits. They vary greatly from state to state as well as by type of local government. Normally, they express the limit as a percent of the property tax base. Often state laws add provisions so that jurisdictions, which tax the same citizens, have lower limits. This avoids greater taxpayer liabilities for citizens from two or more overlapping jurisdictions. Also state laws sometimes establish artificial limits based on the tax imposed for servicing the debt. Another common state limitation is the procedural requirement calling for a referendum on long-term indebtedness bond issues.

Revenue bonds are treated by investors much like corporation bonds. State law often does not prescribe limits and the limits are established by the market. Investors examine forecasts of income to insure debt services will be met and their investments will be safe.

New York City Financial Crisis

In April 1975, New York City hovered on the brink of default on its obligations. With help from New York State, the federal government, and others, default was averted but two significant consequences have emerged:

1. interest rates are higher for state and local government after the crisis;
2. more elaborate financial disclosures are now required.

The effects of the New York crisis were felt throughout the nation and North Carolina is one example. In *Southern City,* Kenneth Murray reported in January, 1976, that:

A recent study by the Municipal Finance Officer's Association (MFOA) shows that the New York City financial crisis has already cost local governments in North Carolina $424,000 in first-year added interest costs on bonded indebtedness and $5.1 million total in interest over the life of municipal bonds issued in 1975.[2]

In the pre-crisis era, state and local governments were able to sell their bonds without revealing much about their financial situation. Since then, investors are demanding greater disclosure of facts about the community and bonds. Appendix 9-A of this chapter explains the Oregon bond disclosure guideline which is a useful model to follow.

EXHIBIT 9-3

**Holders of Outstanding State and Local Debt,
Selected Years, 1950-1975**

Year	Households	Commercial banks	Fire and casualty insurance companies	Other*	Total
1950	40%	33%	4%	23%	100%
1960	44	25	11	20	100
1965	36	39	11	14	100
1966	38	39	12	11	100
1967	33	44	12	11	100
1968	30	48	12	10	100
1969	35	45	12	8	100
1970	31	49	12	8	100
1971	28	51	13	8	100
1972	26	53	14	7	100
1973	27	51	15	7	100
1974	31	48	15	6	100
1975	34	45	15	6	100

*Mainly corporations and life insurance companies.
Source: Advisory Commission on Intergovernmental Relations, *Understanding the Market for State and Local Debt*, M-104, May 1976.

Exhibit 9-3 presents the holders of outstanding state and local debt in recent years. A significant percentage of bond holders are households and many are small investors. Holdings by small investors have grown from $5.3 billion in 1950 to $60 billion by 1975. Inflation has moved more middle class families into the higher tax brackets thus making state and local bonds a good investment for them. In the past, state and local bond investors were large sophisticated concerns capable of hiring the expertise to protect their interests. Now, the New York City crisis plus the large number of small investors have dictated a need for full financial disclosures by governments seeking investors in their bonds.

Full disclosure documents are expensive to prepare. For example, Harris

---

[2]Kenneth Murray, "New York Crisis—Its Effect on North Carolina," *Southern City* (Raleigh, N.C.: North Carolina League of Municipalities, January 1976), p. 6.

County, Texas, had to develop a disclosure statement in 1977 before it went to the market for two issues. The cost was $190,000. The market has been the source of the pressure, but there has been increasing interest in having the government (Securities and Exchange Commission) regulate this market as they do the private security market. The Municipal Finance Officers Association (MFOA) has developed a volunteer "Disclosure Guidelines for Offerings of Securities by State and Local Governments." This guideline is optional in the municipal bond market, but the trend is toward greater disclosure.

In 1933, Congress decided to regulate corporate securities but not state and local bonds. Such regulation was considered unnecessary, especially considering that few cases of abuse were on record. Also there was the constitutional question involving state sovereignty. In the mid-1970s, Congress considered revising the law due to the then crisis of confidence in the market. The arguments against changing the law were the same constitutional sovereignty question and the voluntary measures taken by the MFOA. There has been some but not total local government compliance with MFOA voluntary guidelines.

Government Financial Emergencies

Given the publicity involving the New York City financial crisis, one would begin to assume that municipal bankruptcy was common. It is not. From 1938 to 1945, there were 298 bankruptcy cases filed with the worst year being 104 in 1940. From 1954 to 1975, there were only 18 bankruptcy cases filed with the highest in one year being 3.

There are rather clear warning signs for a municipality which is in financial trouble:

1. an operating fund revenue—expenditure imbalance in which current expenditures significantly exceeded current revenues in one fiscal period (a well managed government, under some conditions such as an excessively large fund balance, could properly have this type of imbalance);
2. a consistent pattern of current expenditures exceeding current revenues by small amounts for several years;
3. an excess of current operating liabilities over current assets (a fund deficit);
4. short-term operating loans outstanding at the conclusion of a fiscal year, the borrowing of cash from restricted funds, or an increase in unpaid bills in lieu of short-term operating loans;
5. a high and rising rate of property tax delinquency;
6. a sudden substantial decrease in assessed values for unexpected reasons;
7. an unfunded or under-funded pension liability unless done over a long period of time such as 40 years;
8. poor budgeting, accounting, and reporting.

Once there is recognition of the financial problems, financial management improvements can be considered. The most common remedy is to eliminate the imbalance between revenue and expenditures. Often, an appropriate remedy is to develop safeguards against misuse of short-term operating funds. The remedy could be to fund the retirement system adequately. Commonly, improvements must be made in municipal accounting and reporting systems.

If self-remedies are ineffective, then more significant steps can be taken. Some states have administrative bodies created to assist troubled local government. If that is inadequate, the courts can demand consultants be hired such as Morgan Guarantee Trust and if necessary arrange for direct agreements with creditors. This is usually adequate for temporary or technical financial emergencies. If the problem continues, states sometimes have the power to force special remedies on a local government. Agreements usually undergo state review, approval, and supervision. The federal role is to provide a means to devise financial adjustments which a majority of the creditors approve.

Under chapter 9 of the federal bankruptcy law, a plan of composition or financial adjustments is developed. First, a voluntary petition for bankruptcy is filed by the eligible local government unit. A plan of composition must be filed with the petition. The plan must be accepted by those holding 51 percent of the securities affected by the plan. Upon filing, an order is entered by the judges either approving or dismissing the plan. If approved, the resources of the debtor come within the jurisdiction of the court and a time and place is fixed for a hearing. Notice is given to the creditors, answers can be filed, and the hearing is held. After the hearing, the court may confirm a plan of composition that has been accepted by the creditors involved in two-thirds of the aggregate amount. The court may but seldom does continue jurisdiction after the confirmation of the plan.

Capital Budgeting

Operating Versus Capital Budgeting

Most local governments have two types of budgets: operating and capital. The operating budget deals with the every day type of activities. The capital budget deals with large expenditures for capital items. They differ in the nature of items purchased, methods of financing, and even the accompanying decision-making process. In most instances, operating expenses are depleted in a single year. Normally, capital items have long-range returns, useful life spans, are relatively expensive, and have physical presences such as a building, road, water supply system, or sewage system.

The most significant difference is the method of financing. Capital budget items are often financed through borrowing, but they can also be funded by saving a period of years for the capital item, grants, special assessment, and the general revenue fund. Because government debts are involved, not surprisingly state laws do establish debt limits (normally associated with the assessed value of property). Also states often require equalization rates to insure consistent treatment throughout each state. The debt limits vary from state to state and there are exceptions to the limit and application of equalization rates.

Some local governments shift as many expenses as possible from operating to capital budgets. For example, in both West Point, Mississippi, and New York City, band uniforms have been called capital budget items by public officials. This tendency can lead to corrupting the concept of a capital item to such an extent that the government has two operating budgets with one financed through borrowing. That situation in turn leads to overuse of bonding, greater government resources used for debt retirement, and proportionately less money used to meet operating budget demands. Eventually the debt can become large enough that payments can not be met and the community must face the possibility of municipal bankruptcy. Traditionally, debt is used to finance items with a life expectance that lasts as long as the debt payments. This practice acts to limit the overuse of debt financing and makes the debt more politically defensible as the future taxpayers are able to identify how they benefited from the decision to finance the item by borrowing money.

In capital budgeting, planning and careful deliberate action are essential. Planning is needed to integrate the capital item with the remainder of the physical structure in the community. Capital improvement plans are essential to coordinate the work by time, funding possibilities, and physical plans. If building is involved, then the process of executing decisions involves studying the possibilities, site selection and acquisition, planning and design as well as construction financing. Delays translate to higher construction costs due to inflation, especially rising labor costs; thus, delays are to be avoided. Also, the increased operating and maintenance expense due to the new facility is an important factor which can be considered in the planning phase. Communities have built facilities they can not afford to operate or maintain (e.g., stadiums).

Capital Facilities Planning

Decisions to add a public facility or make extensive repairs can be made on the basis of understanding the needs of the community and the resources available. The best approach to identifying the resources is to inventory the existing public facilities. The next step is to catalog the proposed public facilities. The key facts in the catalog include: the location of the proposed facility, the year of construction, cost priority, project description, financing schedule, prior or sunk costs, projection of future related fund requests, operating costs, and savings in operating and maintenance costs. The inventory and file of proposed projects can be updated at least once a year to insure that decisions are made on the correct facts.

Making decisions on proposed projects is not easy and can be aided greatly if there are clear detailed answers to the following questions:

1. What is the relationship of the proposed project to the overall development of the city?
2. How many citizens will be helped by the project, and how many citizens will be harmed or inconvenienced if the project is not constructed? What citizens?
3. Will the proposed project replace a present worn out service or structure or is it an additional responsibility of government?
4. Will the project add to the property value of the area thus increasing the value of city property and receipts from property tax? How much increase?
5. Will the construction of the improvement add to the city's operation and maintenance budget? How much?
6. Will the project increase the efficiency of performance? How much and where? What cost savings will result? Will the project reduce the cost of performance for a particular service? How much and where?
7. Will the project provide a service required for economic growth and development of the municipality?
8. Is the estimated cost of the improvement within the city's ability to pay?

Ultimately, priorities have to be decided and judgments have to be made. Sometimes analytical techniques such as cost-benefit analysis are useful but judgment cannot be avoided. Some communities use a point system to establish priorities. One scale used is as follows:

1. urgent (highest priority);
2. essential;
3. necessary;
4. desirable;
5. acceptable;
6. deferrable (lowest priority).

Capital Budget Cycle

The budget cycle for capital budgeting is similar to the operating budget cycle. The phases are identical. A capital budget call and calendar are needed just as in an operating budget. Detailed information must be collected. Illustrations of the forms can be found by consulting the publications of the Municipal Finance Officers Association noted in this chapter's references.

Many governments prepare a multiyear capital improvement program each year. This helps those relying on capital decisions to understand the likely physical facilities in the near future. The program is normally funded through borrowing, grants, and the operating budget. The government formally approves the capital improvement plan and passes an ordinance or law which clearly explains what is approved and the method of financing the program.

Capital budgets are carefully reviewed. Both budget analysts and planners review the plans for possible errors and potential problems. Public hearings are commonly held, especially if revenue sharing money is used to fund the capital budget. Careful consideration goes into deciding the best financing plan. Ultimately, the capital budget is approved by the official government policy-making unit such as the city council and possibly even the electorate if a bond issue is involved.

Bonding

Designing an Issue

Once a government has decided to borrow money, then bonding normally must be undertaken. Normally, competitive bidding is used to seek the lowest bidder. Prior to publishing the invitation to bid, decisions must be made on the maturity, the size of the issue, the call terms, the permissible coupon structures, and the interest cost limit plus the option to reject the bids.

The maturity varies in length and size. Sometimes they are as long as thirty years, but often they are only twenty years. The maturity should not be longer than the useful life of the capital facility which is being financed. Serial bonds sometimes have no payments during the first two to even five years and some have a large final maturity payment. Issues of less that $1 million are not wise because they are not efficient, economical, or appreciated in the market. In 1970, the average issue size was $4.2 million. Large issues require the buyers to form new syndicates. These are merely limited partnerships for the purpose of buying and selling a particular issue of bonds. Syndicates are easily formed and are commonplace in the financial community.

Call provisions and coupon structures are important. A call provision is the right of the borrower to buy back bonds at set prices regardless of current market rate. They do mean that the interest rate is even higher because of the provision. Sometimes the invitation to bid specifies uniform coupons but nonuniform bids exist. They sometimes provide for high coupons for initial periods and low coupons on longer-term bonds thus accelerating the principal repayment. The rate structure depends upon what the buyer believes will sell in the market.

For most bidders, the fact that there is a tax advantage for municipal bonds is significant. The interest income is exempt from federal income taxation and often exempt from income tax in the state of issue. This advantage is lost if the bonds are classified as "arbitrage" bonds. If the state or local government places the loaned funds in revenue-generating investments such as other government bonds, then the Internal Revenue Service would call the bonds arbitrage and would tax the interest income of the bond holder. Without such a rule, local governments would take advantage of their unique lower interest rates to invest in higher interest bearing bonds. That would lead to the absurd situation where much of the nation's debt would be held twice: once by local government and again by local government bondholders. Arbitrage only applies to long-term investments, thus local governments can temporarily invest the funds from bonds and earn extra revenue.

Other factors can also be considered before a bond is offered. The government may wish to establish an interest cost limit to protect itself from bids that are, as a group, unreasonable. Also the government may wish to add a stipulation that all bids may be rejected to further protect itself. Decisions can be made on the type of bond and if it should be registered or not. Will the bond be sold at a public bidding, competitive, negotiated or private placement? When will the bond be dated? What is the best time and place of sale? What are the payment dates for principal and interest? Who will prepare the bond sale documents? Who will receive and read the bids? How will the bids be tabulated and awarded? Who will print the bonds so that the possibility of counterfeiting and theft will be minimized? How will delivery of bonds and receipts be conducted? What will be done if no bids are received? These and other matters are normally considered when an issue is developed.

Many local governments do not have the necessary in-house expertise to handle bonding and therefore seek outside assistance. Some states provide assistance, but normally private advisory services are needed. The amount and degree of assistance varies with the amount and kind of funding contemplated. In moderate size, full-faith-and-credit transactions, groups such as local commercial banks, investment bankers, bond counsels, and state agencies may provide the services at no direct or minimum charge on negotiated sales. However, the services would be minimal and there might be the expectation of developing or protecting an advantageous relationship. Often the government is wiser to contract for consultative services unless adequate in-house competence has been developed.

Purchasers of bonds need to be assured the bond itself is legal and they will not check the public record themselves. Therefore, a bond counsel is needed to certify (1) the legal existence of the government offering the bond, (2) the propriety of authorization of the bond, (3) the correctness of the procedures which have been followed in the conduct of the sale, (4) absence of litigation with respect to the validity of the bond issue, and (5) the correctness of the signatures on the bond. This assurance carries more weight if the bond counsel commands wide respect among investment bankers and investors.

Bond Prospectus, Notice of Sale, and Sale

Since the mid-1970s, a more elaborate bond prospectus is required by investors. The prospectus is merely the information needed by investors to decide whether or not they wish to invest in the bonds. Key information in the prospectus often includes:

1. description of the bonds
2. security for the bonds
3. description of the government
4. financial procedures pertinent to the issue

5. fund revenues and disbursements
6. explanation of the fund's budget
7. local economic factors
8. debt administration applicable to the issue
9. description of the capital improvement program
10. any contingent liabilities
11. tax exemptions
12. ratings
13. certificates from necessary officials
14. assessed valuation and tax rate
15. tax levies and collections
16. fund revenue and expenditures
17. comparative statement of financial conditions.

The MFOA "Disclosure Guidelines for Offerings of Securities by State and Local Governments" is the best guide to prepare a prospectus. It provides essential guidance and is recognized as the authoritative source. An excellent practical digest is presented in the Oregon Bond Disclosure Guidelines in this chapter's appendix.

The prospectus is printed and distributed with the notice of sale. It is sent to investment bankers, a list of large investors, financial newspapers, and ratings and information agencies. The notice of sale includes:

1. the correct legal name of the issuing bond as well as the special law under which the government was organized and which gave it the authority to issue the bonds;
2. the type of bonds to be issued, the amount and purpose of the issue, the maturity schedule, and the call feature;
3. the date, time, and place of sale and the manner in which the bid is to be made;
4. limitations as to interest rate, payment dates of interest, and when and where the principal will be paid;
5. denomination and registration privileges;
6. basis for bidding;
7. amount of good faith check required;
8. bid form and basis for award;
9. name of approving attorney and statement on legality;
10. provisions made for payment of principal and interest;
11. total tax rate in the government unit and legal limits;
12. methods and place for settlement and delivery of the bonds;
13. the right to reject any or all bids.

Some practices are fairly well accepted in the bond market. Bonds are dated as near as possible to the delivery date to avoid improper interest charges. Bonds are normally issued in $5,000 denominations except for odd amounts which should be retired the first year. Interest is paid semi-annually and bond owners often have the option of registering principal only or principal and interest. If the issue is sold on a wide market, then payments are made at large financial centers for the convenience of the bondholders. Payments must be prompt or a default occurs.

Often large issues are bought by highly competitive investment syndicates organized just for the purpose of buying the issue. The practice of these partnerships is to resell the issues as soon as possible to other investors. The syndicate members make their profit on the slight difference of what they bought and sold for each issue. Thus, municipalities selling bonds should be aware of the factors (i.e., maturity, coupon structure, points, rate limits) which permit easy syndicate reselling. If syndicates can easily resell bonds, then the municipality should be able to get a lower interest rate on its bonds.

For larger issues, a government might be wise to contract for a fiscal or paying agent. Paying agents are normally located in large financial centers, and they make the necessary principal and interest payments on the bonds. Fiscal agents have broader powers including replacing lost or destroyed original bonds, exchanging coupons for registered bonds, canceling paid bonds and coupons, cremating canceled bonds and coupons, answering routine correspondence, and signing bonds. The advantage of having an agent at a financial center is the savings of time in the movement of credit, coupons, bonds and checks, thus saving money.

Debt Records and Reporting

Reputation is important. The local government must develop among investors a reputation for accuracy and integrity. A reputation must be established that full trust can be placed in the debt records, reports, and payment calendar. Surprises must be avoided. Scrupulous attention to each detail is essential. If not, the market automatically discounts the credit and higher interest payments result on later issues. Reports are needed by the government bond dealers, bond rating agencies, and, of course, the investors.

Essentially, the investor is interested only in the ability of the issuer to make timely payments of principal and interest. This judgment is made often on the basis of accounting data and reports. The National Committee on Government Accounting in *Governmental Accounting, Auditing, and Financial Reporting* has established basic standards for reporting on debt. This information cannot be segregated from the other financial reports of a government because of the interrelationship of the data and the potential significance of other financial data in understanding the government's debt and financial condition. Briefly, the investor is concerned with the balance sheet, amount of debt outstanding, status of the debt reserves, ability of the government to meet the payments, willingness of officials to use their power to service debt, and the record of community in debt and other financial management. Also the investor is concerned with assessments, the area's economic condition, and the market value of the property, the taxing habits of citizens, and any overlapping of debt with other local governments.

Timely information is important to investors. Therefore, every reasonable effort should be made to provide reports promptly and frequently.

Bond Ratings

State and local government bonds are rated, and this does reflect the likely interest rate for new issues of that jurisdiction. The fact that a government spends less per capita does not necessarily mean higher bond ratings. There is some wisdom in the adage: "Reduce your debt and increase the value of taxable property." Investors do look at such ratios, and both factors may be within the control of the government. The use of budget controls or a certificate from the Municipal Finance Officers Association will not lower rates. However, the use of budgets to plan and manage government does often result in lower rates.

The Standard and Poor's municipal bond rating process involves four broad factors: economic, debt, administrative, and fiscal. Economic factors include the economic diversity of the tax base as well as the diversity and growth of area economic opportunities. Debt factors include debt burden, debt history, trend, and type of security. Administrative factors include tax rate, levy limitations, debt limits, and other information indicating likely ability to meet debt payments. Fiscal factors include the assets and liabilities in the balance sheet as well as trends in assets and liabilities, especially pension liabilities. In the fiscal factors, comparisons are made between assets and liabilities to see if assets exceed expenditure in the present and the foreseeable future. The bond rating process does not proceed without the necessary information (see Appendix 9-B), and after the 1970s, more meetings with issues, extensive field trips, and more extensive analyses are commonly done to rate a state or municipal government. Rating decisions are based, in varying degrees, on the following:

1. likelihood of default—capacity and willingness of the obligator as to the timely payment of interest and repayment of principal in accordance with the terms of the obligation;
2. nature of provisions of the obligation;
3. protection afforded by, and relative position of, the obligation in the event of bankruptcy, reorganization or other arrangement under the laws of bankruptcy and other laws affecting creditors' rights.

Ratings provide the investor and others with an informed opinion of the credit-worthiness of a particular issue. Ratings do not establish interest rates, but higher ratings normally translate to higher interest cost to the issuer. Larger investors conduct their own analysis of issues, but the Moody's and Standard and Poor's rating services provide additional guidance on credit-worthiness.

REVIEW QUESTIONS

1. What is a government debt? What are the various types and forms of debt? Why do they exist? What are the alternatives to debt and why are municipalities likely to incur debt?
2. Contrast revenue bonds, general obligation bond, TANs, RANs, pension liability.
3. What criteria can be used to judge the correct level of state and local debt? Justify the criteria cited.
4. Explain the significance of the New York City financial crisis on (a) New York City, (b) other local governments, (c) the bond market including prospectus requirement (MFOA, federal, others).
5. Why is the term "bankruptcy" inaccurate and misleading for municipal governments? What can be done to anticipate and remedy a financial crisis?
6. How does the decision-making process differ in capital versus operating budgeting?
7. Why is judgment central to any capital budget decision? What analytical questions are especially useful and why?
8. What takes place in designing an issue? What is particularly important and why? Why are syndicates significant? Why is a prospectus important?
9. What can a government do if it gets low bond ratings?

REFERENCES

ARONSON, J. RICHARD and ELI SCHWARTZ. *Management Policies in Local Government Finance*. Washington, D.C.: International City Management Association Municipal Finance Officers Association, 1975.

MOAK, LENNOX L. *Administration of Local Governmental Debt*. Chicago: Municipal Finance Officers Association, 1970.

Municipal Performance Report, 1, 4 (August 1974).

STANFIELD, ROCHELLE L. "It's a Tougher World for City Bonds," *National Journal*, 9, 34 (August 20, 1977), 1300-03.

STEISS, ALAN WALTER. *Local Government Finance*. Lexington, Mass.: D. C. Heath/ Lexington Books, 1975.

U.S. Advisory Commission on Intergovernmental Relations. *City Financial Emergencies: The Intergovernmental Dimension*. Washington, D.C.: Government Printing Office, July 1973.

———. *Significant Features of Fiscal Federalism*, vols. I, II. Washington, D.C.: Government Printing Office, June 1976, and March 1977.

———. *Understanding the Market for State and Local Debt*. Washington, D.C.: Government Printing Office, May 1976.

Appendix 9-A

DISCLOSURE GUIDELINES

BY THE OREGON MUNICIPAL DEBT ADVISORY COMMISSION FOR OREGON GENERAL OBLIGATION BOND SALES UNDER $1,000,000

The Present Legal Requirements

With the passage of SB 867, as of July 1, 1977 all general obligation municipal bond issuers in Oregon must comply with ORS 287.018 which requires the preparation of a preliminary official statement to be available upon the date of first publication. The statute, as amended, will read:

ORS 287.018. For general obligation issues:

(1) The issuer shall prepare and make available upon request to bidders and investors a preliminary official statement that includes the following:

(a) Past and current financing and estimated future financing of the issuer;

(b) Brief description of the financial administration and organization of the issuer;

(c) Brief description of the economic and social characteristics of the issuer which will permit bidders and investors to appraise the issuer's ability to assume and service adequately the debt obligation; and

(d) Any other information the issuer may provide or which the Oregon Municipal Debt Advisory Commission may require by rule.

(2) The preliminary official statement described in subsection (1) of this section shall be available not later than the date of first publication of the notice of bond sale.

(3) The preliminary official statement shall contain the best available information which shall be accurate to the best knowledge of the issuer. However, any errors or omissions in the preliminary official statement shall not affect the validity of the bond issue.

Clarification

The statute thus sets forth the legal requirements for Oregon for a preliminary official statement. The generality of the subsections leaves some questions as to acceptable types and amounts of information, especially in light of present disclosure standards presented by the Municipal Finance Officers Association in its *"Disclosure Guidelines . . ."* published in December 1976. The Municipal Debt Advisory Commission is attempting to clarify the minimum levels of disclosure required for issuers; this clarification is based on the assumption that the requirements will vary according to the size of the bond issue. These guidelines address the "small" issues (defined as under $1,000,000). Disclosure for issues $1 million or over should conform to the standards set forth in the Municipal Finance Officers Association Guidelines. A differentiation by issue size is made as a reflection of the common practice whereby smaller issues are bought by Oregon underwriters who are familiar with the general nature of the issuer and who need less information to evaluate the issue. These guidelines were primarily designed to meet the informational needs of these local underwriters and *not* to meet the needs of a non-local investor. Issuers, regardless of size, are encouraged to review the Municipal Finance Officers Association Guidelines and to include the additional pertinent information as feasible.

The Commission intends, by these Guidelines, to increase the flow of information to the bond underwriters without creating an unreasonable burden in time or cost upon the issuing municipality. It is anticipated that this increased flow of information will result in market benefits, especially in lower interest rates, provided the information reflects sound financial management and economic stability for the issuing municipality.

Sources for Guidelines Items

The following guidelines were obtained from interviews with several Oregon bond underwriters, bond counsel and financial advisors, as well as from the Municipal Finance Officers Association *Disclosure Guidelines . . .* and an article in the Duke Law Journal, Volume 1976, No. 6, by Petersen, Doty, Forbes and Bourque entitled, *"Searching for Standards: Disclosure in the Municipal Securities Market"* (hereinafter referred to as the *"Municipal Credit Project"*).

Ranking

Items in the prior Guidelines were ranked; however, the Commission felt that issuers should attempt to provide all items if possible. Those items included primarily for their marketing value have been starred (*) so as to provide some indication of priority. Those items not starred presently constitute the Commission's recommended *minimum* level of disclosure for issues under $1 million.

Responsibility for Full Disclosure

The presentation of the information should be brief and concise. However, any material adverse condition that could affect the sale or servicing of the debt should be fully and clearly disclosed, even if not required by a specific guideline. Disclosure must assure a possibly unsophisticated investor of the financial and economic viability of the issuer.

The *"Municipal Credit Product"* (Duke Law Journal) discusses the potential liability of the municipal bond issuer:

> *"Investors have become increasingly aware of the availability of* [the anti-fraud provisions of the federal securities laws] *as a means of recouping losses incurred in municipal securities transactions. In actions brought under section 17 of the Securities Act of 1933 and rule 10b-5, promulgated under section 10(b) of the Securities Exchange Act of 1934, attention will likely focus on the issuer's official statement, which provides information about the particular debt issue being offered as well as a history and overview of the issuer's financial and economic condition.*
>
> *The court reviewing the statement will first be required to determine whether the issuer has misstated or omitted any material fact with regard to the issue. The task of determining what facts are "material" poses considerable problems. The leading cases in the area of corporate securities approach the problem from the viewpoint of the investor. In* Affiliated Ute Citizens v. United States, *for example, the Supreme Court defined as "material" all information which "a reasonable investor might consider in the making of* [a] *decision . . ."*
>
> *. . . voluntary disclosure by issuers is, to a large extent, a response to a perceived investor demand for certain kinds of information. . . . It could be inferred that information which is not normally disclosed is simply not considered important by most investors, . . . A knowledge of what facts municipal issuers normally disclose will therefore be of considerable probative value to a court in determining whether a particular omission was material.*
>
> *Once the court has determined that a material fact has been misstated or omitted, it must then determine whether the issuer's conduct was sufficiently culpable to constitute a violation of the anti-fraud provisions. Recent Supreme Court decisions indicate that plaintiffs will be required to prove at least gross negligence or recklessness on the part of the issuer in order to recover. Under any standard of culpability short of absolute liability, however, the court will need to compare the defendant's conduct with that of others in its position. For example, the fact that an issuer failed to disclose a significant item of information that is routinely disclosed by a vast majority of municipal issuers would clearly tend to show at least negligence on its part. In addition, if it were shown that the item was included in a widely circulated list of suggested items for disclosure, the defendant's omission could be more readily cast as gross negligence."*

Therefore, these Guidelines have taken into account the results of the national survey undertaken by the Municipal Finance Officers Association to determine what kinds of information municipal issuers are presently disclosing (as cited in the Duke Law Journal article), plus the personal recommendations of the Oregon bond market professionals discussed earlier.

Audits

Since all issuers will be requested to provide most underwriters copies of the most recent audit along with the official statement, municipalities anticipating a bond sale should request that the auditing firm print ten to twenty extra copies when printing the usual annual audit. It also is helpful to request preparation of the financial tables for the official statement by the issuer's annual auditing firm, or to request a review of the tables for accurate reporting of the audit figures.

Comments Sought

Further discussion regarding the Guidelines is sought by the Commission and a public hearing will be held in the Fall for this purpose. Time and place will be announced. In the interim, comments should be directed to the Commission at 159 State Capitol Building, Salem, Oregon 97310; phone (503) 378-4930.

User Manual and Sample Statement

A manual providing definitions, data sources, methods of calculation and manners of presentation is available as well as sample official statements. The recommended guidelines and notes are provided in this newsletter for general review. However, issuers preparing statements are urged to obtain, free of charge, the user manual and samples.

The Commission is actively seeking data sources and compiling financial, demographic and economic data which it will provide issuers upon request for a reasonable charge. Contact the Commission for a schedule of rates and available data.

Advisory Guidelines by
The Oregon Municipal Debt Advisory Commission

Several items are further explained in a set of notes following the informational items listing. The listing and notes comprise the body of the Guidelines. The starred items are considered helpful for marketing.

Informational Items and Ratings

I. *EXTENT OF DISCLOSURE:*[1] Any material adverse condition that may affect the sale or servicing of the debt should be fully disclosed, even if not required by a specific guideline. These guidelines are not intended to exclude informational items covered in the Municipal Finance Officers Association Guidelines, which should also be consulted for relevant material.

II. *BOND INFORMATION:*[2]
   A. Amount of Sale
   B. Date and Time of Sale

---

[1]*Extent of Disclosure:* This section applies to all sections following it. No reference to this section is needed in the statement.

[2]*Bond Information:* Although many of these items are present in the notice of sale, it is important to clearly lay out the items indicated in the event this document is passed along to the investor.

    C. Issuer Name, Type of District (if not in name), County

    D. Type of Bonds (General Obligation, Revenue, Bancroft, etc.)

    E. Security[3] (from what sources will bonds be paid)

    F. Date of Bonds

    G. Payment Dates of Principal and Interest

    H. Place of Payment; paying agent

    I. Denominations ($5,000 or $1,000)

    J. Redemption (callable?)

    K. Registration (Coupon? Registered?)

    L. Tax Exempt Status

    M. Pending Litigation (state if there is or is *not* any litigation pending which would affect the issuer's ability to issue bonds or service the debt)

    N. Rating (if rated)

    O. Purpose (briefly)

    P. Authority to issue
       1. Statutory authority (ORS or Charter citation)
       2. *(if election):* date of election and total amount authorized
       3. Date resolution or ordinance passed by governing body

  *Q. Statutory Debt Limit (ORS or Charter Percent or True Cash Value; include citation)

    R. Bond Counsel and Statement that Legal Opinion will be offered

    S. Maturity Schedule

    T. Name of Preparer(s) of Statement; their title, address and phone number[4]

    U. Attach the Notice of Sale—state that it is attached

III. *PROJECT INFORMATION:*

    A. Purpose[5]

    B. Sources for Financing[6] and Application of Funds

  *C. *If the project is a new construction or improvement of a facility:* describe condition and development plans

    D. *If issuer is a school district:*
     *1. General physical condition of all schools
      2. Plans for further construction or improvement of all schools, if anticipate future bonding
      3. Enrollment for district
        (a) prior five years
       *(b) future five years
      4. Is the district approved by the State Department of Education as a "standard district"? *If not,* has the Department of Education approved the bond sale? State which situation.

    E. *If these are water or sewer bonds:*
      1. Schedule of rates and service charges
     *2. General physical condition of entire system and significant present or projected development plans

---

[3]*Security:* If there are any plans to use non-tax revenues, whether pledged or not, it will be beneficial to the sale if this intention is mentioned.

[4]*Statement Preparor:* It is most helpful to give the name of the person or persons who actually compiled the information and can answer detailed questions about the items.

[5]*Purpose:* What is the total project? (Note: This may be the same as the purpose of the bond issue or may be the total project of which the bonds finance a portion.)

[6]*Source for Financing:* Total project financing. If other monies are to be used such as federal or state grants, state how much, from where and how they will be allocated. If the total financing of the project is from bond proceeds, so state. Indicate amount of unallocated proceeds, if any.

3. *If the issuer is NOT in compliance with the State Department of Environmental Quality or the EPA regulations,* why not? What steps are planned?
4. *If any system revenues pledged to payment of bonds:*
    *(a) 5 year record of revenue support for other sewer or water bonds outstanding
    (b) Present number of connections
    (c) Number of connections broken down by Industrial vs. Commercial vs. Residential
        *(i) present
        *(ii) projections
5. *If anticipate any changes in rate level or structure which would significantly affect revenues, explain.*

F. Other Material information

IV. DEBT INFORMATION:
A. Outstanding Debt (as of date of sale)
    1. Gross Direct Debt[7] (including this issue)
    *2. Reserve Fund dedicated to payment of General Obligation bonds which are not self-supporting
    3. Net Direct Debt[8] (including this issue)
    4. Authorized Debt, not yet issued—amount, date authorized, purpose
    5. Short term debt: warrants, notes, loans, leases. *If substantial:* describe amount, date, maturity, and source of payment
    *6. Revenue bonds outstanding (amount outstanding, date, source of payment)
    *7. Limited Tax Bonds Outstanding (Tax Increment Bonds, as in Urban Renewal)
B. Future Debt Plans
C. Debt Limitation and Capacity, including this issue
D. Overlapping Debt[9]
*E. Debt History (5 years)
*F. Debt Ratios and Per Capita Figures[10]

---

[7]*Gross Direct Debt:* The sum of all outstanding general obligation bonded debt (principal only). This includes all "general obligation" bonds whether self-supporting or not and all Bancroft Bonds. This figure represents all bonded debt which obligates tax monies of the issuer, whether presently applied to debt service or pledged in the case that non-tax revenues are insufficient.

[8]*Net Direct Debt:* Net Direct Debt is calculated from Gross Direct Debt by subtracting self-supporting debt. *Self-supporting debt* includes Bancroft Bonds and any General Obligation Bonds (such as Water and Sewer Bonds) which are 100% supported from system revenues and no tax monies have ever been used for debt service or operating expenses. Also subtracted are the total monies accumulated in a reserve fund dedicated to payment on the non-self-supporting General Obligation Bonds.

[9]*Overlapping Debt:* is that portion of the debt obligations of other governmental units for which the issuer's residents are responsible. Debt figures preferably should be as of the date of sale; the figures should not exceed three months prior to the sale. (The Commission can assist issuers with this calculation.)

[10]*Ratios and Per Capita Figures:* These are figures widely used to market the bonds. Present:
Total Net Direct and Overlapping Debt
Ratio Net Direct Debt to True Cash Value
Ratio Net Direct and Overlapping Debt to True Cash Value
Per Capita Net Direct Debt
Per Capita Net Direct and Overlapping Debt

    G.   Default Statement—state if ever have defaulted on any type of debt and, if so, explain

  *H.   Debt Service Schedule,[11] (future debt requirements)

    I.   Other material information

V. FINANCIAL INFORMATION

    A.   Attach from audit reports the following schedules for the General Fund and any relevant funds, e.g. sewer or water fund if sewer or water bond issue

        1. Operating Statement (Revenues and Expenditures)

           3 years

           *5 years

        2. Statement of Changes in Fund Balances

           3 years

           *5 years

        3. Balance Sheet (Assets & Liabilities)

           1 year

           *3-5 years

        4. Basis of Accounting

    B.   As applies to total revenues (all funds) of issuer, provide:

      *1. Total revenues and expenditures as of current date

      *2. Summary of current budget

        3. *If a revenue source is unusual or comprises a significant portion (over 10%) of the total,* explain (indicate which fund or funds handle accounting of this source).

        4. Amount or percent of total revenues which are derived from each non-local source (federal, state or county, etc.)

          *(a) present year budget

          *(b) prior 3 years

      *5. Percent of total revenues from property taxes

    C.   *If any relevant fund has a deficit in the most recent audit report, give amount and explain.*

    D.   *If significant federal, state or other grants have been obtained or are expected, explain.*

    E.   Audit Note[12]

        (NOTE: *Many underwriters will require complete copies of the most recent audit. Be sure to have copies available.)*

    F.   Other material information

VI. PROPERTY TAX INFORMATION *(all available from County Assessor and/or Tax Collector)*

    A.   Tax Collection Record including Assessed Valuations—5 fiscal years

    B.   Largest Taxpayers, their Assessed Valuations, and type of business (if not clear)

        1. 5 taxpayers for small issuers

           10 taxpayers for large issuers

        2. Major utilities

  *C.   Consolidated Tax Rate of Issuer

---

    [11]*Debt Service Schedule:* Present for all General Obligation Bonds (including Bancroft Bonds) combined and for the proposed issue.

    [12]*Audit Note:* Offer the following statement:

"(Issuer) is audited annually and its conformance to generally accepted accounting principles is evaluated. Complete copies of the most recent audit are available from (audit source name and address)." *Note:* If the Auditor's Opinion letter indicates a major defect or deficiency, mention should be made of the problem and the proposed remedies.

VII. GENERAL ISSUER INFORMATION *(brief narrative)*
  *A. Date of Incorporation
  B. Purpose of Function (if not clear)
  C. Population
    1. Current
    *2. Trend (1950, 1960, 1970, 1974-77)
  D. Location
    1. General location in state
    *2. Approximate boundaries
    *3. Proximity to major cities
    *4. Map
  *E. Area (square miles)
  F. Government
    1. Type
    2. List of members of governing body and major department heads:
      *(a) names and positions
      *(b) occupations, terms of office, expiration date of terms
    3. *If County or City:* Do you operate under home rule? So state.
    *4. Name of accounting firm
    *5. Name of legal counsel
  G. Pension Fund
    1. Oregon Public Employes Retirement System
    2. No fund—so state
    3. Other pension funds: give name, assets, unfunded liability, address and phone number of fund
  H. Employee Relations
    1. Method and status of contract negotiations
  *I. History of Budget, Bond, and Serial Levy Elections—5 years
  J. Significant Future Plans—for expansion of district functions or service, for cutbacks, for construction, or for any other major change
  K. Other material information

VIII. ECONOMIC INFORMATION *(supply data, if available, to substantiate statements)*
  A. Major Economic Base(s) (What makes the area function economically?) Provide for lowest level of government available which includes issuer.
    1. Categories (e.g., agriculture, forest products, tourism, manufacturing, services, etc.)
    2. Major employers within boundaries of issuer (include governmental units)
      (a) type of product
      (b) number of employees (approximate)
      (c) *If portion of firm extends outside district, indicate approximate portion within or without boundaries*
      *(d) future plans of firm—expected areas of expansion or reductions— plans for pollution control development
    *3. Major firms outside issuer which employs residents of issuer *(if any)*
      *(a) product
      *(b) number of employees (approximate)
      *(c) future plans (see 2d above)
    4. Major crops, if appropriate
      *(a) percent each type comprises of overall agriculture
  B. Significant Features—anything outstanding about issuer—what makes it different from other issuers (economically or socially)

    *C. Transportation—major sources of access

    *D. Utilities—major types and how supplied, indicate if public or private

    *E. Growth—Describe expansions of business, of construction, of population, etc. either occurring or expected. Present any data available to substantiate trends (5 to 10 years) and projections (identify source of data)

    *F. Economic Indicators—data which presents economic viability of district
- *1. Bank Deposits and outstanding loans
- *2. Construction starts—past year
- *3. Retail sales—past year
- *4. Unemployment rates
- *5. Per capita income
- *6. Building permits
- *7. Effective buying income
- *8. Value of agricultural products
- *9. Value added by manufacturing
- *10. State level of comparison of above data

    G. Other material information

IX. OTHER

    A. Identity of financial advisor, if used

    B. Any economic or other interest of any authorizing official of the issuer in the acquisition or use of the proceeds of the issue

    C. Any contingency fee arrangements of the issuer with:
1. Bond counsel
2. Underwriters
3. Other professionals

    made in conjunction with the issuance or use of the proceeds of the issue.

Appendix 9-B

Municipal Credit Documentation

by Standard and Poor's (1978)

Data may be found in various sources but our files should contain the following information:

Last three annual audit reports
Current budget document
Current capital improvement program
Official statements for new financing
Planning document
Zoning or land use map
In case of interim borrowing, cash flow statement
Statement of long & short term debt with annual and monthly maturity dates as appropriate
Indication of appropriate authority for debt issuance
Files should contain documentation of charter, constitution or law concerning debt issuance
Statement concerning remaining borrowing capacity and tax rate and levy capacity
Statement regarding sources and allocation of funds for project being financed
Description of project being financed
Will additional funds be required to complete project?
If yes, from where will funds be derived and under what conditions?

The nature of the security for the debt should be concisely but accurately defined.

If the debt is guaranteed by another person (in legal terms), full credit review of such other person must be done unless we have current rating for such person.

We should measure credit impact potential of guaranteed or debt service reserve makeup provision debt upon obligor. Full schedule of such debt must be in our file. In case of a guarantor or insurer, what may be asserted as a defense in a suit on the guarantee or insurance?

Description of the remedies of default and whether the issuer can be sued for failure to perform and whether any judgments resulting from such suit are enforceable against the issuer.

Issuer's range and level of services and capacity to provide such services are to be documented. Such data would cover the type of government, the relationship to and areas of shared responsibilities with other governments.

The manner in which principal officials are chosen and the authority and method by which policy and program decisions are made.

Recent additions or losses of major industrial commercial or governmental entities or other employers or major taxpayers.

In enterprise financing, a description of the location and general character of the principal facilities should be provided. Is project land owned or leased by issuer?

Indicate any lease obligations, their nature and term.

Engineering and/or feasibility report. How many of such reports on the project under review were done? If such reports were not done, so indicate and reasons therefore.

In enterprise financing the service area, monopoly or competitive nature of service in area.

Ten year trend of customers and five year forecast by categories of major revenue producers. List ten leading customers by revenues and usage.

List any governmental program providing an important part of enterprise revenues.

Indicate party responsible for rate determination and whether it is subject to outside review.

Sources and availability of raw materials essential to present and proposed operations of an enterprise.

Status of licenses, permits and franchises required to be held by enterprise including EPA, environmental impact, etc. Indicate status of labor relations.

Debt trend for last ten years long-term and short—include lease rental obligations, guaranteed debt and other contingent debt.

Ten-year trend of assessed values with basis of assessment noted.

Ten-year trend of net direct debt ratios—per capita. True value and income—where available.

Statement of debt remaining authorized and unissued.

Description of accounting practices of the issuer and any deviation from generally accepted accounting principles. Indicate any accounting change in last three years and impact thereof upon financial results as reported.

For enterprises, the major revenue and expenditure categories should be indicated for ten years and current budget as well as most recent 12-month period available.

Key balance sheet data for three years. Fund balances and year-end adjustments thereon should be noted.

Ten-year trend on annual debt service as a percent of expenditures.

If issue is payable from a special tax—ten-year trend of such tax.

Describe issuer's property valuation and assessment procedure, tax collections, enforcement and changes in such policy in last five years.

Describe priority of tax claims of issuer over other indebtedness of taxpayer.

Five-year trend of valuations by category—industrial, commercial, utility and residential.

Indicate status of borrowing against delinquent taxes and policy regarding write-offs on such taxes.

Describe borrowing for operating expenses and deficits in last five years—other than RAN or TAN against current revenues.

Indicate whether debt service in past five years has been met through loans from other governments—indicate source, amount and any commitment to repay.

Describe any legislation or procedures—federal, state or otherwise which would apply to issuer in case of a financial emergency.

Regarding financial reports—where transfers occur among enterprise and general funds—both funds must be analyzed for the indicated time frame.

Full reading and comprehension of footnotes in financial statements is mandated.

Indicate whether consultants on engineering, feasibility etc, were employed on a contingent basis and if so, the nature of such contingent basis. Also indicate if any such person was or is connected with issuer as underwriter, financial advisor, bond holder, member of governing body or employee.

Statement regarding any pending litigation affecting status of debt, governmental structure or fiscal condition of issuer.

Statement regarding public employee pension funds—status and funding.

For revenue bonds—the bond resolution, trust indenture, lease if appropriate.

For hospitals—historical and projected occupancy and utilization—5 years.

Necessary approvals and accreditations.

Detail of third-party payors.

Evidence of community support.

TEN

Revenue Systems

There are two sides to every budget. One is expenditure and the other is revenue. This chapter discusses intergovernmental revenue systems, property tax, and other revenue sources. The revenue side of budgeting is explained in an intergovernmental context involving the growth of government and the current patterns in government revenue. The most controversial but yet most important local tax is the property tax. This chapter explains the tax, the controversy, and the administration of the tax. The same is done for income and sales taxes. At the completion of this chapter, the reader should know:

1. how much government has grown;
2. the increasing significance of the intergovernmental transfer payments;
3. which taxes are most significant and what taxes are becoming more important;
4. a definition of property tax and the major criticisms of the tax;
5. the major suggested property tax reforms including the *Serrano v. Priest* decision and its implication;
6. how property is assessed as well as means to test assessments;
7. the assessment cycle, application of tax rates, and foreclosures;
8. the definition, significance, issues, and administration of both income and sales taxes.

Intergovernmental Revenue Patterns

Government Growth[1]

There are various means to indicate government growth, but they all show an upward trend in the size of the public sector. The conclusions concerning this trend vary. Former conservative Republican Treasury Secretary William Simon said in August 1975: "The threat to free enterprise is the growing dominance of government spending within our economy. Back in the 1920s, 12 cents out of every dollar spent in the United States was spent by government. Today 33 cents out of every dollar is spent by government."[2] Blechman, Gramlick, and Hartman of the Brookings Institution concluded that "Although there are many possible ways of measuring the growth of the federal sector, by most measures, there has been relatively little change in the share of total output consumed by the federal government in the past 16 years."[3] Exhibit 10-1 illustrates the diverse results of the measures.

With due respect to William Simon, 1949 is a much more meaningful year with which to compare our present economy. In the 1920s, we were an isolationist, laissez-faire nation. By 1949, we were an active world power and our view of the role of government in the society had shifted. Still using that basis, government did grow with the only exception somewhat ironically being the number of federal public sector employees per 1,000 population.

Patterns in Government Revenue

An interesting trend in intergovernmental finance is the relative mix among the three levels of government. There has been a relatively modest trend to centralization but much of that increase can be attributed to the depressed economy. The states have maintained a relatively constant share of domestic expenditures since 1974. However, the local level—even after deducting transfers—has decreased from 38.9 percent in 1954 to 33.5 percent in 1975. There has been a movement toward centralization especially in the areas of social service benefits and grants-in-aid. This has led to local governments becoming increasingly dependent upon transfer payments from the federal and state levels.

---

[1]Portions of this chapter have been published previously in *The Bureaucrat*, vol. 6, no. 1 (Spring 1977).

[2]Michael Bell and L. Richard Gabler, "Government Growth: An Intergovernmental Concern," *Intergovernmental Perspective*, 2, 4 (Fall 1976), 8.

[3]Barry M. Blechman, Edward M. Gramlick, and Robert W. Hartman, *Setting National Priorities: The 1976 Budget*. Washington, D.C.: Brookings Institution, 1976, p. 7.

EXHIBIT 10-1

An Elastic Yardstick for Measuring the Growth of Government, 1949-76

	1949	1976	Percent Change from 1949 to 1976
Dollar Expenditures *(in billions)*			
Federal	41.3	390.6	845.7
State-Local	18.0	185.0	927.3
Total	59.3	575.6	870.7
Public Expenditures *as a Percent of GNP*			
Federal	16.0	23.2	45.0
State-Local	7.0	11.0	57.1
Total	23.0	34.2	48.7
Public Sector *Employees* *(in millions)*			
Federal	2.075	2.850	37.3
State-Local	3.906	12.229	213.1
Total	5.981	15.079	152.1
Public Sector *Employees* *per 1,000 Population*			
Federal	13.9	13.2	-5.1
State-Local	26.1	56.8	117.6
Total	40.0	70.0	75.0
Public Expenditures *as a Percent of GNP* *adjusted for price* *changes*[1]			
Federal	17.6	22.8	29.5
State-Local	9.3	10.9	17.2
Total	26.9	33.7	25.3
Tax Burden for the *Middle Income* *Family*[2]	*1953*	*1975*	*From 1953 to 1975*
as percent *of income*	11.8	22.7	92.4

[1]Expressed in 1972 dollars.
[2]$5,000 in 1953 and $14,000 in 1975, assuming all income was based on wages and salaries.
Source: ACIR Staff Compilations, 1976.

Exhibit 10-2 illustrates the relative mix of revenue and expenditures among the three levels of government:

EXHIBIT 10-2

Expenditure and Revenue Totals by Percent Distribution
1929-1975

| | REVENUE | | | EXPENDITURES | | | |
	Total Tax Revenue	Total General Revenue	Total Revenue	Total After Transfers	Total Before Transfers	Domestic After Transfers	Domestic Before Transfers
Federal Level							
1929	29.2	32.3	31.1	23.5	25.5	14.3	16.5
1949	70.6	71.4	67.9	65.9	69.6	45.8	51.7
1954	73.9	72.8	70.1	69.0	72.0	39.7	45.5
1959	67.5	65.0	64.2	64.2	60.5	30.2	48.2
1969	65.6	63.1	63.9	58.9	66.0	38.2	48.9
1971	59.1	57.2	59.4	56.3	64.8	40.2	51.9
1972	58.6	56.3	58.7	55.9	66.0	40.6	54.2
1974	58.6	56.8	59.5	56.0	65.6	42.8	55.3
1975*	57.6	55.3	58.7	57.6	68.0	45.8	59.0
State Level							
1929	20.3	19.3	19.2	16.7	20.9	18.7	23.1
1949	14.6	12.8	16.1	31.0	15.0	20.6	23.9
1954	13.1	13.0	14.7	11.9	13.1	21.4	25.5
1959	15.9	15.9	17.2	13.4	14.3	22.6	24.2
1969	18.8	19.2	19.1	15.5	17.4	23.4	26.1

1971	22.2	22.1	21.3	16.7	18.2	22.9	24.9
1972	22.8	22.8	22.0	17.0	17.6	22.8	23.7
1974	23.5	23.2	22.2	16.8	18.7	21.8	24.3
1975*	23.9	24.2	22.8	16.2	17.6	20.7	22.5

Local Level

1929	50.5	48.4	49.7	59.8	53.6	67.0	60.4
1949	14.7	14.8	16.0	21.1	15.4	33.5	24.4
1954	13.0	14.2	15.2	20.0	14.0	38.9	29.0
1959	16.6	18.2	18.6	22.4	16.2	38.0	27.5
1969	15.6	17.8	17.0	25.6	16.7	38.5	25.0
1971	18.7	20.7	19.3	27.0	17.0	36.9	23.2
1972	18.6	20.8	19.3	27.2	16.4	36.6	22.1
1974	17.9	20.0	18.2	27.2	15.7	35.4	20.4
1975*	18.4	20.6	18.5	26.2	14.5	33.5	18.5

*Estimated.
Source: U.S. Bureau of Census, Department of Commerce, Governmental Finances, Selected Years. 1972 Census of Governments, vol. 6, no. 4, U.S. Bureau of Census, Department of Commerce.

There is a growing state and local dependency on outside aid. Exhibit 10-3 shows the rather dramatic trend.

At the state and local level, the importance of all the revenue sources have shifted with transfer payments being one of the dramatic changes. The property tax is less significant now although it is still an important revenue generator. The income tax has become more significant as have the numerous changes and miscellaneous revenues including revenue sharing. The net result is that state and local governments are moving toward a more balanced revenue system. Exhibit 10-4 shows the shift from 1954 to 1976.

At the federal level, the federal individual income tax and the social security tax now dominate. The social security and related trust fund revenue has grown remarkably. Corporate income tax and sales, gross receipts and customs revenue have significantly dropped. Exhibit 10-5 shows these developments.

Five tax concerns or questions frequently asked about revenue systems are (1) the relative tax burden among income classes, (2) the relative tax burden by state, (3) the mix of revenue sources, (4) the relative revenue strength of state versus local government, and (5) equity features of taxes. The relative tax burden among income classes is not progressive as only five state-local tax systems can be so classified. Of the remainder, only 15 are proportional and the rest are regressive. There is a dramatic range in relative tax burden among the states with the southeast states being the lowest. Regional differences are also apparent in the state-local revenue mix. States in New England and Great Lakes regions have made relatively greater use of the property tax whereas the southeastern and Rocky Mountain states get an above average share of their revenue from federal aid. New England and the mideastern states tend to put more emphasis on taxes and less emphasis on user charges. The opposite is true in the rest of the country. States have emerged as senior partners in state-local finance with only seven exceptions in the mid-1970s. Equity features are particularly striking among states. Most northeastern and north central states exempt food sales from sales tax, but this pattern does not apply in the southeast and southwest. Support for circuit-breaker property tax exemptions is found in the Great Lakes and plains regions but not in the southeast where property tax burdens are relatively low. However, that region does apply the homestead exemption.

Exhibit 10-6 is a summary table for governmental revenue in 1974-75. It shows the relative importance of each revenue source by level of government.

Property Tax and Controversy

A Simple Idea

Property tax is a simple revenue-generating idea. First, property is assessed locally so that property value is determined. Second, a tax rate is determined and applied on the basis of the property value. If the property owner fails to pay the

EXHIBIT 10-3

The Growing State and Local Dependency on Outside Aid, Selected Years 1948-1976
(dollar amounts in millions)

Fiscal Year	Federal Aid to States		State and Federal Aid to Local Governments	
	Amount	As a Percent of State General Revenue from Own Source	Amount	As a Percent of Local General Revenue from Own Source
1948	$1,643	21.9	$3,501	44.5
1954	2,668	21.5	$5,933	43.5
1959	5,888	32.4	8,739	42.2
1964	9,046	32.1	13,829	45.7
1969	16,907	34.1	26,082	56.9
1970	19,252	33.5	29,525	57.5
1971	22,754	37.1	34,473	60.0
1972	26,791	37.9	39,694	60.6
1973	31,361[1]	39.0	47,866[1]	67.9
1974	31,632[1]	35.5	54,752[1]	71.3
1975 est.	35,500[1]	36.1	60,900[1]	72.8
1976 est.	42,750[1]	40.1	68,750[1] [2]	75.5

[1]Includes the following Federal general revenue sharing payments (in billions): 1973—state $2.2, local $4.4; 1974—state $2.0, local $4.1; 1975—state $2.0, local $4.1; 1976—state $2.1, local $4.2.

[2]The $68.8 billion of intergovernmental aid received by local governments in 1976 can be broken down as follows: $14.3 billion direct Federal aid, approximately $12 billion indirect Federal aid (passed through the state—estimated on basis of 1967 data, latest available), and $42.5 billion direct state aid.

Source: ACIR staff compilation based on U.S. Bureau of the Census, *Governmental Finances,* various years; and ACIR staff estimates.

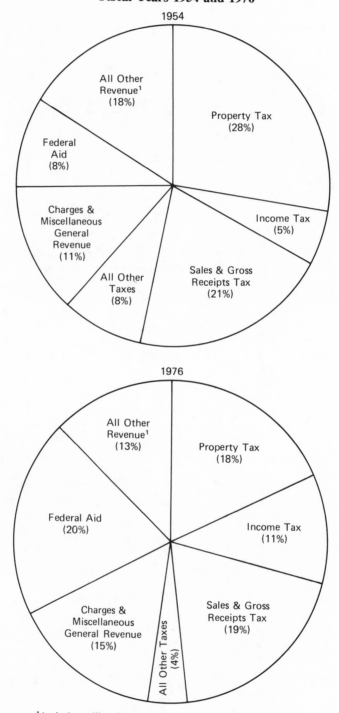

EXHIBIT 10-4

The State and Local Revenue System Becomes More Diversified with the Relative Decline in Property Taxes and Relative Increase in State Income Taxes and Federal Aid, Fiscal Years 1954 and 1976

1954

All Other Revenue[1] (18%)

Property Tax (28%)

Federal Aid (8%)

Charges & Miscellaneous General Revenue (11%)

Income Tax (5%)

All Other Taxes (8%)

Sales & Gross Receipts Tax (21%)

1976

All Other Revenue[1] (13%)

Property Tax (18%)

Federal Aid (20%)

Income Tax (11%)

Charges & Miscellaneous General Revenue (15%)

All Other Taxes (4%)

Sales & Gross Receipts Tax (19%)

[1] Includes utility, liquor store, and insurance trust revenue

Source: ACIR staff compilation based on U.S. Bureau of the Census, *Government Finances*, various years; and ACIR staff estimates.

EXHIBIT 10-5

The Federal Individual Income Tax and the Social Security Tax Now Dominate the Federal Revenue System, Fiscal Years 1954 and 1976

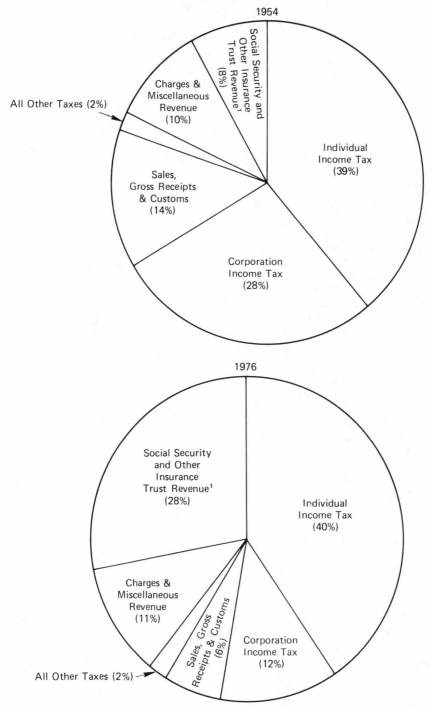

¹ Mainly Social Security receipts (26 percent of total revenue in 1976).

Source: ACIR staff compilation based on U.S. Bureau of the Census, *Government Finances,* various years; and ACIR staff estimates.

EXHIBIT 10-6

Governmental Revenue, by Source, by Level of Government: 1974-75

Sources	All governments	Federal Government
TOTAL REVENUE	517 175[1]	303 857
TOTAL GENERAL REVENUE	403 208[1]	223 311
INTERGOVERNMENTAL REVENUE	—	1 244
FROM FEDERAL GOVERNMENT	—	—
FROM STATE GOVERNMENTS	—	1 244
FROM LOCAL GOVERNMENTS	—	—
REVENUE FROM OWN SOURCES	517 175	302 613
GENERAL REVENUE FROM OWN SOURCES	403 208	222 067
TAXES	331 650	190 185
PROPERTY	51 491	—
INDIVIDUAL INCOME	143 840	122 386
CORPORATION INCOME	47 263	40 621
SALES AND GROSS RECEIPTS	70 905	21 090
CUSTOMS DUTIES	4 289	4 289
GENERAL SALES AND GROSS RECEIPTS	29 102	—
SELECTIVE SALES AND GROSS RECEIPTS	37 514	16 801
MOTOR FUEL	12,799	4 475
ALCOHOLIC BEVERAGES	7 396	5 331
TOBACCO PRODUCTS	5 710	2 315
PUBLIC UTILITIES	5 935	2 875
OTHER	5 675	1 805
MOTOR VEHICLE AND OPERATORS LICENSES	4 243	—
DEATH AND GIFT TAX	6 029	4 611
ALL OTHER	7 879	1 477
CHARGES AND MISCELLANEOUS GENERAL REVENUE	71 558	31 882
CURRENT CHARGES	45 268	19 680
NATIONAL DEFENSE AND INTERNATIONAL RELATIONS	4 559	4 559
POSTAL SERVICE	9 552	9 552
EDUCATION	9 102	51
SCHOOL LUNCH SALES	1 672	—
INSTITUTIONS OF HIGHER EDUCATION	6 331	—
OTHER	1 099	51

Note: Because of rounding, detail may not add to totals: Local government amounts are estimates subject to sampling variation.
— Represents zero or rounds to zero.
[1]Duplicative transactions between levels of government are excluded.
[2]Minor amount included in individual income tax figures.
[3]Minor amount included in "All other" taxes.

Source: U.S. Bureau of the Census, Governmental Finances in 1974-75.

| Amount (millions of dollars) | | | Per capita | | |
| State and local governments | | | | Federal Govern-ment | State and local govern-ments |
Total	State	Local	Total		
261 616[1]	154 632	159 731[1]	2 426.67[1]	1 425.75	1 227.55[1]
228 195[1]	134 611	146 331[1]	1 891.92[1]	1 047.81	1 070.73[1]
47 054	37 827	61 975	(1)	5.84	220.79
47 054	36 148	10 906	(1)	—	220.79
(1)	—	51 068	(1)	5.84	(1)
(1)	1 680	(1)	(1)	—	(1)
214 562	116 805	97 757	2 426.67	1 419.91	1 006.76
181 141	96 784	84 357	1 891.92	1 041.98	849.94
141 465	80 155	61 310	1 556.16	892.38	663.78
51 491	1 451	50 040	241.60	—	241.60
21 454	18 819	2 635	674.92	574.26	100.67
6 642	6 642	(2)	221.77	190.60	31.17
49 815	43 346	6 468	332.70	98.96	233.74
—	—	—	20.12	20.12	—
29 102	24 780	4 322	136.55	—	136.55
20 713	18 566	2 147	176.02	78.83	97.19
8 324	8 255	68	60.06	21.00	39.06
2 065	1 963	102	34.70	25.01	9.69
3 395	3 286	109	26.79	10.86	15.93
3 060	1 740	1 319	27.85	13.49	14.36
3 870	3 821	549	26.63	8.47	18.16
4 243	3 941	302	19.91	—	19.91
1 418	1 418	(3)	28.29	21.64	6.65
6 402	4 538	1 864	36.97	6.93	30.04
39 676	16 629	23 047	335.76	149.60	186.17
25 588	10 437	15 152	212.41	92.34	120.06
—	—	—	21.39	21.39	—
—	—	—	44.82	44.82	—
9 051	5 751	3 301	42.71	0.24	42.47
1 672	—	1 672	7.85	—	7.85
6 331	5 625	707	29.71	—	29.71
1 048	126	922	5.16	0.24	4.92

EXHIBIT 10-6 (*Continued*)

	All govern-ments	Federal Govern-ment
HOSPITALS	6 037	39
SEWERAGE	1 964	—
SANITATION OTHER THAN SEWERAGE	578	—
LOCAL PARKS AND RECREATION	493	—
NATURAL RESOURCES	3 472	3 125
HOUSING AND URBAN RENEWAL	1 289	495
AIR TRANSPORTATION	1 037	18
WATER TRANSPORT AND TERMINALS	725	269
PARKING FACILITIES	251	—
OTHER	6 210	1 572
MISCELLANEOUS GENERAL REVENUE	26 290	12 202
SPECIAL ASSESSMENTS	825	—
SALE OF PROPERTY	1 133	793
INTEREST EARNINGS	10 368	2 525
OTHER	13 963	8 884
UTILITY REVENUE	10 867	—
LIQUOR STORES REVENUE	2 468	—
INSURANCE TRUST REVENUE	100 632	80 546

taxes, then the owner can be fined and, as a last resort, the property can be taken by the government to pay the taxes.

This form of taxation is still nearly the most significant revenue source for most state and local governments. At one time, property reflected wealth, thus a real estate property tax could have been a progressive tax. Today, wealth is not reflected in real property; therefore, this form of taxation cannot be used to tax the wealth uniformally and progressively. There has been a decline in the relative significance of property tax as a revenue generator because it has not provided sufficient revenue by itself. Property tax is less significant today, but it is still highly important as a revenue generator.

Property tax is placed on personal and real property. Tangible personal property includes machinery, equipment, and motor vehicles. Intangible personal property includes stocks, bonds, mortgages, and money. Real property includes land as well as improvements to the land such as buildings. Normally, property taxes are administered locally. Not all property is taxed at a universal rate. In some cases, the tax is regressive but special features can be added to minimize regressive burdens. Another interesting fact is that one person can be held responsible for taxes on both personal and real property. Also a citizen may live in overlapping local governments and, thus, be taxed on the same property by two common jurisdictions.

Amount (millions of dollars) State and local governments			Per capita		State and local governments
				Federal Government	
Total	State	Local	Total	ment	ments
5 998	1 750	4 248	28.33	0.18	28.14
1 964	—	1 964	9.22	—	9.22
578	—	578	2.71	—	2.71
493	—	493	2.31	—	2.31
347	318	29	16.29	14.66	1.63
794	37	757	6.05	2.32	3.73
1 019	98	920	4.87	0.08	4.78
456	131	325	3.40	1.26	2.14
251	—	251	1.18	—	1.18
4 638	2 352	2 286	29.14	7.38	21.76
14 088	6 193	7 895	123.36	57.25	66.10
825	30	796	3.87	—	3.87
340	68	273	5.32	3.72	1.60
7 843	3 731	4 112	48.65	11.85	36.80
5 079	2 365	2 714	65.52	41.69	23.83
10 867	—	10 867	50.99	—	50.99
2 468	2 129	338	11.58	—	11.58
20 086	17 892	2 194	472.18	377.94	94.25

Criticisms

John Shannon of the Advisory Commission on Intergovernmental Relations pointed out that the property tax is considered to be the most onerous tax. A 1972 poll showed that 45 percent of the nation's citizens regard property tax as the worst or least fair tax. Taxes are never popular, but property tax beat the others in nonpopularity by margins of two to one. Why?

1. This form of taxation bears down harshly on low-income households. Lower income families must pay a higher percentage of their incomes for real estate taxes as illustrated in Exhibit 10-7.
2. Property tax is an antihousing levy. It discourages home ownership and does not provide preferential treatment for shelter cost as commonly found in income and sales taxes. Also, as taxes increase, property tax is viewed by many as a threat to their continued home ownership. Property taxes increase as values go up, but the owner does not benefit from the "paper profit" as it is rarely converted to spendable income. This means that taxes are increased but the property remains the same.
3. The administration of property tax is difficult and often poorly done. At best, the assessment is an informed estimate, that is, a subjective judgment of market value. At worst, the assessment can be used for political or economic advantage.
4. The infrequent mass reappraisals in periods of inflation result in severe taxpayer shock and hardship. Taxes go up radically, and taxpayers may not be in economic

EXHIBIT 10-7

Real Estate Taxes as a Percentage of Family Income, Owner-Occupied Single-Family Homes, by Income Class and by Region, 1970

Family income [a]	United States Total	North-east Region	North-central Region	South Region	West Region	Number and distribution of homeowners	
						No. (000)	% dist. [b]
Less than $2,000	16.6	30.8	18.0	8.2	22.9	1,718.8	5.5
$ 2,000- 2,999	9.7	15.7	9.8	5.2	12.5	1,288.7	9.7
3,000- 3,999	7.7	13.1	7.7	4.3	8.7	1,397.8	14.1
4,000- 4,999	6.4	9.8	6.7	3.4	8.0	1,342.8	18.5
5,000- 5,999	5.5	9.3	5.7	2.9	6.5	1,365.1	22.8
6,000- 6,999	4.7	7.1	4.9	2.5	5.9	1,530.1	27.8
7,000- 9,999	4.2	6.2	4.2	2.2	5.0	5,377.4	45.0
10,000-14,999	3.7	5.3	3.6	2.0	4.0	8,910.3	73.6
15,000-24,999	3.3	4.6	3.1	2.0	3.4	6,365.6	94.0
$25,000 or more	2.9	3.9	2.7	1.7	2.9	1,876.9	100.0
All incomes	4.9 [c]	6.9 [c]	5.1 [c]	2.9 [c]	5.4 [c]	31,144.7	

[a] Census definition of income (income from all sources). Income reported was received in 1970.

[b] Cumulated from lowest class.

[c] Arithmetic mean—median for U.S. is 3.4.

Source: U.S. Bureau of the Census, *Residential Finance Survey, 1970* (conducted in 1971), special tabulations prepared for the Advisory Commission on Inter-governmental Relations. Real estate tax data were compiled for properties acquired prior to 1970 and represent taxes paid during 1970.

positions to absorb sometimes doubling and tripling of tax bills. No other tax has such severe hikes.

5. Property taxes can be painful to pay. Often the property taxes are collected with the monthly mortgage payment charge. Such a "pay-as-you-go" technique is less painful for most taxpayers. Often, however, local government does not permit such practices, and payments must be made on a yearly basis, thus causing hardships.
6. Property tax does contribute to urban blight. If some houses must be foreclosed due to nonpayment of taxes, such houses are likely to be in marginal neighborhoods. The long foreclosure process will probably stimulate extreme negligence to the house, thus harming an already weak housing market. Values will drop, and the neighborhood will deteriorate.

One very complex problem is the perennial conflict between state valuation and local assessment practices. The property tax laws of most states require all classes of property be assessed at the same percentage of current market value. This sounds reasonable, but most state tax administrators are unable to hold county assessment at any uniform percent of current market value. The most frequent beneficiaries—not victims—of the extralegal assessment practices are farmers and homeowners. Farmland tends to be assessed at a lower percentage of market value than residential property. Income-producing property such as a factory site tends to be assessed at a higher rate. There are examples of the company in a "company town" benefiting, but that is not the common pattern.

There is a natural reluctance of state officials to raise the assessments of all classes of property to the state valuation standard. Such reforms are politically grim to those officials. Local rate makers should cut back tax rates if the state hikes local assessment, thus each taxpayer would pay about the same tax amount. However, local governments are pressed for added revenue so by not lowering the tax rate they can generate more income while placing the tax hike blame on the state. Another problem for state leaders is a uniform tax policy, which means that they will be repealing the popular "little assessment break" given farmers and homeowners. Both headaches are political liabilities which state officials do not wish to bear. Tax reform designed to bring the law and practice into reasonable alignment does require heroic action. Thus such reforms—when they do occur—take place normally because of court rather than legislative or administrative action.

Property Tax Reforms

Given the number of criticisms of property taxes, no one should be surprised to find an active reform movement involving property tax. Few argue that the tax should be eliminated because it does generate large quantities of tax revenue. Many do argue for the less radical reforms designed to improve the process.

Some obvious improvements are to have better assessors and to use better assessment techniques. Better pay would attract a more qualified person. Persons hired should be given added training. Also, selection of assessors should be on the basis of professional merit, not ability to win local elections. Assessment can be improved by using cadastral maps and parcel information files. The work of assessment lends itself to data processing; thus, much routine work can be done by computers. Another technique is to use building permit data to alert assessor's to important changes. Another useful device is to enact a real property transfer tax act which includes a provision to automatically notify the assessor of changed market value. Statistical techniques like multiple regression analysis can be useful to identify market data which best indicates rapid changes in market value. Other reforms are to use professional consulting firms, especially for major reassessments.

Another reform involves government reorganization. Assessment districts often can be consolidated. This would lead to some economies of scale. It also would permit more specialization, better job development for assessors, and the use of sophisticated equipment which could not be justified in small operations.

A reform addressed to correcting the regressive character of property tax is called circuit breaker. A typical circuit breaker in the mid-1970s covered only the aged, aided renters as well as homeowners, limited benefits to households with incomes below $5,000 with no asset test, and imposed a maximum total relief of $500 or less. The details of circuit breakers vary from state to state. Circuit breakers are normally designed to aid the families with the lowest incomes or the elderly. They mitigate against some of the harsh realities shown in Exhibit 10-1.

More radical reforms are advocated. One is the site value approach which exempts reproducible capital from the property tax base. Proponents argue that there would be no tax loss but taxing would be done in a different way. They say taxing the building as improved property tends to slow down renewal while only taxing land does the opposite. Thus, urban areas would be improved. These debates will continue as long as there are legitimate criticisms of the property tax.

In 1978, the people of California voted overwhelmingly to support Proposition 13 which limits the property tax collected to 1% of the market value and moves back the property assessments of the 1975-76 rolls. In addition, it provides for a 2% growth rate annually. This cuts property tax collection from $12 billion per year to $5 billion per year. In other states, similar measures are being considered to limit taxes and the size of government. This desire to cut taxes reflects a general negative attitude toward government and a concern for rising costs, especially property taxes.

Serrano v. Priest

A particularly significant reform is shifting the property tax to the state level. Reformers point out that this would solve many of the problems most commonly cited.

In 1971, the State of California Supreme Court ruled in *Serrano v. Priest* that the relationship between a district's property tax wealth per pupil and its educational expenditure must be broken. In other words, the property tax may be administered locally, but the funds must go into a state-wide pool. The level of spending for a child's education may not be a function of wealth other than the wealth of the state as a whole.

This decision has remarkable property tax implications. At least in education, there is no longer such a thing as a rich or poor district. The Serrano decision, strictly applied, would invalidate many existing patterns of real property school financing. The decision does not void real estate property tax, but does require a major design constraint on the tax.

In 1973, the U.S. Supreme Court in *San Antonio Independent School District v. Rodriguez* did not extend the Serrano decision to the national level. In a five-to-four opinion, the court ruled that education was not one of the fundamental rights; thus, it was not covered under the equal protection clause of the Constitution. Interestingly, the lawyers for Rodriguez could have argued discrimination and equal opportunity and the court decision might have been otherwise. However, the court ruling meant that the Serrano decision did not apply on a national level.

More states are following the California reasoning, normally by court ruling. Some call this a Robin Hood approach as the state serves to equalize the tax among the local districts. The Serrano decision continues to be influential and property tax is being revised around the country due to that decision.

Assessment and Taxation

Taxable Property and Assessment

Real estate property normally is defined to include the land, structures, and fixtures. The key test is "Is the item fixed?" (For example, the item nailed to the wall is "fixed.") If the answer to the test is yes, it is considered part of the real property for tax purposes. Repairs are not considered to add *per se* to the property value, but improvements do. Here the test is: "Is the change an addition or alteration versus restoring it to a previous condition?" Both tests are difficult to apply and much controversy arises out of using them. One common problem is how to handle mobile homes because, as the name implies, they are not fixed to the property. Most states supplement the test of being fixed by using the length of time the mobile home is on the property or other actions taken to indicate fixture such as removing wheels.

The first step in property taxation is to determine the tax base. An inventory must be taken. This is done normally using owner declarations, surveys, and building permits. Care must be taken to record properly all relevant details, especially improvements to the property.

The assessment process is complex. It must be accurate and uniform or charges of unfairness can be made resulting in possible court action. Normally, assessment is based on a uniform fraction of or full market value. Classes of property (e.g., farms, vacant land, one-family residences, multiple residences) are taxed at different rates. Sometimes tax exemptions exist such as homestead, elderly, sovereignty (e.g., Indian tribe or foreign embassy), or meritorious service (e.g., religious, charitable, educational, or veterans).

The assessment is normally made on market price. Whenever possible, the test used is the market price for the property. That is defined as the price at which a willing seller will sell and a willing buyer will buy where the seller is not forced to sell and the buyer is not forced to pay. If the property was recently sold, then that price would probably constitute market price. Normally, the assessor does not find such a situation, and judgments are based on sales information. A sales ratio, that is, the ratio between price and assessed value, is developed based on sales reports. If the assessment is accurate, the ratio would be one for full market value assessment. Statistical measures, such as central tendency and dispersion, are applied to the sales ratios. This helps the assessor isolate current assessed value inaccuracies as well as determine the quality of assessment. These ratios can then be used to develop a percentage factor to adjust improper assessments. A more sophisticated approach is multiple regression analysis which identifies variables which reflect market value. This approach could be used to find property value indicators and use them to update assessments. Another approach is to analyze market data to select independent variables which help to predict, or estimate sales prices accurately, or identify comparable properties to determine property value.

In some situations, other market approaches must be used in making an assessment. One is the cost or replacement cost approach. This approach is a particularly useful means of valuating large numbers of buildings. The stress is on how much it would cost to replace the building at the time of assessment. Data can be gathered from builders and others to determine reproduction cost of the building. Then age and condition can be determined to recognize the depreciation factors. Next, land value is estimated. Finally, the replacement cost minus depreciation is compared against the recent sale price of similar property.

A third approach is the income approach, and it is seldom used as the sole basis for assessment. It is particularly useful where the market for the property is imperfect (e.g., no willing buyer). Net income for the property is first calculated and then divided by the current discount rate to arrive at an estimated property value. This value should be validated by using the income approach on similar property which can be assessed by the market approach. The results should be comparable.

Assessments should be done frequently enough so that the assessment is comparable with the market price. In many assessing jurisdictions—which are sometimes not the same as taxing jurisdictions—the practice is to have extremely infrequent reassessments. This leads to the "welcome stranger distortion."

Those that move into an area are assessed automatically at the market price when their house is bought. The residents who do not sell their homes are assessed at the lower past assessment. Thus newcomers pay higher property taxes for comparable property. A hardship sometimes caused by reassessment involves circuit breakers. As inflation occurs, an owner can move from nearly zero property taxes to significant taxes because the property exceeds the relief level. However, the circuit breaker can be carefully worded to provide a gradual increase in property taxes rather than a harsh drastic increase.

So-called tax havens do exist. Let us say a family owns an expensive, even highly assessed home. Normally, this would mean high property taxes. If that home is in a tax district which has a great deal of industry, then the tax rate may be low on residential property because enough revenue to run the government is generated from the industrial property tax owners. This would be a tax haven for the residential property owners. Taxes paid depend on both the assessment and the tax rate.

A state requires that a uniform property tax assessment exist throughout the state, but the practical problem is that there are many local assessing jurisdictions. One means to achieve the desired objective is for a state board of equalization to convert each local assessment into a uniform statewide assessment. This conversion process can be done by multiplying the local assessment by a ratio or rate much like the one used in the sales ratio assessment approach. The state equalization rate is the ratio of assessed value of real property and market value. Exhibit 10-8 explains how a state determines the equalization rate.

EXHIBIT 10-8

State Equalization Rate Determination

Step 1: The assessed value of the property is established by using the local government assessment rolls.

Step 2: The market value of all property is established. This is done by examining sales information. An estimate for all the property is based on the sales information.

Step 3: The ratios are determined for all classes of property based on the assessed and market values.

Step 4: For each class of property, the total number of taxed properties and market to assessed value rate are determined for each county. The computation appears as follows for one class of property.

	Market Value	Assessed Valuation	Ratio	Number of Taxed Properties	Products
Taxing District A	A_m	A_r	$A_m{:}A_r$	A_p	$(A_m{:}A_r)A_p$
Taxing District B	B_m	B_r	$B_m{:}B_r$	B_p	$(B_m{:}B_r)B_p$

cont.

Taxing District C	C_m	C_r	$C_m{:}C_r$	C_p	$(C_m{:}C_r)C_p$
Taxing District N	etc.	etc.	etc.	etc.	
				T_p	P

$$P \div T_p = \text{state equalized ratio}$$

Step 5:   Inform each taxing district of the state equalization ratio for each class of property. They are required to apply (multiply) this ratio to the determined full market value in determining the state uniform percent of full market value applicable to the taxing district.

The equalization rate serves as a measure of assessment equality. If the market value of a house is $40,000 and the equalization rate is 50 percent, then the assessment should be about $20,000. If it is not, then the house is either under- or overassessed.

Testing Assessments

The assessment process is often highly controversial. People do not want to pay any more taxes than necessary, especially if the tax is increased due to a recent tax reassessment. Taxpayers "rebellions" occur when a large number of property owners protest increased reassessments. Considering the subjective nature of assessment, mistakes can easily be made and differences of opinion can make a difference in the tax due. Individual taxpayer complaints and appeals are common. This section discusses several tests which can be applied to test the assessment process.[3] There are three key questions:

1. Has the assessor apportioned the property tax burden among owners on the basis of their value?
2. Does the assessor tend to favor or to discriminate against certain types of property?
3. Are the higher-priced properties underassessed?

The test for apportioning the tax burden on the basis of value is the coefficient of dispersion for the district. The coefficient reflects how closely the assessment values are to each other relative to market value. The steps for calculation are as follows:

1. Determine the assessment ratio for each of a sample of properties sold. Let us say there are three parcels. Each sold at $10,000 and assessed separately at $5,000 $6,000, and $7,000. The separate assessment ratios are:

    50%   60%   70%
2. Determine the average of these assessment ratios for the sample of transactions. Average (or median) assessment ratio:

    60%

---

[3]This section draws heavily from Arnold H. Raphaelson, "Property Assessment and Tax Administration," in J. Richard Aronson and Eli Schwartz (eds.), *Management Policies in Local Government* (Washington, D.C.: International City Management Association, 1975).

3. Compute the average deviation of the separate assessment ratios from the average or median assessment ratio. Average deviation:

$$(10\% + 0\% + 10\%) \div 3 = 6.6\%$$

4. Relate the average deviation to the median or average assessment ratio. Coefficient of dispersion:

$$6.6\% \div 60\% = 0.11 \text{ or } 11\%$$

Note: Margin of 10% expected given imperfection in data.

In the above explanation, the test tells us the assessor has *not* apportioned the property tax burden among the owners on the basis of their property's value. The coefficient of dispersion was 11 percent which is 1 percent over the excusable margin. The problem is probably not significant, but a problem does exist.

The test for determining if the assessor is discriminating against some types of property is made by substituting above each category the average assessment ratio for each coefficient of dispersion category assessment ratio. This relates the average category assessment ratio to the overall ratio, thus relating the shares of the property tax burden of the different categories. The calculations are similar to the ones cited previously. For example:

1. The assessment ratios for each category are:

$$40\% \qquad 60\% \qquad 80\%$$

2. Average of median assessment ratio:

$$60\%$$

3. Average deviation:

$$(20\% + 0\% + 20\%) \div 3 = 13.3\%$$

4. Coefficient of dispersion:

$$13.3\% \div 60\% = .22 \text{ or } 22\%$$

The coefficient of dispersion indicates definite discrimination.

The test to determine if higher priced properties are underassessed is done by calculating the price-related differential. It is a measure of the relative accuracy of higher and lower priced property assessments. The steps for calculation are as follows:

1. Calculate the aggregate assessment-sales ratio which is weighted by the values of the parcels in the sample. Let us say the following example exists:

Sale Price	Assessed Value	Assessment Ratio
$100,000	$20,000	20%
10,000	4,000	40%
10,000	4,000	40%
10,000	4,000	40%
$130,000	$32,000	140%

The aggregate assessment-sales ratio is:

$$(\$32,000 \div \$130,000) = 0.246 \text{ or } 24.6\%$$

2. Calculate the average of the assessment ratios of the separate parcels. The average assessment ratio of properties is:

$$140 \div 4 = 0.350 \text{ or } 35\%$$

3. Divide the mean of the assessment ratios by the aggregate assessment-sales ratio to determine the price-related differential. The price-related differential is:

$$35.0 \div 24.6 = 1.42 \text{ or } 142\%$$

The deviation from 100 percent is the key concern in this analysis. If the calculations result in about 100 percent, then there is no under- or overassessment. If the calculations result in above 100 percent, then there is underassessment of higher priced properties. If the calculations result in below 100 percent, then there is underassessment of lower priced properties. In the above example, 142 percent is significantly over 100 percent; therefore, there is underassessment of the $100,000 property.

There are three types of improper assessment situations: illegal, inequitable, and overvaluation. Illegal assessment is when some specific legal rule or law was violated in the assessment process. Inequity is when assessed value exceeds the uniform percentage for the class of property. Overvaluation is when assessment exceeds the actual market value. The following illustrates the concepts:

	House A	*House B*	*House C*
Current market value	$20,000	$20,000	$20,000
Equalization rate	.50	.50	.50
Calculated assessed value	10,000	10,000	10,000
Actual assessed value	25,000	10,000	15,000
	over valuation	equitable assessment	inequitably assessed

The assessor can expect complaints from the owners of both Houses A and C.

Assessment Cycle, Taxation, and Foreclosure

The assessment cycle is built upon an assessment calendar much like the budget calendar. By the taxable-status day, the assessor must determine the value of the property. By the tentative completion date, the assessment role is considered complete and legal copies are filed. By the grievance day, formal petitions for change of assessment to the review board must be filed. The final completion day is the beginning of court reviews of review board decisions. Eventually, the state or local legislative body must certify the assessment. The final step is that the assessment roll becomes the tax roll. All this must be done each year.

The state or local government now must calculate how much revenue it needs and the tax rate needed to generate that amount of revenue. The government computes estimated expenditures and subtracts other revenue. The remainder must be generated by the so-called tax of last resort—the property tax. The needed revenue is divided by the assessed valuation which is converted into a rate per thousand assessed value. The tax rate is determined by the tax base and the amount of money needed to run the government.

The process does have its constraints. Often a law establishes a maximum tax rate. Certainly there are economic constraints because high rates discourage commerce and people living in an area. There are also political constraints because high tax rates can lead to taxpayer rebellions which can force some officials out of office.

The yield from property tax is due both to the tax rate and the assessed value. The tax yield can increase if the assessed value goes up or the tax rate is increased. If the local government is at the maximum tax rate, then pressures increase for reassessments, which is an often neglected task. If a community has a growing tax base, then it has the advantage of getting a greater yield without necessarily increasing the tax rate or reassessing the established property. However, if a community has a shrinking tax base, then it has the unfortunate prospect of reaching its tax rate limit and reassessing its property as much as possible. This tends to discourage commerce and to encourage greater flight from the community.

Taxes are collected in a variety of ways. Some governments demand a yearly or possibly a quarterly payment directly to the government. Most people must borrow money from a bank to buy a home, and they have monthly mortgage payments to make to the bank. Often the bank will also collect the property taxes as a part of the monthly payment. The tax amount goes into an escrow account until payment is due to the government. If the government does not receive payment, there is an extra interest charge or penalty amount added on to the already delinquent tax obligation.

If no payment is made, then a long, complex foreclosure begins. The process varies from state to state, but the following illustrates a typical situation. First, a tax lien is imposed which includes the interest and the penalties. Tax liens are in the form of tax certificates. They are negotiable securities and can be sold as they represent a debt which must be liquidated before clear title can be conveyed. The property serves as the security for the debt.

The whole process is designed to give the taxpayers a fair opportunity to save their property. Public notice on major foreclosure actions on the property in question must be given, but often individual notice is not required. At the sale, certificates on the title are given and the owner has one year to redeem or to lose the property. If it is not redeemed, then title is conveyed to the owner of the tax certificate unless there is actual occupancy of the property or the property is also subject to a mortgage. If those conditions exist, the tax certificate owner can foreclose. The process involves years. Often the property in question is neglected during this period. Its value goes down, and it becomes an eyesore to the neighborhood.

Other Revenue Sources

Income Tax

Income tax is thought of as a federal tax, but it is also a revenue source for state and local government. For example, in 1974-75 $143,840 million in individual income tax was collected in the United States of which $21,454 million was state and local income tax revenue. About 12 percent or $2,635 million was local income tax revenue. At the federal level, income tax is collected on both corporations and individuals, with the latter being much more significant. The federal tax is collected on all types of income, but there are many complex exceptions which are beyond the scope of this text. The state income taxes are normally related closely to the federal tax with some specific changes desired by each state's legislature. Local income taxes are normally flat-rate taxes on wages and salaries.

Like the property tax, the income tax is not without its issues. The complexity of the federal tax and the related "tax loophole" are now common issues. At the state and local level, taxation of nonresidents and taxation of nonlabor income are frequent controversial subjects. Most agree that tax should be a means to redistribute revenue among classes and among localities, but disagreement exists on how much should be redistributed and which localities should receive the benefit. One particular concern to state and local governments is that the tax can produce an out migration of individuals and businesses to lower tax areas.

The details of income taxation administration vary, but the major features are rates, base, withholding, administrative staff and equipment, revenue potential and implementation. Rates can provide the progressive feature of the tax because higher income persons are taxed at a higher rate. Federal and state income taxes have progressive rates, but most local income taxes are done on a flat rate. The base is that to which the rate is applied in order to arrive at the tax. At the local level, it is simply the wages and salaries earned. At the federal level, the base is difficult to calculate, but it is the net taxable income after various adjustments are made. The withholding is a key administrative feature of this tax because it makes tax payment less painful to the average taxpayer. Employers are required to deduct specific amounts from each employee's paycheck for taxes. Thus, an amount is set aside for the yearly taxes. The income tax is difficult to administer and qualified staff plus sophisticated equipment, such as electronic data processing, are needed. The revenue potential is quite good for this tax, and sophisticated revenue estimating procedures are often important as explained in an earlier chapter. Tax administration involves maintaining a bookkeeping and audit staff, reporting forms, the continuing surveillance of tax collections, and prosecution of tax evasion and fraud cases.

Sales Tax

The sales tax is primarily a state tax, but some local governments use it. Out of $29,102 million collected in 1974-75, $24,780 went to the state level, $4,302 to the local level, and none to the federal level. A sales tax applies to goods and services normally levied at the retail stores and expressed in percentage terms. Sales tax can be general (i.e., broadly applicable) or selective (i.e., limited to a few items). The use of this tax expanded due to the need for greater revenue than the income or property tax alone could provide. It has proven to be a highly successful tax.

The policy issues related to sales tax include jurisdictional liability, loss of business, and compliance. Should sales tax liability for a particular transaction be established at the *place of delivery* or *at the location of the vendor*? The *place of delivery* answer would result in added tax revenue but also added administrative headaches. One way to deal with the problem is the use tax. It is a tax levied in lieu of the sales tax on an item purchased outside the sales tax jurisdiction but still used and enjoyed in that jurisdiction. In practice, use taxes are poorly enforced and the *location of the vendor* is the most practical jurisdictional liability test to apply. A government does lose retail business if their sales tax is higher than adjacent areas. The best policy is to have sales tax uniformity throughout a county or metropolitan area. Compliance problems always exist with contractors, itinerant sellers, installation work, and multiple operations having locations in different cities.

Three other policy issues are regressivity, overlapping governments, and allocation. Sales tax applies mostly to the consumers and the poor must consume all of their resources. Therefore, the sales tax will affect the poor more. Sales taxes are regressive. One attempt to lessen regressivity is to exempt food and similar vitals from the tax. Often more than one government unit covers an area and each imposes sales tax. Thus there is an overlapping of local sales taxes. A potential sales tax policy conflict exists and certainly confusion for the retailers collecting the tax exists. Another issue is allocation because of the lack of correlation between sales tax base and revenue needs. Areas with concentrations of retail stores such as shopping centers will benefit greatly from the tax, but the greater tax needs may be in the poorer neighborhoods with fewer stores. If the tax is statewide and placed in a general fund, then this is not a significant problem. However, there are many local governments which collect sales taxes themselves.

These issues are implicit in state and local sales tax. Approaches can be taken to mitigate the problems, but they do remain and must be weighed when deciding upon how to administer this tax.

There are four steps in administration of the sales tax. First, a list of vendors must be prepared and updated. Second, return forms explaining the tax collected by vendors must be prepared. Third, the returns or collections are mailed with stress placed on speed. Return lists must be compared with the vendor list so that delinquents can be isolated. Sometimes court action is necessary to get the returns. The fourth step is to have trained auditors examine a sample of vendor accounts and records. This is essential to maintain successful retail sales tax administration. Each step requires expertise and careful attention to detail.

Other Taxes

There is a large variety of other taxes and government revenue sources, each with its unique issues and administrative difficulties. User charges exist for government services provided much like private industry. Tolls, fees, and license fees are charged. Transfer taxes and other legal transaction charges also exist. Special assessments and utility service taxes are also common. The relative significance as generators of revenue can be judged by examining Exhibit 10-6.

REVIEW QUESTIONS

1. Explain why it is difficult to explain how much government has grown.
2. What are the major intergovernmental revenue system trends? Explain the implication of those trends.
3. Explain some of the major differences in the revenue systems in the various regions of the country.
4. Why is the property tax considered to be the most onerous tax?
5. Explain why achieving a uniform, full-market-value property tax is extremely difficult.
6. What are the most easily adopted property tax reforms, and why is it difficult to achieve those reforms?
7. Why is *Serrano v. Priest* an important case?
8. Explain why judgment is important in applying the key tests associated with property tax.
9. Explain the various approaches to assessment and why it is a difficult judgment to make.
10. What are equalization rates in real property tax? How are they applied?
11. What aspects of the assessment process should be tested, and how is that done?
12. How is the tax rate determined?
13. How are property taxes collected, and what happens if taxes are not paid?
14. Compare and contrast the issues involving income and sales taxes.
15. Compare and contrast income and sales tax administration.

REFERENCES

Advisory Commission on Intergovernmental Relations. *Significant Features of Fiscal Federalism, 1976-77.* Washington, D.C.: Government Printing Office, March 1977.

ARONSON, J. RICHARD and ELI SCHWARTZ (eds.). *Management Policies in Local Government Finance*. Washington, D.C.: International City Management Association, 1975.

ARRON, HENRY J. *Who Pays the Property Tax*. Washington, D.C.: Brookings Institution, 1975.

BLECHMON, BARRY E., GRAMLICK, EDWARD M., and HARTMAN, ROBERT W. *Setting National Priorities: The 1976 Budget*. Washington, D.C. Brookings Institution, 1976.

BLINDER, ALAN S. et al. *The Economics of Public Finance*. Washington, D.C.: Brookings Institution, 1974.

BREAK, GEORGE F. *Agenda for Local Tax Reform*. Berkeley: University of California, Institute of Governmental Studies, 1970.

DORSEY, THOMAS A. *Understanding the Real Property Tax*. Syracuse, N.Y.: Syracuse Governmental Research Bureau, 1974.

ECKER-RACZ, L. L. *The Politics and Economics of State-Local Finance*. Englewood Cliffs, N.J.: Prentice-Hall, 1970.

MAXWELL, JAMES and ARONSON, J. R. *Financing State and Local Governments*. Washington, D.C.: Brookings Institution, 1977.

PETERSON, GEORGE E. (ed.). *Property Tax Reform*. Washington, D.C.: Urban Institute, 1973.

ELEVEN

Analysis for Budgeting

Budgeting requires analysis, and this chapter introduces a wide variety of analytical techniques useful in public budgeting. This is not a "how to do it" chapter, but rather it shows what kinds of analysis relate to budgeting. The first section focuses upon the conceptual foundation upon which analysis can be applied. The next section explains productivity analysis. The last two sections explain benefit-cost analysis. At the completion of this chapter, the reader should know:

1. a conceptual means to relate input, process, outcome, and output;
2. the significance of the cause and effect assumption and its relationship to justifying a budget;
3. a criteria for measurement selection and mistakes commonly associated with that selection;
4. performance budgeting;
5. the simple analytical techniques which help us understand key relationships;
6. the basics of marginal analysis and discounting to present value;
7. the basics of productivity analysis and how it can be used to strengthen budget requests;
8. the difference between benefit-cost and cost-effectiveness analysis;
9. the fundamental concepts associated with benefit-cost analysis;
10. the analytical limitations to the benefit-cost technique.

Conceptual Foundation

Input, Process, and Output Variables

Jesse Burkhead developed the material cited in Exhibit 11-1. It is divided into three parts: input variables, process variables, and output variables. This system's conceptual approach is central to much of the analytical thinking in public budgeting. The government is viewed as a system with resources needed to run it and specific outputs and outcomes resulting from the government's activities. The input is viewed largely in terms of dollars, but other factors are also significant. The output is what results. People in budgeting focus their attention on both input and output information in trying to determine if given government activities are worthwhile.

Professor Burkhead defines output variables in terms of benefits to individuals and society. This treatment has strong merits because this focuses the decision makers upon the ultimate results rather than the intermediate effects. However, one can define output in terms of the specific unit produced by the governmental unit. For example, the exhibit could have cited the number of graduates as well as the increase in knowledge and skill levels. From the perspective of public administration, both types of outputs are useful conceptually. The former shall be called *outcomes* in this book so that a conceptual distinction can be maintained.

Three types of output and outcome indicators are volume, quality, and ratio. Volume indicators display the quantity of service such as the number of graduates. Quality indicators show characteristics, duration, content, extent, or

EXHIBIT 11-1

**Input, Process, and Output Variables
in the Educational Process**

Input Variables (land, labor, capital)	*Process Variables (current expenditure policies)*	*Output* Variables (benefits to the individual and society)*
Student time 　in the classroom 　at home	Class size	Increased intellectual 　curiosity
extracurricular	Size of the school	Social adaptation
Personnel time	Teacher-pupil ratio	
administrative 　teaching		Development of 　creativity
clerical 　maintenance	Ratio of administrative 　and clerical personnel	
auxiliary	to students	Increase in skills and 　earning ability
Materials and supplies	Use of personnel for 　guidance of remedial 　instruction	Increased lifetime 　earnings
Buildings and Equipment		Growth of informed 　electorate
		Increased national growth

*Called "outcomes" in this text.
Source: Based on materials developed by Professor Jesse Burkhead of the Maxwell School, Syracuse University.

degree. Ratio indicators show the quantity of service in some larger perspective such as population or area. For example, out of 70 potential graduates, a total of 68 were graduated.

In analysis, the problem is taking the conceptual tool illustrated in Exhibit 11-1 and applying it to given governmental situations. What are the input variables of an agency? The variables (e.g., dollars, expertise) under the control of government decision makers are the most significant. What are the process variables which tend to describe the administrative condition? Of course, if those conditions help shed light on greater government effectiveness or efficiency, then the data are of particular value. What are the outcome variables, or what is being specifically produced? In government agencies with tangible products such as highway construction, this is easier to answer than in programs involving promoting individual or community development. Even the latter can often be quantified, but not always. What are the output variables, or what changes have occurred in society due to the government program? Government programs are created to make some differences due to their existence. What are those differences? These questions are not easily answered, but they represent the first steps toward useful analysis. Exhibits 11-2 and 11-3 illustrate some common indicators.

Bases for Measures

Almost all government programs are intended to affect society or individuals in some way or the necessary legislation would not have been passed. Often, the exact desired impacts on society are vague and even internally contradictory, but there almost always is some purpose behind each law and government program. There is an assumed cause-and-effect relationship in which the government program is to cause an effect on society. This assumption is central to much of the analysis useful in budgeting. Often budget analysts try to determine if a resource request and even the program itself is "worth it" given the results of that program.

The burden of proving the worth of a program and a specific resource request is placed on the agency. The agency must justify the budget to the department, the executive, and the legislative body. Often those involved act as if an absolute proof exists that a given program is worthwhile. Unfortunately, those holding such a view are not sensitive to the philosopher Descartes—absolute proof for any subject other than one's own existence (cogito ergo sum) is not possible; therefore, we must use other criteria.

In public administration, the criteria of necessary but not sufficient cause is normally the best. For example, if the ultimate desired effect is to reduce the crime rate, holding the police force responsible for that effect may seem reasonable until one realizes that crime results from more than poor police work. Good police work may be necessary, but it alone is not sufficient to reach a low crime rate. Too often analysts and decision makers apply the harsher necessary and

EXHIBIT 11-2

Trend Charts for Individual Activities

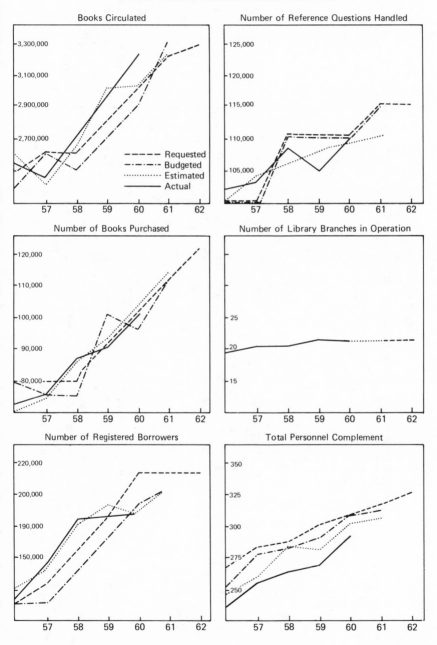

Source: Moak and Killian, *Operating Budget Manual*, p. 149.

EXHIBIT 11-3

Continuing Record of Complement of Permanent Full-Time Personnel

Sub-Unit or activity		1956	1957	1958	1959	1960	1961	1962	1963	1964	1965
Circulation	Requested	130	135	135	140	142	145	150			
	Budgeted	120	130	130	130	140	140				
	Authorized (7/1)	120	130	135	130	145	145				
	Actual (7/1)	112	127	132	129	144					
Book Purchase	Requested	35	35	35	45	45	50	50			
	Budgeted	30	35	35	45	45	50				
	Authorized (7/1)	30	32	35	40	40	45				
	Actual (7/1)	27	32	32	36	36					
Reference	Requested	100	110	115	115	120	120	125			
	Bugeted	100	110	115	115	120	120				
	Authorized (7/1)	95	95	110	110	115	115				
	Actual (7/1)	96	94	98	103	112					
Total personnel complement	Requested	265	280	285	300	307	315	325			
	Budgeted	250	275	280	290	305	310				
	Authorized (7/1)	245	257	280	280	300	305				
	Actual (7/1)	235	253	262	268	292					

Note: Using 1962 as an example, the number "requested" would have appeared in the data prepared in mid-1961 for the 1962 budget; the budgeted would represent the number of full-time men that could be paid upon the basis of the 1962 budget as adopted; the "authorized" would represent the authorization at a given date in the middle of the year by whatever process formal authorization is provided. In some cities, the authorized number would have to be the same as the allotted number; in others, this would not be so due to flexibility available or to amendments that may have been made to the budget since original adoption. "Actual" provides an at-date figure of the number filled and is taken from the budget request for 1963.

Source: Moak and Killian, *Operating Budget Manual,* p. 148.

sufficient criteria in juding the worth of government programs. This unfortunate conceptual mistake merely leads to false expectations and frustrated administrators and citizens.

Conceptually, an analyst should be able to develop a program impact theory. Given a set of resources and the conditions in society, a government program can produce outputs which in turn will lead to outcomes. The resources, in part, are reflected in the budget request. The outputs are the achieved objectives of management. Those objectives provide guidance to the lower officials and administrators in the bureaucracy. The outcomes are the achieved objectives one cites in program evaluations. Those impacts or outcomes are what higher-level decision makers should view in judging the government program.

The program impact theory is the heart of any good budget justification. The person justifying the budget should be arguing that the agency will achieve the legally stated desired effects (such as the law's purpose) on society or individuals if the agency is given the requested resources. The program impact theory should be the conceptual means to relate the resource requests with the stated end results caused in society.

If the desired end results do not occur, then two types of failures are possible: (1) the agency did not do its job correctly or (2) the theory was incorrect. If the agency conceptually separated outputs and outcomes correctly and gathered the necessary data, then the type of failure can be determined. If the objectives of management were met, then one type of failure can be eliminated. This permits proper focus upon the theoretical failure, which is the responsibility of the highest level decision makers for using poor theory or the academic community for not developing adequate theories. Once the failure is identified, then attention can be focused upon discarding faculty theories and researching to develop more useful theoretical understandings. This identification of failure is particularly significant and helps us understand the relationship of social science research and the needs of higher level administrators.

Criteria for Measurement Selection

Budgeting is highly practical. Data used must be relevant and relatively simple. Sophisticated data can be used to develop thoughts, but presentations are made in a political arena where analytical sophistication often does not exist. Therefore, the persuasive data must not only be consistent with the program impact theory, but it must also be simple enough to be usable in the political arena.

Three common mistakes should be avoided in selecting measurements. First, do not count the uncountable. Sometimes in our desire to be quantitative we try to measure attributes which do not lend themselves to being counted. For example, a surrogate measure for "increased intellectual curiosity" can be developed, but its relationship to the attribute might be highly questionable.

Second, recognize that the data may be unavailable. In analytical work we often use data because it is there and not because it has real analytical worth. The third mistake is counting—it can lead to improper program direction and misinformation. If the top officials judge success by numbers, then the lower ranks will try to show success with those numbers. Sometimes an appearance of success is artificial such as improper body counts in war or failure to resolve welfare cases so that case loads appear artificially high.

Measurement selection requires judgment. A knowledge of data is critical. Equally critical is a knowledge of public administration and the unintended consequences of each selected measure.

Performance Budgeting

Earlier we discussed line-item and program budgeting. The line-item budget focuses upon the detail so that control can be insured. If a worker violates the line-item budget, then blame can be fixed. The program budget arranges the budget material in such a way as to aid the executive and legislator in understanding the broader policy implications of their decisions.

A third approach is performance budgeting in which the budget material is arranged so that the existence of economy and efficiency can be ascertained easily. The ultimate policy direction is considered only in terms of the economy and efficiency of the program itself. The budget is classified in terms of performance units and detail. The keys are accomplishment and linking achievement to resources (input).

Many of the difficulties with performance budgeting relate to measurements. Some types of activities, such as labor mediations, cannot be measured accurately. Sometimes the measures that do exist are inadequate. Without good measures, performance budgeting is meaningless.

Another difficulty is the common problem of mixing work performed with measuring accomplishment. This important conceptual distinction must be understood and used correctly. Work performed would be the hours of time spent in collecting the garbage. Measuring accomplishment would be the actual tons of garbage collected. The latter should be used not only as the management objective but also as the measure in performance budgeting. The work performed is a useful statistic but only in the context of the other information.

In government, economy and efficiency are often of secondary importance. For example, winning a battle is more important than conducting the battle efficiently.

There is no one best budget approach for all types of government situations. Possibly, the important stress in a particular government should be placed upon policy choices. Control may not be critical as it can be achieved in other ways, and efficiency is not a critical issue for the officials. However, in other government situations productivity and efficiency may be the central concern. In such circumstances, a budget focus upon performance might be best. Each situation should be judged in terms of what is best for the agency under those circumstances.

Elementary Analysis

Defining Relationships

Most analysis used in budgeting is not complex. Trend charts, scatter diagrams and simple regression, marginal cost, and discounting to present value are all relatively simple analytical techniques. Often relationships involving budget requests, final budgets, year-end estimates of current expenses, and actual performance are important. If relationships can be established, then the budget analyst's job is made easier. Normally, relationships are best described using a conventional scale, but sometimes a logarithmic scale or index numbers can be employed to better highlight the significance of the data. One common relationship is to show a given variable as it changes over time. This is the highly useful trend chart illustrated by Exhibits 11-2 and 11-3. If a trend is apparent, then low-term forecasting is made easier and future consequences become more predictable.

In many situations the relationship between two variables is more difficult to determine. One approach is to place the two variables on two axes as illustrated in Exhibit 11-4. The analyst then places a dot representing each simultaneous occurrence of the two variables. This results in a scatter diagram which may

EXHIBIT 11-4

Illustration of Statistical Analysis

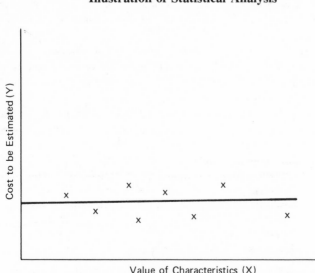

Value of Characteristics (X)

indicate a relationship between the two variables. Exhibit 11-4 shows such a relationship for a car between maintenance cost and miles driven. The line is a simple regression analysis defining that relationship.

Marginal Cost and Discounting

Another useful technique is marginal cost. In conducting the affairs of government, the initial cost of a program is often expensive while further effort leads to less unit costs. This means that in many circumstances the analyst should understand that marginal costs are lower. This might prove to be highly significant data. For example, if an agency is asking for a proportionate increase in funding, the analyst might question this request in that marginal costs should not increase proportionately.

In order to perform marginal cost analysis, the data must be separated into one-time fixed costs and recurring costs. Common one-time fixed costs include research, project planning, engineering, tests, evaluations, land purchases, facility construction, equipment, and initial training. Common recurring costs include personnel expenses, employee benefits, maintenance, direct contributions to people, payments for services, and overall and replacement training. The fixed costs remain the same, but the recurring costs increase with added units. Thus, as the units increase the unit cost decreases. This data can be plotted on a simple chart or described in simple statistical expressions.

Another technique is discounting to present value. A dollar received or spent in the future is not equivalent to a dollar received or spent today. Therefore, adjustments should be made if comparisons are to be made. The technique is similar to the statistical concept used to compute compound interest at the bank. This technique is useful when comparisons must be made, but the two subjects must not occur during the same time period or involve different financing methods.

Fred A. Kramer has cited a simple but common situation to illustrate the use of this analytical technique.[1] A city must choose between contracting with a private garbage collector for $65,000 per year or doing it themselves. The latter option would require a $40,000 truck and a $55,000 yearly operating expense. Without discounting, the best option is doing it themselves because $10,000 can be saved by that approach. With discounting, the best option is the contract. The following shows the arithmetic:

Year	Savings in the Year	× 8% Discount Factor	= Present Value
1	$10,000	.926	$ 9,260
2	10,000	.857	8,570
3	10,000	.794	7,940
4	10,000	.735	7,350
5	10,000	.681	6,810
	Total Present Value of Annual Savings =		$39,930

[1]Fred A. Kramer, "The Discounting to Present Value Technique as a Decision Tool," *Special Bulletin* 1976E (November 24, 1976), Municipal Finance Officers Association.

In the example, the private contract is the best buy because the total present value of annual savings is less than the capital investment.

Caution must be stressed in using the discount technique. Numbers have a way of seeming so final and clear. Realistically, the ingredients in the question should be carefully weighed in terms of their sensitive character. An output of a problem is sensitive when the results can be altered by minor changes in a variable. If the analysis is highly sensitive, then any recommendations due to the analysis should be questioned because the technique does not warrant the implied certitude. This technique can be abused by changing the annual returns or savings, the life of the asset, the amount of the investment, the discount rate, or the annual returns in the earlier years. This does not mean the technique should not be used, but it should be used with a complete understanding of the possible distortions.

Productivity Analysis

Productivity

Productivity is a measure of efficiency usually expressed as the ratio of the quantity of output to the quantity of input used in the production of that output. Productivity does not involve effectiveness, but it does involve efficiency. Commonly, productivity focuses upon output per man hour of change or changes in cost per unit of output. It does not measure the work completed versus the work needed to be completed.

The concept of productivity is often misunderstood. It is falsely tied to harder physical work, when it is in fact tied to doing the work with less effort but still increasing output. This is normally done by better work procedures, better use of machines, or better worker attitude toward the job. In quantifying productivity, the mistake is made of using outcomes (benefits to individuals and society) instead of outputs (products of the program). There are normally too many intervening variables between outcomes and outputs to permit a meaningful usage of outcomes. Another conceptual confusion is that an increase in productivity may reflect a cost reduction, but that a cost reduction is not always a result of an increase in productivity. Other reasons for cost reduction can exist such as a simple budget cut. However, too often we do equate productivity and cost reduction.

A study on productivity in the federal government was conducted in the mid-1970s, and its findings on the reasons for increases in productivity are enlightening. A commonly cited reason for a productivity increase was an increase in the work load, thus allowing the agency to lower its unit cost. Fixed and variable costs explain how productive advantages can result from increased work loads. In other cases, productivity increased because of improved training, increased and better use of job evaluations, greater upward mobility, or the use of a career ladder to develop the work force. In some instances, greater productivity was due to automation and the use of new labor-saving equipment.

Although productivity is a simple concept, there are no simple uniform answers for increasing productivity. Each situation must be examined separately. The federal study illustrates this point by saying the greater productivity resulted from (1) improved morale resulting from job redesign and enrichment, and (2) reorganization and work simplification. The study seems to say that making a job more complex and simple both result in greater productivity. This apparent contradiction can be resolved by understanding the human factor related to the job situation. For some people, the job is too complex and beyond their abilities. The answer is work simplification. For some people, the job is too simple and their boredom leads to poor work habits. The answer is job enrichment such as rotation or a larger range of responsibilities. Sound increased productivity recommendations must be based on a knowledge of both management science as well as human behavior.

The same federal study also cited some common reasons for declines in productivity. Increased product complexity cannot always be factored out of the measurements, and that complexity can mean less productivity. For example, increased environmental, safety, and legal requirements mean added work steps, equipment, or additional features. This may be in the public interest, but one of the disadvantages is increased production costs; thus a loss in productivity. Another reason for loss is a steady and sharp decline in work load which is not matched by staff reductions. Either human compassion or labor agreements can mean lower productivity, but again other practical reasons supersede the desire for efficiency. A third common reason for a decline is, ironically, the installation of a new or automated system. For a period of time during the installation, both the automated and old system must be operated, thus decreasing productivity until the old system is phased out. These reasons are significant and suggest the complex issues which prevent us always achieving increased productivity.

Productivity and Budgeting

Agencies can strengthen their budget requests by citing productivity measures. Reviewing authorities normally more readily accept cost estimates based upon data involving productivity. Those requests are more impressive and help establish agency creditability. Exhibit 11-5 is extracted from the 1975 U.S. Budget Appendix. It illustrates how hard facts strengthen the agency's justification of its budget even in an agency such as the mediation and conciliation service. Exhibit 11-6 illustrates how productivity measures can be melded into a budget justification document. The most helpful data and measures are:

1. productivity indices which relate end products produced to manpower or cost measures;

2. unit cost ratios which relate work performed to all or a part of the cost of performing the work;
3. work measuring ratios which relate work performed to manpower needs in carrying out the work;
4. program or work load data which show trends in the program work;
5. statistical data, such as regression analysis, which relate experience data to manpower.

EXHIBIT 11-5

Selected Illustration of a Presentation of Output Data in the 1975 Budget Appendix

Federal Mediation and Conciliation Service

Salaries and Expenses

The Service, under title II of the Labor Management Relations Act of 1947, assists labor and management in mediation and prevention of disputes affecting industries engaged in interstate commerce and defense production, other than rail and air transportation, whenever in its judgment such disputes threaten to cause a substantial interruption of commerce. Under the authority of Executive Order 11491 of October 29, 1969, as amended by Executive Order 11616, dated August 26, 1971, the Service also makes its mediation and conciliation facilities available to Federal agencies and organizations representing Federal employees in the resolution of negotiation disputes.

1. *Mediation Service.* During 1973, dispute notices and other notifications affecting 117,884 employers were received by the Service. Cases totaling 21,745 were assigned for mediation, and 21,032 mediation assignments were closed during the year. About 89% of the mediation assignments closed which required the services of mediators were settled without work stoppages. A total of 26,973 mediation conferences were conducted by mediators during 1973. The workload shown above includes assignments closed in both the private and public sectors. Cases in process at the end of 1973 totaled 5,449; this is the normal carryover of open cases from month to month, with seasonal fluctuations. The following chart shows a 5-year comparison of workload data:

DISPUTE WORKLOAD DATA

	1969	1970	1971	1972	1973
Cases in process at the beginning of the year	5,260	5,113	5,020	4,889	4,736
Mediation assignments	21,839	19,769	21,727	19,308	21,745
Mediation assignments closed	21,986	19,862	21,858	19,461	21,032
Cases in process at end of year	5,113	5,020	4,889	4,736	5,449
Mediation conferences conducted	31,605	30,334	32,293	29,223	26,973

Source: Extracted from p. 878 of the 1975 Budget Appendix

EXHIBIT 11-6

Illustration of Selected Agency Productivity Trends
The Defense Supply Agency

Since the activation of DSA, constant management attention to the basic goal of maximum efficiency has produced significant operating economies. In the early years of DSA, 1962-1966, increased productivity was realized through manpower reductions as numerous organizational and procedural improvements were effected. However, it was not until FY 1967 that a formal output and productivity evaluation system was installed. Since that time, overall output per man-year has increased almost 30 percent.

Chart 1 depicts the composite productivity trend for the agency from FY 1967 through FY 1973. The index shown was derived from the basic data which constituted DSA's input to the Government-wide productivity project. Improvement has averaged about 5 percent per year for the past six years. DSA currently employs about 52,000 military and civilian personnel in performing its assigned mission. Had the increase in productivity reflected on this chart not been realized, today's job would require about 10,000 more personnel than are currently employed.

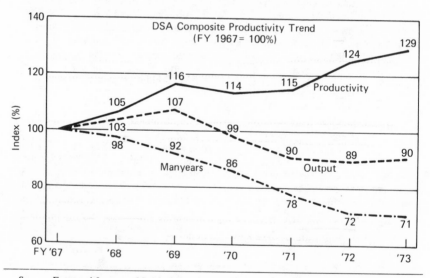

Source: Extracted from pp. 35–36 of the Joint Financial Management Improvement Program "Report on Federal Productivity, Volume II, Productivity Case Studies" (June 1974).

The Benefit-Cost Concept

Concept: What and Why

Benefit-cost analysis is based on the rather simple belief that projects should be judged on the basis of project cost versus project benefits. At best, benefit-cost analysis is a guide for investment decision. It can help decision makers decide if specific expenditures should be undertaken, if the scale of the project is appropriate and what the optimum project size should be. Some claim and treat benefit-cost as a framework for a general theory of government investment.

Cost-effectiveness is sometimes confused with benefit-cost analysis, but there are advantages to maintaining the distinction. Cost-effectiveness assumes benefits and does not compare them with cost as in benefit-cost analysis. In cost-effectiveness analysis, the analyst wishes to determine the least costly means to achieve the objective. Frequently, all methods of analysis using inputs, alternatives, and outputs mean cost-effectiveness analysis including benefit-cost. However, cost-effectiveness can often be the more effective analytical technique and blurring the distinction between the techniques tends to blind practitioners to the comparative advantages of the two techniques. Both have their advantages, but often cost-effectiveness can be used where benefit-cost is a meaningless technique.

The sophisticated benefit-cost analysis is useful. It can establish a framework for reasonably consistent and uniform project evaluations at the staff level. This can lead to added discipline of the political process because weak projects will appear inferior, thus making their funding difficult in an open political setting. The technique is most useful when the choice set is narrow and the decision involves economic alternative investments. The technique draws increasing criticism when intangibles and complex social values are present in the analysis. Value perspectives such as reallocation of wealth are not addressed well with benefit-cost analysis.

Benefit-cost analysis involves defining a choice set, analytical constraints, measurements, and a choice model. Analysis must be made manageable so that the work can be done within a reasonable time frame. Thus, parameters or range of projects must be established. Analytical constraints, e.g., legal, political, distributional, financial, and physical, must be understood, stated, and treated either as side considerations of the analysis or included into the analytical objective functions. Benefit-cost analysis involves measurements, therefore, all the challenges and analytical limitations of data apply to benefit-cost analysis. Those challenges and limitations must be understood or serious analytical mistakes will be made and decision makers will be given misleading advice. A full treatment of this topic is beyond the scope of this text, but is covered in books concerning research methods. The choice model is the means used to relate the estimated costs and benefits. It is the formula. The model (formula) is used to decide how the measures will be incorporated into the overall analysis.

Procedures

The procedures of benefit-cost analysis involve defining the objective functions, benefits, and costs as well as calculating present value. The objective functions specify without weighing the ultimate values used in the analysis.

Examples include increasing national income, aggregate consumption, supply of foreign exchange, and employment. The functions must be quantifiable, or they cannot be treated in the analysis. Benefits are defined normally as present value of the contributions in relationship to the objective function. Costs are sometimes defined in terms of reducing the objective function. They are also the present value of the resources that are employed and are valued at opportunity costs as a consequence of implementing the project.

The calculations in benefit-cost analysis are complex due to several factors. Both benefits and costs must be measured over time in order to permit a broad view of project impacts, especially economic consequences. Benefits are measured by the market price of the project outputs or the price consumers are willing to pay. Costs are measured by the monetary outlays necessary to undertake the investment. Both occur over time. Unlike the private sector, externalities—i.e., project effects on others which occur because of the project's existence (such as down-stream pollution from a plant)—are calculated into public sector benefit-cost analysis. Also, opportunity costs are valued because full employment and scarce resources are assumed to exist. This means that some worthwhile choices are forgone once the decision is made to undertake the project, and this is a project cost. If the assumption is incorrect, e.g., full employment does not exist, then costs should be revised downward.

Alternative Choice Models

The decision on projects is often done by ranking alternative projects. The ranking depends on the choice model (formula) used. The various models do not give the analyst the same results. The four models are:

Benefit-cost	Based on discounted present value
Benefit/cost	Ratio of present value of benefits and costs
Rate of return or marginal investment efficiency	Discount rate which puts the benefits and costs at equilibrium
Payout period	Number of years of benefit needed so that the benefit equals the cost

Each model has its inherent bias. The benefit-cost model biases the decision in favor of large projects due to the manner in which the figures are calculated. Any deductions from benefits rather than adding to costs would affect ratios and thus the second benefit/cost model. If benefits or costs do not occur evenly over the streams of time, this may not be properly computed in mathematical models unless special provisions permit this unevenness.

Virtually all practitioners prefer the benefit-cost (discounted present value) model. It focuses on explicit treatment of budgetary and other constraints as well as project indivisibility and interdependencies. This model forces the separate treatment of those matters without confusing them with the determination of the proper discount rate. Also, calculation of present value is not a behind-the-scenes adjustment because it must be treated openly in the analysis.

Benefit-Cost Ingredients

A purpose of this chapter is not to explain how benefit-cost analysis is done but rather to stress the sophisticated analytical nature of the technique as well as the inherent limitations of the technique. Too many professionals advocate and even use the technique without understanding its true analytical sophistication. It is a worthwhile technique, and it should be studied by those interested in public budgeting. However, the first step is to recognize the complex nature of this type of analysis and to be especially sensitive to its limitations.

The remainder of this section examines key factors associated with benefit-cost analysis. Stress is placed on the limitations and cautions which should be associated with this technique. This stress is meant to sensitize the reader to the analytical problems associated with the technique. A full explanation of how to apply the technique is beyond the scope of this text, and readers are encouraged to learn more about this and other analytical techniques in further study.

Benefits and Estimation

Benefits are classified as primary, secondary, and intangible. Primary benefits are the values of goods or services resulting from project conditions. They are included in the analysis. Common examples are additional crops due to irrigated lands and annual savings in flood damages. Associated costs, e.g., seed for irrigated land, are subtracted from primary benefits. Secondary benefits either stem from or are induced by the project, but are not directly resulting from the project. Their inclusion as benefits is subject to controversy. Intangibles are nondollar-value benefits, e.g., aesthetic quality of the landscape, which by definition cannot be included in the benefit-cost calculations.

What gets counted as "benefits" is important. Therefore, if the major benefits are intangibles, then the analysis often loses much of its worth. Also if the major benefits are secondary, the inclusion of them is controversial and the resulting analytical conclusions would be subject to a complex debate involving the technique more than the project. The purpose of analysis is to aid decision makers, and the result of using controversial techniques is to confuse further the decision-making process.

Benefit-cost analysis is almost always used prior to the project's existence; therefore, costs and benefits are estimated over the projected life of the project.

Cost estimates include construction engineering, relocation of households, erosion, and third-party effects. Benefits are harder to estimate, especially if they do not occur evenly over time. Decisions must be made on when to stop counting, what not to count, how to count, and how to aggregate benefits. These decisions may greatly affect the analysis; therefore, controversial decisions may lead to controversial analytical conclusions.

One commonly voiced concern is how to handle costs which have already been made, i.e., sunk costs. This is not a controversial subject because they are almost uniformly treated as not relevant to the project cost and not calculated. Sunk costs may be of significant political concern, but they are not added into the project cost.

Discount Rate

The most controversial ingredient of benefit-cost analysis is the discount rate. The controversy centers not on its proper role in the analysis, but on how it should be determined. It is significant because a higher rate means that fewer projects will be justified, especially if they have costs accumulating over a long period of time. The rationale for a discount rate is that the resources used in a particular project could have been invested elsewhere to yield future resources larger than the amount invested; therefore, this should be taken into consideration in the analysis.

Several approaches to determine discount rates are advocated. One says that a discount rate should bias toward present goods over future goods, whereas another argues for higher value to future goods. Others argue opportunity cost should be based upon equivalent private investments, whereas still others say external effects should be added and subtracted from those private opportunity costs. The debate is endless and most end up by using an arbitrary interest cost of federal funds in a certain period to select a rate.

If the projects analyzed are similar in size and time stream, then the rate used is not significant as long as the same approach is used for all projects. If not, then the analytical results become controversial.

Externalities, Risk, and Other Considerations

Externalities are included in benefit-cost analysis, but they are difficult to determine. Technological externalities involve the physical input-output relationship of other producing units. Pecuniary externalities involve the influences of the project on the prices of other producing units. For example, a public recreation facility may affect demand and thus price on nearby private facilities. Measurement of externalities is treacherous. Ideally, only "important externalities" are included in the analysis. Interestingly, the influence on the local wage rate is normally not included as "important." Controversy can easily exist on the inclusion of externalities as well as the measurement of them.

Often benefits and costs involve risk and uncertainty. Risk can be described by a probability function normally based on experience. Uncertainty, in its purest meaning, is not subject to probability determination. This means that risk can be included in the analysis, but uncertainty cannot be included. How to calculate risk and uncertainty varies. Some establish a higher permissible rate than 1.0. Some use a higher rate of discount, and some rationalize the arbitrary benefit stream cutoff by referring to risk and uncertainty. An analyst can deal with risk by including a probability function in an already complex formula, but uncertainty by definition must be treated arbitrarily. Such treatment leads to controversy over the analytical results.

Two other considerations illustrate the complexity of this technique. As was pointed out, sometimes private opportunity costs are used to determine public project opportunity costs. The danger is private market costs are higher due to the different tax statuses and costs of financing. Another consideration is when user charges are not independent of the benefit measures. User charges will restrict use, thus benefits will be reduced. Benefit-cost analysis requires a great deal of thought and care. If that professional treatment is not afforded, then embarrassing controversy can develop over the analytical quality of the analysis.

Benefit-cost analysis is biased toward values associated with money. It does not work well with projects concerning social equality, and the poor tend to be discriminated against with this technique. For example, the value of life is often computed in terms of earning power, thus an airplane passenger is treated as worth more than a bus rider. Values such as equality of opportunity cannot be treated well with this technique. If the project involves such values, then the use of the benefit-cost technique itself will be controversial.

Conclusion

Analysis is only ammunition for the political debates and administrative decisions, but the ammunition can be significant. Benefit-cost is a highly sophisticated analytical technique. If controversy over the technique can be avoided, then the technique can become significant.

REVIEW QUESTIONS

1. Explain how the conceptual input, process, output, outcomes model is useful to practitioners working with public budgets.
2. What conceptual and practical assumptions are highly useful in establishing a means to use measures in budgeting? Explain why each is useful.

3. Why is the program impact theory the heart of any good budget justification? Explain how this theory helps conceptually link program planning, budgeting, progress reporting, and evaluation.

4. Explain why measurement selection involves judgment.

5. Contrast and compare line-item, program, and performance budgeting.

6. Justify the statement: "There is no one best budget approach for all types of government situations."

7. Explain how any two simple analytical techniques can be useful to the budget analyst.

8. Contrast discounting to present value with marginal analysis.

9. Misunderstanding the productivity concept can lead to what types of difficulties?

10. Justify the statement: "There are no simple uniform answers for increasing productivity."

11. What are some of the most common reasons for government not to increase productivity?

12. Why is benefit-cost analysis at best only a guide for investment decisions?

13. Compare and contrast benefit-cost and cost-effectiveness analyses.

14. Explain why benefit-cost is a sophisticated and difficult technique to apply.

15. Explain how benefit-cost analysis can be abused as a technique.

16. Benefit-cost analysis can be dysfunctional to decision making. How?

REFERENCES

BURKHEAD, JESSE and JERRY MINER. *Public Expenditure.* Chicago: Aldine-Atherton, 1971.

Committee for Economic Development. *Improving Productivity in State and Local Government.* New York: Committee for Economic Development March 1976.

HARTY, HARRY P. "Overview of Modern Program Analysis Characteristics and Techniques: Modern Program Analysis—Hero or Villian?" Washington, D.C.: Urban Institute, 1969.

————. LOUIS BLAIR, DONALD FISK, and WAYNE KIMMEL. *Program Analysis for State and Local Governments.* Washington, D.C.: Urban Institute, 1976.

ISAAC, STEPHEN, in collaboration with William B. Michael *Handbook in Research and Evaluation.* San Diego: Edits Publishers, 1971.

KRAMER, FRED A. "The Discounting to Present Value Technique as a Decision Tool," *Special Bulletin* 1976E (November 24, 1976).

MOAK, LENNOX L. and KATHRYN W. KILLIAN. *Operating Budget Manual.* Chicago: Municipal Finance Officers Association, 1963.

ROSS, JOHN P. and JESSE BURKHEAD. *Productivity in the Local Government Sector.* Lexington, Mass.: D.C. Heath, 1974.

U.S. Joint Financial Management Improvement Program. *Productivity Programs in the Federal Government* (July 1976) U.S. Joint Financial Management Improvement Program. Washington D.C.

Urban Institute and International City Management Association. *Measuring the Effectiveness of Basic Municipal Services* (February 1974). Washington D.C.: International City Management Association.

WRIGHT, CHESTER and MICHAEL D. TATE. *Economics and Systems Analysis: Introduction for Public Managers*. Reading, Mass.: Addison-Wesley, 1973.

TWELVE

Financial Management

This chapter covers two important financial management topics: (1) purchasing and inventory, and (2) risk management. Both subjects are not central to public budgeting but are highly useful knowledge for a person working in budgeting. At the conclusion of this last chapter, the reader should know:

1. what purchasing is and why a specialist in purchasing is useful to a government;
2. what competitive bidding is and its disadvantages;
3. the importance of standardization and specifications;
4. the usefulness of preventative group replacement, computing maintenance and equipment cost on purchasing decisions, and cooperative intergovernmental arrangements;
5. the usefulness of central stores and the challenge of inventory management;
6. the significance of property control;
7. what risk management is and why it is an important concern;
8. what exposure identification is and how one goes about risk evaluation;
9. what risk control is and its significance;
10. what self-insurance is and when it is appropriate;
11. what insurance is, how it is selected, and some general standards applicable to it;
12. the elements of administration related to proper risk management;
13. the significance of retirement plans to public budgeting.

Purchasing Inventory

Objectives and Realities

In an organization, goods and services must be acquired. This activity is called purchasing. Materials, supplies, and equipment must be procured which best suit the job to be done by the operating unit. Ideally, the correct quantity should be ordered and in the hands of the operator when the units are needed. This proper timing of orders should also anticipate potential emergency shortage situations. The goods, services (including technical services), or equipment should be purchased at the lowest possible price. Last, unneeded inventory must be disposed of appropriately.

A central purchasing agent should be in charge of the above. Purchasing requires a knowledge of supply sources, pricing, business practices, market conditions, and appropriate laws, ordinances, and regulations. The procurement system should be devised to insure that discounts are taken, quality is tested, items are properly received and stored, and deliveries are prompt. Expertise is needed in dealing with salespersons, contractors, and people in the government seeking goods and services to get their jobs done. In other words, procurement is a separate administrative specialty and often can best be done by a central purchasing agent.

In spite of the obvious advantages, there are serious problems in properly conducting purchasing operations. Political pressures sometimes award favorite persons or groups contracts on the basis of political influence. Because of the enormous amounts of money involved, corruption is always a threat. Another problem is the procurement approaches—discussed later—because they do not lend themselves to undisputed proper purchases of services, especially if high levels of talent are being acquired. Also, the process can be so involved that quick purchases are simply not possible. In other words, procurement is not an easy administrative undertaking.

Procurement

Centralized and sometimes cooperative approaches to procurement are often taken. Centralization and cooperation lead to sufficient enough activity to justify hiring a specialist purchasing agent. A specialist can take the time to better monitor delivery services, develop a list of qualified vendors, and improve purchased items through standardization, use of standard specifications, better inspections, and testing. Responsibility for procurement can be more easily established in problem cases. Also greater fiscal control over expenditures for materials, supplies, and equipment can be achieved. These benefits are not automatic. Often central purchasing can mean friction between the ordering departments and the purchasing department as well as other problems if the purchasing department is inefficient, corrupt, or lacks sufficient budget authority.

In most governments, the law requires most purchases to be made with competitive bidding in order to minimize cost and to avoid corruption. Advertising for many bids and maintaining up-to-date lists of suppliers are essential if the spirit of the law is to be kept. The opportunity to bid should be unrestricted in most circumstances. The invitation or requests for bids should involve related items and specify the conditions of delivery. The sealed bids should be opened publicly and awards to other than the lowest bidder must be clearly explained in terms of the previously stated criteria. Awards must be in accordance with the stated specifications. Care should be taken to discourage and, if necessary, to prosecute seller collusion.

Competitive bidding has its disadvantages. It is inflexible and takes a great deal of time to process. It does not lend itself to small purchases, emergency buying, or contracts for professional services. If only one or even a few bids are received, then the government must be able to refuse the bid, or the process may result in higher prices rather than lower ones. In such circumstances, a negotiated bid may be a better purchasing process.

Standardization and specification are important procurement activities. Standardization of purchased items can lead to reducing the number and kinds of items purchased, thus reducing cost through quantity buying. Exceptions to standardization exist especially with highly specialized and technical goods. However, standardization is often desirable as it leads to price savings, quality improvements, and lower administrative costs. A procurement specification is a product or material description upon which bids are solicited. An adequate specification must be accurate and complete, but not overspecific. It must describe the methods of inspection and testing; state special requirements such as packing; conform, if possible, to national standards; and be internally consistent and simply stated. Good specification should place all bidders on an equal basis, minimize disputes, and avoid expensive brand-name buying. Both standardization and specification require enormous work and a highly qualified staff. If they serve no practical purpose in a given context, they should be avoided as they should serve to increase and not lower efficiency.

Goods should be inspected and tested. Were the goods delivered on time and in good condition? Were the goods received those that were ordered? Are the goods of the quality ordered? Inspection and testing answer these vital questions. Not all items need be inspected, but a random sample should be taken.

Another purchasing department responsibility is disposal of property. If possible, reassignment of items should be made. However, the time comes when the item such as an automobile should be traded, sold at auction, or sold as surplus. The objective should be to save the government money by using the items as much as possible and recovering any value for the goods after they have ceased being useful to the government.

Selected Purchasing Challenges

One purchasing challenge is deciding if particular items should be replaced as a group or individually. A preventative maintenance program can sometimes result in overall savings by replacing all of an item (e.g., light bulbs) at one time rather than individually. Group replacement can be cheaper due to the efficiency in scheduling labor and quantity price discounts. If this is to be done, then a replacement cycle must be established so that buying and labor scheduling can be properly coordinated. Also, some research is needed to decide the expected life of the item and the best replacement time.

Another challenge is including maintenance cost with the equipment cost so that total cost can be computed. The maintenance cost can be estimated by the supplier or the government. In fact, the contract with the supplier can include a proviso guaranteeing the maximum maintenance cost and any excessive maintenance cost would be reimbursed by the seller. Exhibit 12-1 is an illustration cited in chapter 14 of *Management Policies in Local Government Finance.*

EXHIBIT 12-1

Total-Cost Purchasing or Least-Cost Purchasing

Three suppliers bid as follows on heavy equipment:

Supplier	Purchase Price	Total Five-Year Guaranteed Maintenance Cost	Repurchase Price
A	$23,000	$11,000	$ 2,000
B	30,000	5,000	15,000
C	26,000	12,000	10,000

Supplier C has specified a five-year guarantee of $800 times the age of the machine each year. Suppliers A and B have agreed to apportion their guarantees evenly over the five years (i.e., $2,200 per annum for A and $1,000 per annum for B).

The formula to calculate total cost is as follows:

$$K = P + \left[\sum_{i=1}^{5} R_i \left(\frac{1}{1.2}\right)^i \right] - T \left(\frac{1}{1.2}\right)^5$$

where

K = net present value R_i = maintenance cost in year i

P = purchase price   T = repurchase price

Using a 20 percent discount, the formula results in the following:

Supplier	Purchase Price	+ Present Value of Maintenance Cost	− Present Value of Repurchased Price	= Net Present Value
A	$23,000	$6,579	$ 804	$28,775
B	30,000	2,991	6,029	26,962
C	26,000	6,318	4,019	28,299

The least expensive total cost bid is B.[1]

A third purchasing challenge is cooperative intergovernmental arrangements. Such arrangements can mean cost savings, but they should be undertaken with a clear understanding of all the factors involved. A basis for cost sharing must be negotiated. The level of service should be the same; or, if reduced, then this must be accepted. Labor disputes can sometimes arise when jobs are eliminated. Also the parties must understand who controls the planning, specifications, and service availability. Cooperative arrangements are normally difficult to apply due to disagreements over uniform items, the need for detailed records, and the allocation of shared costs. Beside cost-savings advantages, cooperative programs lead to a better sharing of ideas and greater personnel growth opportunities. Some important services that can be contracted or shared include street lighting, garbage disposal, sanitation services, health services, tax assessment and collection, water supply, law enforcement, and street and highway maintenance.

Central Stores and Inventory

Central warehousing, including tanks and storage yards, can foster significant savings since it makes possible quantity buying at the right time and price. Central stores permit better use of lead time to stock for emergencies and to allow the management of uneven requirements for goods. The disadvantage of central stores is the administrative cost of operation. Thus, the warehousing should be minimized. Problems to avoid include:

1. overstocking, especially if the goods can become obsolete;
2. a nonrestrictive inventory, not limited to substantial demand items;
3. not balancing stocking cost against value of having the item in stock when needed;
4. failure to consider the full range of cost elements.

The critical challenge of inventory is to calculate and to achieve the optimum amount of commodities so that necessary goods are available but storage costs are minimized. If supplies were available instantly and if purchase unit price did not vary by such factors as size of purchase, there would be no need for inventory. However, inventory is needed to reduce the likelihood of being out of needed goods and to achieve the lower price by bulk purchase and by taking advantage of fluctuations in market price. Those "savings" must be balanced against storage costs. This calculation is much like the decisions on investing idle cash discussed in an earlier chapter.

---

[1]A. Wayne Corcoran, "Financial Management," in J. Richard Aronson and Eli Schwartz (eds.), *Management Policies in Local Government Finance* (Washington, D.C.: International City Management Association, 1975).

Safety stock must be determined. There are various ways to determine that level of stock, but they all should recognize the various inventory costs:

1. ordering cost—preparing specifications, obtaining competitive bids, negotiating, receiving items;
2. incremental cost—unique extra costs due to specific order;
3. carrying cost—deterioration, obsolescence, storing, issuing, theft, handling, interest, and insurance;
4. shortage cost—associated with disappointing a client, legal settlements, lost labor costs, other costs due to delay or failure to provide service.

The solution for optimal safety stock is where the total of holding costs and expected shortage costs are minimal. These calculations assume sound estimates, but once those costs are determined, the actual calculation for optimal safety stock is relatively simple, especially with a computer. Rules of thumb can be developed in terms of days of normal use. Ideally, these rules of thumb should be checked against the more sophisticated calculations.

Another calculation involves ordering cost. For this, the economic ordering quantity (EOQ) model is used. The ordering costs must be weighed against the holding costs which arise due to the size of the order. The calculation is similar to the optimal safety stock determination. The optimum ordering quantity is where the total of two types of costs are at a minimum. The following EOQ model is used:

$$Q = \sqrt{2C_0D \div C_H}$$

where

Q = the optimum (i.e., most economic) quantity to order

C_0 = the cost of ordering per order

C_H = the cost of holding per unit per time period

D = the quantity of units used or demanded each time period

An example is as follows:

D = 110 cubic yards of gravel used per day

C_0 = \$20.00 per order (ordering costs)

C_H = \$0.02 per yard per day (holding costs)

$$Q = \sqrt{2(20)110 \div .02} = 469 \text{ yards}^2$$

---

[2] This explanation and example are from Corcoran, "Financial Management."

Again, most analysts develop simpler rules of thumb. However, the results of those casual estimates should be tested against the more sophisticated approach discussed here.

Total desirable inventory is calculated by adding the EOQ and safety stock solution. A more accurate solution would use a simultaneous solution, but that higher degree of accuracy is not normally warranted.

The above uses quantifiable costs, but often important government or society costs cannot be reduced to numbers. This should be understood when applying the techniques.

Property Control

A property control officer is needed to insure that personal property and the equipment of government is being efficiently managed. No operational control is necessary, but procedures must be devised and practices must be monitored to insure efficient management. This type of control should only be applied to items where poor use can easily mean inefficiency or corruption.

Records control fixes responsibility. It fixes who has actual control and is reponsible for the care of the item. Periodic reports are needed on the condition of the item. Records help on insurance loss claims, preventative maintenance decisions, and reordering. Records should use identifying numbers, acquisition purchase orders, transfers, and repair and disposal orders.

An option to owning goods is leasing. This is an alternative which may be the best economic investment. The calculations to determine this are similar to the ones involving present value discussed in an earlier chapter.

Risk Management

A Practical Necessity

Forbes magazine reported the following true account:

On a clear, dry night in 1974, 26 year old Thomas J. Garchar cruised down a straightaway on Broadway County's (Fla.) University Drive and smashed his car headlong into a 560 pound decorative limestone boulder lying on the road's median. Paralyzed from the neck down as a result of the accident, Garchar sued the retirement town of Tamarac (population: 31,000), essentially on the grounds that Tamarac's city fathers knew that the boulder was there, but had not removed it.

In court Garchar admitted to having been up 18 hours straight and to having downed three drinks just prior to the accident. Yet last November, a local jury found Tamarac guilty of negligence and awarded Garchar and his wife $4.7 million in damages. (Broward County, responsible for placing the boulder on the median, settled out of court for another $1.15 million.) The town is appealing the case, and

$1 million of the judgment is covered by liability insurance, but meanwhile Tamarac faces the prospect of raising taxes to pay the award."[3]

In *Governmental Finance* the following case was cited.[4] A 23-year-old patrol officer was hired. He was in generally good health when hired, but after 18 months he suffered a lifting injury to his lower back. This led to two months lost work time, surgery, and two more months of operative recovery. The officer returned to work but was extremely bothered by back pain due to work activities. This led to more lost time, medical bills, and physical therapy. After two-and-a-half years service, he stopped working due to his back problem and was retired one year later on a disability pension at age 26. The cost was:

Medical expenses for disc surgery	$ 6,300
Lost time compensation costs	5,500
Ongoing medical expenses	4,000
Retirement benefit (two-thirds average monthly salary which was $620 with projected mortality of 50 years)	372,000
Cost to hire and train replacement patrol officer	2,000
Estimated partial disability settlement by compensation carrier	15,000
Other hidden costs estimated	2,000
Total Cost	$406,800

Both public and private concerns are subject to significant risks which could be costly to the government. Risk management is merely deciding how best to deal with those risks and to manage the problem accordingly. The above cases dramatically point out that risk is a significant consideration in good financial management. Insurance is one way to deal with risk, and the costs of insurance are rising dramatically. The League of California Cities in 1975 surveyed municipal liability insurance premiums, and they discovered a one-year increase of 96 percent as well as many nonrenewals of insurance. In other words, risks are significant and the traditional solution—insurance—is becoming more expensive and harder to acquire.

The risks or liabilities for government include civil damages, breach of contract, dishonesty protection, workmen's compensation, activity interruption, and even health protection. What losses can take place? Property can be damaged. People can be hurt. Property can be stolen. People can get sick. Each represents a loss which can cost a government significant sums of money.

The most serious loss exposure concerns third-party liabilities. In the first

---

[3]Lawrence Minard, "The Premiums of City Life," *Forbes,* 119, 6 (March 15, 1977). p. 96.
[4]Edward G. Lengyel, "Controlling Risk: The Safety Factor," *Governmental Finance,* 6, 33 (May 1977). p. 47.

case cited above, the town of Tamarac has been held liable for not removing a traffic safety hazard. This resulted in a large award damage. Similar awards can occur if a public employee is involved in an accident. Suits can be brought for environmental pollution. For example, the town of Hopewell, Virginia was sued in the mid-1970s for either actively or passively condoning the contamination of the James River by a small firm connected with Allied Chemical Company. New loss exposures are being defined in the courts today: Jail inmates have sued Dutchess County, New York for providing inadequate medical treatment. The City of Los Angeles was sued by property owners near the airport because aircraft noise reduced their property value. The potential cost to state and local government is high.

Exposure Identification and Risk Evaluation

The first step in risk management is the identification of government resources and the losses that are possible. What kind of damages to people and property could take place? What type of damage can result if that responsibility is not met? What happens if someone is in an accident, is sick, or is dishonest? This step requires an inventory of the government's resources and a careful evaluation of responsibilities and potential damages. This evaluation can be helped by knowing the types of risk liabilities governments commonly experience and the types of claims currently found in the courts. This step must be done on a continuing basis by using checklists, questionnaires, interviews with employees, physical inspections, and a careful monitoring of the contemporary risk management literature.

Part of exposure identification must be a full understanding of the tort doctrine of government immunity. This doctrine gave government immunity from many civil tort actions such as negligence. However, this doctrine has been reconsidered since the 1940s, and governments are increasingly vulnerable. This means, for example, that governments can be sued for not maintaining property to prevent injuries. Care must be taken in these areas by governments, or costly judgments can occur. An awareness of state law is necessary to understand the status of the doctrine of government immunity in each particular state.

Information is the key to exposure identification. Accurate and timely data on costs must be available so that costs can be identified with specific departments and activities. Financial statements, especially involving capital projects, help identify property exposures and areas of new activity not analyzed for risks. Another useful source of data is analyses of operations. By following through the process, the risk manager can identify services that could be disrupted, potential hazards in procedures, health dangers, and equipment safety concerns. In looking over such data, the manager is particularly concerned with the likely frequency and severity of the exposure potential. Other concerns include neat storage of goods and equipment, storage proximity to fire sources, free movement so danger can be escaped and gotten to quickly by proper officials, and special handling of flammable liquids.

Exhibit 12-2 is a useful risk and insurance checklist. This checklist can help to review systematically the exposures facing a government unit.

EXHIBIT 12-2

Risk and Insurance Check List

I. Real Property
  A. Buildings owned
    1. Nature, use and location
    2. Value replacement and actual cash value
    3. Rental value of space used
    4. Income from space rented to others
    5. Laws and ordinances for demolition and for replacement standards
  B. Buildings rented from others
    1. Nature, use and location
    2. Value of improvements and betterments made by tenant
    3. Total rent paid by tenant
    4. Rental income derived from subletting space to others
    5. Value of the lease (is the lease favorable?)
    6. Type of insurance clauses and hold harmless agreements in the lease
  C. All buildings and other real property (includes A and B above)
    1. Alterations and additions in progress or contemplated
    2. Boilers and pressure vessels in operation
    3. Power machinery in operation (switchboards, motors, engines, generators, etc.)
    4. Cold storage vaults and other special provisions for maintaining controlled temperature or humidity
    5. Electric or neon signs
    6. Plate or ornamental glass
    7. Elevators and escalators
    8. Possible fire department service charges
    9. Fire and other protection (sprinklers, alarms, watchmen)
II. Personal Property
  A. Stock, including packaging materials (each location)
    1. Peak value and low values (month by month)
    2. Susceptibility to crime loss
    3. Values dependent on parts difficult to replace
    4. Values susceptible to damage by lack of heat or cold
  B. Furniture and fixtures attached to the building
    1. Those permanently attached to the building
    2. Unattached furniture, fixtures, machinery, office equipment
    3. Supplies and prepaid expense items
  C. Personal Property belonging to others
  D. Personal property in the custody of others

Source: Gerald M. Surfus, "Identifying and Evaluating Potential Risk," *Governmental Finance,* 6, 28 (May 1977), 28–29.

    E. Coins and currency (maximum amounts)
       1. Payroll cash (when)
       2. Other cash
       3. Cash in custody of each bank messenger
       4. Cash in custody of each truck driver or collector
       5. Cash kept in safes overnight
       6. Liability limit or armored car carrier
    F. Incoming checks (maximum amounts)
       1. On premises
       2. In safes overnight
       3. In custody of each bank messenger
       4. In custody of each truck driver or collector
    G. Bank accounts (locations, amounts, uses)
    H. Securities (maximum amounts)
       1. In safes
       2. In custody of each bank messenger
       3. In safe deposit vaults
       4. At other locations (specify)
    I. Especially valuable property (maximum amounts) (e.g., precious stones, fine
      arts, antiques, rare metals, isotopes, radium)
       1. In safes
       2. Elsewhere on premises
       3. In custody of each truck driver
       4. In safe deposit vault
       5. At other locations or in transit (specify)
    J. Valuable papers, documents, records
       1. Kind
       2. Where kept
       3. Value
       4. Protection afforded
    K. Accounts receivable
       1. Maximum and minimum values
       2. Where account records are kept
       3. How protected
    L. Automobiles, airplanes, boats, trains, buses (owned or used)
       1. Ownership
         a) Owned
         b) Non-owned
       2. Value and extent of concentration in one place at one time
III.   Operations
    A. Central operations: principal services
       1. Nature of all services regularly provided
       2. Sources of materials and supplies used
       3. Flow of goods, steps or processes in provision of services: any bottlenecks
       4. Extent, nature, and location of goods on installment or similar credit
         arrangements
       5. Installation, demonstration, or servicing away from premises
       6. Quality control
    B. Service for employees
       1. Operation of a hospital, infirmary, or first-aid station
       2. Operation of a restaurant for employees
       3. Sponsorship of employee athletic teams

    C. Operation of a medical facility or other service in which a malpractice hazard exists

    D. Operation of a restaurant for the general public

    E. Work let out under contract

    F. Advertising signs, vending machines, booths, etc., owned or operated away from the premises

    G. Sponsorship of outside athletic team

    H. Liability assumed under contract
1. Sidetrack agreements
2. Leases
3. Hold harmless agreements
4. Purchase orders
5. Elevator or escalator maintenance agreements
6. Easements
7. Service agreements (for or by the entity)
8. Other contracts
9. Warranties

    I. Shipments (values shipped annually and the maximum value of any one shipment, both incoming and outgoing)
1. Own trucks
2. Truckmen
3. Rail
4. Railway express
5. Air
6. Parcel post prepaid and C.O.D.
7. Registered mail
8. Inland or coastal water
9. Foreign
10. Marine cargo

    J. "Time element" exposures
1. Payroll: key persons; "ordinary" payroll
2. Cost of merchandise
3. Cost of heat, light, and power
4. Trend of revenue for current year; estimate for next year
5. Maximum time required to replace facilities subject to damage
6. Percentage of revenue that would be affected by a business interruption loss
7. The availability and probable cost of substitute facilities to reduce loss of revenue in case of damage to present facilities
8. Extra expense to maintain operations following loss
9. If plans are interdependent, the percentage of revenue affected by a stoppage at each such plant or location, assuming damage at only one location
10. Extent to which operations are dependent on outside sources of heat, light, or power

IV. Personnel

    A. Home-state employees
1. Duties
2. Use of automobiles
3. Estimated annual payroll

    B. Employees in other states
1. Residence state and states traveled

2. Duties
3. Use of automobiles
4. Estimated annual payroll
C. Employees annual payroll
D. Employees required to use or travel in aircraft
E. Classification of employees according to duties
F. Key individuals (individuals whose loss might seriously affect operations)
V. Principal Property Hazards (Probable Maximum Loss)
A. Fire and allied lines
B. Earthquake
C. Flood
D. Other
VI. Data Processing Machines
A. Owned or leased
B. Protection
C. Lease to others?
D. Disaster plan
E. Analysis of extra expense costs

The measurement of potential losses is not easily accomplished. A complete inventory of property is needed, including building location distance to hazards; proximity to highway, air, or rail traffic; available fire protection including quality indicators such as water pressure; and a description of the surrounding property. The inventory should also include the construction details, specifics on safety protections used, and building and equipment replacement costs. In measuring liability exposure, an evaluation of the law including government immunity, current history of local claim awards, and review of all contract terms are essential. In measuring fidelity exposure, an examination of cash receipts, opportunities to convert assets to cash, and potential for dealings with high officials with vendors or grantees must be reviewed carefully. Periodic outside audits are essential. Risk managers must review (1) the audits, (2) accounting reports which show balances, (3) purchasing procedures, (4) electronic data processing concerning money, (5) the location and volume of cash, and (6) cash internal control procedures. Losses must be weighed in terms of exposure and severity.

Given the difficulty of gathering information and other aspects of risk management, not surprisingly the previous government practice was to buy insurance and transfer the risk. This permitted the government officials to forget about the risk and pay attention to other more pressing problems. Today, government cannot afford to handle risk in that manner because:

1. premiums are expensive and increasing in price;
2. some forms of coverage do not exist;
3. government immunity is shrinking;
4. damage awards are radically increasing beyond maximum insurance award limits;
5. preventative and safety programs can dramatically reduce exposure risks;

6. self-insurance is often a cheaper alternative than insurance;
7. knowledge of insurance and exposure risks can translate into better insurance coverage at less cost.

Risk Control

Risk control is the reduction of risk or loss through careful procedures and practices in security, personnel safety, fire prevention, auto safety, product safety, environmental protection, and emergency planning. For the most part, state and local governments do not perform adequate risk control. In 1975, the National Safety Council said the national average lost time personnel rate was 13.1 (lost time accident per million man hours worked). Some claim a lost time injury rate of over 41 can be accused of inaction bordering on criminal negligence. The chemical, aerospace, and automotive industries all rate less than 4. Federal civil employees rate 6.5. The rate for municipalities was 41.3. Police, refuse, and fire rates were 54.8, 98.7, and 149 respectively. In 1975, 1 out of 14 municipal employees, 1 out of 10 police employees, 1 out of 6 refuse handlers, and 1 out of 4 fire fighters were involved in a lost time accident. This is a record of inaction and inadequate attention to safety. However, the problem is being recognized due to social, economic, and legal pressures. Sound risk control programs include:

1. *Security*—preventative techniques and procedures for theft, burglary, and vandalism;
2. *Personnel safety*—meeting occupational safety and health standards, setting work safety standards, monitoring work environment and recordkeeping on accidents, safety training, safety committees;
3. *Fleet safety*—systematic review of driving records and implementation of stringent defensive driving courses;
4. *Property conservation*—regular inspection by fire, electrical, police, and others to identify and to correct physical property;
5. *Environmental protection*—procedures to dispose of solid, liquid, and gaseous wastes in accordance with state and federal standards;
6. *Emergency preparedness*—plans for and practice in dealing with a wide variety of emergencies such as bomb threats, national disasters including fires and floods, and nuclear war;
7. *Contract liability*—procedures to review likely contracts so that the government will not assume the liability of others as well as care to get contractors for public authorities to sign a stiff hold-harmless agreement with evidence of adequate insurance.

Over the years the following safety beliefs have proven to be helpful: (1) Unsafe acts and conditions lead to accidents and injuries; (2) reducing the frequency of injury will also lessen the severity of injury; (3) safety means education, engineering, and enforcement. The key person for safety is the first line supervisor. Post-injury investigations are essential to identify and remove unsafe acts and conditions. Safety programs translate to actively caring about safety and implementing the proper remedies. Safety plans should reflect those beliefs in most instances.

Risk control costs money as does insurance. A public authority can approach risk control insurance mix decisions on the basis of lowest cost to the government. Exhibit 12-3 illustrates how the cost can be charted. The cost of risk control is calculated and related to the likely cost of insurance and self-insurance.

EXHIBIT 12-3

Risk Control Plus Insurance

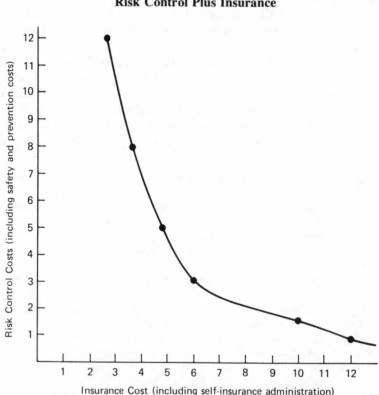

Insurance Cost (including self-insurance administration)

The solution is the lowest joint risk control and insurance cost. Obviously, human compassion must be considered, and those values dictate that higher sums of money be spent for risk control than our economic analysis suggests. However, the chart does help us see the relationship between safety and insurance costs.

Risk Funding and Self-Insurance

Risk funding is providing for sufficient funds to meet loss situations if they occur by the most effective use of internal and external financial resources. A public body can retain the risk and pay losses through extraordinary means or the regular budget. Another option is to transfer the risk through a pooling of insurance. The self-insurance or partial self-insurance option is often desirable because it is the most economical approach for a public body. Even the insurance industry is encouraging the use of high deductibles—that is, partial self-insurance—today.

Insurance is merely pooling risks plus an administrative charge to administer that pooling. Insurance companies will generally collect from $1.50 to $2.00 in premiums for every dollar spent in claims. Some governments are larger than insurance companies and are in a better position to fund the potential losses than are the companies. A guideline to help decide the proper risk retention amount is that a government body should be willing to accept up to one-tenth of one percent of its operating budget in uninsured losses arising out of a single occurrence, or up to one percent of the operating budget as the aggregate of all such self-insured losses in a single fiscal year.

The following corollary objectives exist in risk funding: (1) sufficient funds must be provided to meet the worst possible loss event. Some use a "maximum foreseeable loss" criterion and others also use a "maximum probable loss" estimate for the loss. (2) The management of risk funding should include proper use of idle cash reserves. (3) The maximum stability of risk funding should be maintained over time. (4) Administration should be both as efficient and effective as possible.

Governments are in much better position to absorb losses than most private concerns. They can use the following special factors:

1. federal disaster assistance (Public Law 93-288);
2. funded reserves or especially created insurance company for that purpose;
3. spreading judgments over, say, a 10-year period;
4. bond issues;
5. special tax levies;
6. citizen or group donations;

Another type of self-insurance option is pooling on a local, regional, or state basis. For example, the cities in Contra Costa County California have pooled together their liability and property risks. Pools for workers' compensation claims have been set up in Alabama, Texas, and Maine. This alternative does work well; and as the liability insurance marketplace deteriorates, this joint action may become the only practical alternative. The biggest problem with pooling is the challenge of reaching administrative consensus on such matters as the cost allocation system. The accompanying chart is a useful guideline on risk retention.

Type of Risk	*Retention Policy*
Low frequency and low severity	This risk should be retained due to the low exposure.
High frequency and low severity	Normally, this risk should be retained as self-insurance.
High frequency and high severity	Handling this risk depends on the size of the government and insurance marketplace. Worker's compensation is a typical loss exposure of this type.
Low frequency and high severity	This risk cannot normally be absorbed; risk transfer by insurance is wise. An alternative is to partial self-insurance. This can reduce insurance and total risk costs. Property and liability exposures are prime examples of this type.

Partial self-insurance can be practiced through high deductibles and special insurance plans which permit a sharing of risk with the insurance company. The decisions on this subject should weigh premium credits and administrative savings. Do not risk a lot for a little. A deductible should result in commensurate savings compared to the risk which is retained. However, the government should set the deductible at the level it can afford based on its own financial ability and not on the saving generated in any one year. An annual aggregate deductible should be used rather than a single occurrence deductible because this provides greater budgeting certitude. The following addresses common practices by type of insurance:

1. *Fire insurance*—high deductibles are often used. Normally the deductible should be on a "per occurrence" basis and not on a "per loss" basis because a single windstorm is one occurrence but many losses. Also an aggregate deductible should be used.

2. *Workers' compensation*—most private and increasingly public bodies self-insure with insurance for catastrophic loss, e.g., over $100,000 on a per occurrence basis.

3. *Public liability*—the use of insurance above set limits is critical, but such insurance is getting increasingly more difficult to obtain. The following are two examples of coverage used in the state of California:
   a. In the mid-1970s, the county of Orange went from a per loss of $25,000 self-insurance to $500,000 on any liability loss.
   b. The city of San Diego increased its liability self-insurance retention from $500,000 to $5 million.

The planning process for self-insurance takes about six months. The first month is spent gathering data especially on premiums and losses as discussed earlier. In the second month, the maximum amount which can be retained should be determined. In the third month, the insurance bidding process should begin. In the fourth month, the bids should be reviewed or costs negotiated. In the fifth month, the contracts should be awarded.

A true self-insurance program means that the government performs all the various functions which would have been handled by an insurance carrier. These functions include accounting for premiums, a safety and loss control service, adjusting services, legal services, and funding for losses. A fund, from which losses will be paid up to the retained limit, must be established. Such funds are accumulated on a gradual basis, and the idle funds are invested. Also, the department incurring the loss should be charged back a predetermined amount of each loss. This serves to encourage department heads to be sensitive to their risks and the importance of risk control.

Insurance

Many public authorities require bidding for insurance. There is some controversy associated with bidding. Advocates point out that open competitive bidding gives every company a fair opportunity to receive the contract, and the process leads to the best price for the government. Those against the process point to several problems. Yearly bidding discourages long-term company-to-client relationships, thus negating a potential advantage and adding to the cost of overhead in the insurance industry. Increasingly fewer companies are willing to bid, thus artifically high bids do exist. If individual negotiations occur instead, they might result in lower bids. An alternative approach is limited competitive bidding where focus is placed upon selecting qualified agents or brokers. Two or three are selected and asked to submit firm quotations. The contract is awarded on the basis of those bids.

The forms of insurance include property insurance, crime coverage, liability coverage, and employee benefits. Property insurance includes both fire, "all risk" contracts on buildings, contents, and property, and other coverages. Crime coverages include employee dishonesty, faithful performance bonds, and protection against burglary, robbery, and theft. Liability coverages include all forms of public liability insurance, automobile insurance, and workers' compensation. Umbrella protection is essential and should include the governing body, all boards, commissions, elected officials, employees, and even volunteers. Employee benefits is often a labor-management negotiated subject, but it can include health insurance, major medical insurance, long-term disability income insurance, accident insurance, group life insurance, and pension plans.

A few general standards apply to all insurance contracts. The named insured group should be consistent on all policies. Property limits should be updated to actual cash or replacement value. All insurance contracts should have a 60-day written notice cancellation, nonrenewal, or material reduction clause. Retention and participation in risk should be carefully spelled out in the contract.

Proper notification of loss should begin after the risk manager is aware of the loss, and payments on losses should be to the governmental body. Normally, the contracts should all, or as many as possible, expire at the end of the fiscal year. Cash flow arrangements should be made to the advantage of the government's idle cash plans.

Some general suggestions on content can be made. Coverage should be very broad due to the variety of risk exposures found in government. Large maximum limits should be used. For example, in the mid-1970s, a limit of $5 million was appropriate for small governments and $10 to $20 million or more for larger entities. Umbrella coverage is getting more difficult to obtain so some risks must be insured separately such as airport liability, aircraft, and bus lines.

Administration

A risk management program requires continuous direction and careful attention. For larger governments, a full-time risk manager is essential and an additional safety staff would be wise. For smaller governments, this activity can be part of the budget office responsibilities. For both large and small governments, outside assistance can be quite valuable at times due to the complex nature of this subject.

A formal risk management policy should be developed which sets out important understandings. The policy must have active top legislative and executive support. The policy should establish the goals of the program as well as define authority and responsibility in this area. The necessary types of interdepartmental coordination should be spelled out. Guidelines on risk retention should be stated in the context of the risk management philosophy of loss reduction and prevention. Insurance purchasing should be centralized. A model policy statement is presented in Exhibit 12-4.

EXHIBIT 12-4

Risk Management Policy

1. The function of risk management has as its purpose:
   a. Protecting the municipality from catastrophic losses
   b. Minimizing the total cost of accidental loss to the municipality
2. Risk management is to place the greatest emphasis on reduction rather than reimbursement of loss, through professional attention to loss control techniques, motivational incentives, prompt claims payments, and other loss prevention measures.
3. All insurance shall be purchased through the city risk management department.
4. Subject to the risk manager's discretion, the amount of insurance purchased shall provide protection whenever a single accidental loss would result in property loss in excess of $50,000 per incident or liability judgment that would potentially exceed $50,000 per incident. Lesser amounts may be retained if financially feasible.

Source: "Risk Management in Local Government," *Government Finance*, 6, 2 (May 1977), 44.

Two keys to risk management are communication and cooperation. Risk identification depends on getting the necessary information for the governing body, the legal staff, the program units, the personnel department, purchasing, and others. A government has outstanding in-house expertise which must be tapped. The expertise includes the fire department, police, inspection units, attorney's office, finance, personnel, and others. Each can be quite helpful. For example, the fire department can help devise a fire loss prevention effort, and the finance office can help devise the best means to deal with idle cash resulting from the risk management program.

The risk managers should report annually on their program to top management. The report should point out major changes in the program, the outline of new program departures in the future, and comparisons to programs with other similar governmental units. The loss prevention program should be presented and total cost savings stated. The report should also contain an analysis of claims paid, reserves, administrative, and legal costs.

In conclusion, the risk manager should have responsibility for:

1. aiding units in analyzing risks, including accidental losses;
2. advising and adjusting major losses for all units on loss prevention, safety, and self-insurance levels;
3. allocating insurance and risk costs to the units;
4. maintaining records of losses, loss costs, premiums, and related costs;
5. reviewing all new contracts for hold-harmless requirements;
6. purchasing insurance;
7. coordinating all activities involving risk.

Retirement Programs

A complete treatment of retirement programs is beyond the scope of this text and may more properly be covered in other books. However, retirement programs do have a significant impact upon government budgets at all levels. Many retirement plans call for pension in 20 years with generous provisions. Many governments have discovered the cost of such plans are very high in future years, especially if a cost-of-living provision was added. When labor negotiations are occurring, a government would be wise to analyze the implications of the various proposals to be sure that the policy can be afforded in future years.

REVIEW QUESTIONS

1. Explain why "professional" procurement is difficult to perform.
2. Explain how "competitive bidding" can be corrupted and why it can be dysfunctional. Explain this also in terms of insurance.

3. Explain the balance desired in warehousing and why this is difficult to achieve.
4. Explain the relationship between risk control and insurance.
5. What type of knowledge and skill is needed for exposure identification and risk evaluation?
6. Explain what factors should be weighed in deciding how much risk should be retained.
7. What types of continuous direction and careful attention connote excellent risk management?

REFERENCES

CORCORAN, A. WAYNE. "Financial Management," in J. Richard Aronson and Eli Schwartz (eds.), *Management Policies in Local Government Finance.* Washington, D.C.: International City Management Association, 1975.
International City Management Association. *Municipal Finance Administration,* 6th ed. Chicago: International City Management Association, 1962.
MOAK, LENNOX L. and ALBERT M. HILLHOUSE. *Local Government Finance.* Chicago: Municipal Finance Officers Association, 1975.
"Risk Management in Local Government," *Government Finances,* 6, 2 (May 1977).
ROSS, NESTOR R. and JOSEPH S. GERBER. *Governmental Risk Management Manual.* Tucson, Ariz: Risk Management Publishing Company, 1977.

Glossary

Accounting: Technique consisting of recording transactions of an agency in financial terms including the classification of those transactions, summarizing, reporting, interpretation, and analysis for the user of the data. It is merely keeping track of and analyzing the transactions by using summaries and classifications.

Accrual method of accounting: In this method, revenues are recorded when they are earned or billed and expenditures are recorded when they are obligated. This method permits accountability but it also distorts the revenue and cash position of the government.

Allotment: The primary budget control method used by agencies. It provides authority from the agency head to the operating officials to incur obligations or expenditures within prescribed amounts for a specific period of time.

Annual budget: Revenues and expenditures presented for one fiscal year period.

Apportionments and allotments: An executive branch mechanism to regulate the rate and actual spending of authorized funds.

"Arbitrage" bonds: The exemption from income tax is lost with this type of bond. This classification occurs if the state and local governments place the funds from the bonds in other investments rather than the prescribed activities.

Assets: Include cash, short-term investments, property tax receivables, amounts due from other funds, and inventory.

Auditing: System which checks on the accuracy of the accounting system, the correct operation of the system including validating inventories and existing equipment, proper legal authority to perform the activity, adequacy of the control system, fraud, waste and mismanagement, and the effectiveness of the program.

Backdoor spending: The commitment of federal funds outside the appropriation process.

Balance sheet: Accounting statement designed to balance total assets, total liabilities, and fund balance.

Benefit-cost analysis: Technique based on the belief that project should be judged on the basis of project cost versus project benefits.

Bond: A written promise to pay a specific sum of money (called the face value or principal amount) at a specified date or dates (called the maturity dates) together with periodic interest at a specific rate.

Bond maturity: The period of time established at the end of which a bond principal is completely paid. The length of the maturity normally is not longer than the useful life of the facility which is being financed.

Bond prospectus: The formal information used by sellers to help investors decide whether or not they wish to invest in bonds.

Borrowing authority: Government official can borrow money and the Congress must pass subsequent appropriations to liquidate the debt.

Budget: Plan for the accomplishment of programs related to objectives and goals within a definite time period, including an estimate of the resource required, together with an estimate of the resource available, usually compared with one or more past periods and showing future requirements. Request for funds to run the government.

Budget and Accounting Act of 1921: provided for an executive national government budget and an independent audit of government accounts.

Budget and Accounting and Procedures Act of 1950: President was given the authority to prescribe the contents and budget arrangements, simplification of presentations, broadening of appropriations, and progress toward performance budgeting.

Budget call: Guidance provided by the Budget Office to all the departments and agencies informing them to prepare the budget and how to go about preparing the budget. Much of the guidance is standardized and established in official bulletins and circulars.

Budget Execution System: Should be established to give direction to on-going agency activities and permit continuous and current reviews to determine if planned objectives are being met. One approach is to link an operating budget with management-by-objectives.

Budget-wise model: Awareness of all the forms and tables, but discounting them almost completely because the government's decisions are perceived to be all political and other factors are not significant. A person following this model stresses such decision-making is inevitable and all that a budget staff can do is to react and watch the political events unfold.

Call provision: The right of the borrower to buy back bonds at set prices regardless of current market rate.

Capital budget: This budget deals with large expenditures for capital items normally financed by borrowing. Usually capital items have long-range returns, useful life spans, are relatively expensive, and have physical presence such as a building, road, sewage system, etc.

Cash method of accounting: Income is recorded when it is received and expenditures when they are paid. This method is easy to administer and the cash balance is easily determined. However, expenses and revenues cannot be related to the budget and its fiscal year. Therefore accountability is impossible.

Circuit breakers: A reform recommendation for property taxation, which would reduce the regressive nature of the tax. They often give exemptions to families with the lowest income or elderly to relieve them of paying some of their property taxes.

Clientele group: This group is perceived to be affected by the agency's programs and takes an active interest in the agency's policy and actions.

Comprehensive budget: All revenues and expenditures included in the budget.

Congressional Budget and Impoundment Control Act of 1974:   One aspect of several reforms directed toward strengthening the legislative branch. Made such changes as creating the new Senate and House Budget Committees, creating a new Congressional Budget Office, requiring a current services budget, and requiring various reforms addressed to the Presidential budget and impoundment powers. It created a unified congressional budget reform and it strengthened Congress as a co-equal branch with the executive on budgetary matters.

Congressional Budget Office: Responsible for presenting the Congress with respectable and viable alternatives on aggregate levels of spending and revenue. The office must also make cost estimates for proposed legislation reported to the floor and provide cost projections for all existing legislation.

Continuing resolution: If a decision has not been reached on appropriations prior to the beginning of the new current year, then Congress can pass a resolution which says the government can continue to obligate and spend at last year's budget levels of the lowest level passed by a chamber of Congress. The wording is usually framed to permit spending at the lowest amount the legislature is likely to pass.

Contract authority: Condition in which government officials can obligate the government through legal contracts and the Congress must pass subsequent appropriations to fulfill the obligation.

Cost-effectiveness analysis: This method assumes benefits and does not compare them with cost as in benefit-cost analysis. In cost-effectiveness analysis, the analyst wishes to determine the least costly means to achieve the objective.

Crosswalk: One of most useful analytical tools for the budget examiner. It serves as a conceptual bridge between two organizational means to describe and control agency activities. Example: A common crosswalk is between the so-called program structure and the appropriation structure.

Current services budget: This executive budget projection alerts the Congress, especially the CBO, the Budget Committees, and the Appropriation Committees, that they should be anticipating specific revenue, expenditure, and debt levels, assuming current policy is unchanged. It also provides a baseline of comparison to the later Presidential budget.

Debt: It is a government credit obligation.

Decision Packages: Self-contained units for budget choice containing input and output data (resources to operate the program and the products of the program) as well as the expected levels of performance for each defined level of expenditure. Program and higher level managers then rank those decision packages in order of priority. The lowest levels don't get funded.

Default risk: The possibility that a borrower will fail to pay the principal or interest on a loan. All other factors constant, the greater the possibility the borrower will fail to meet the obligation, the greater the premium or market yield on the security.

Detailed line items: Presenting the exact amount planned to be spent for every separate thing or service to be purchased.

Discounting to present value: A dollar received or spent in the future is not equivalent to a dollar received or spent today. Therefore, adjustments must be made if comparisons are to be made.

Discount-rate policy: The interest rate the Federal Revenue charges member banks for loans. This is an economic stabilization tool. An increase in interest charges normally leads to a rise in the rates charged others. Thus, money becomes more expensive and fewer people borrow. This contracts the economy.

Earmarked revenue: Funds from a specific source can be spent only for designated activity. Example: gasoline taxes can only be spent for highway construction and maintenance.

Economic ordering quantity: A means to determine the total desirable inventory. Ordering costs must be weighed against the holding cost which would arise due to the size of an order.

Electronic funds transfer system: A system that provides the capability for automatic receipts of funds as well as computer assisted generation of fund transfers among treasury, Federal Reserve Banks, member banks, etc. Thus processing of checks can be done instantly instead of taking several days thus virtually eliminating the float.

Employment Act of 1946:   Called for economic planning and a budget policy directed toward achieving maximum national employment and production.

External audits: Carried out by independent separate agencies. This type of audit examines accounts, checks on the accuracy of recorded transactions and inventories, on-site review of stocks, verifies physical existence of equipment, and reviews operating procedures and regulations.

Federal Anti-Deficiency Act: This act is designed to focus responsibility for budget control. It states that any person knowingly and willfully violating the appointments can be fined and imprisoned.

Federal Reserve: The U.S. central banking system which operates to control the economy's supply of money and credit.

Fixed costs: Those costs in any project or program which remain constant regardless of the increase or decrease in units produced.

Float: The difference between the total amount of checks drawn on a bank account by the government and the amount shown on the bank's books for that account.

"Full-faith-and-credit-debt":   Long term debts in which the credit (including the implied power of taxation) is unconditionally pledged by the government.

Fund accounting: A sum of money is set aside for a particular purpose and accounted for separately from the other monies of the government. The purpose is to control the handling of money to insure that it will be spent only for the purpose intended.

General Accounting Office: The congressional audit agency for the U.S. Federal government. This agency reports directly to and is responsible to the Congress. GAO investigates fraud, waste, and mismanagement. Their audits focus upon delegation of responsibility, policy direction including program evaluation, budget and accounting practices, and the adequacy of internal controls including internal auditing.

Government Corporation Act of 1945:   Directed the GAO to audit public corporations in terms of their performance rather than mere legality and propriety of their expenditures.

Gross national product: The GNP is the total productive activity in a country during a certain period of time. It equals personal consumption plus gross private domestic investment plus government purchases of goods and services plus net exports of goods and services.

Identification of all transactions: Recording every obligation and transfer of money, and liquidation of obligation.

Income tax: Revenue source used at all levels of government, principally at the federal level. The tax is levied on the income of both corporations and individuals.

Incremental budgeting: Focuses upon the current year budget request with emphasis on increases from the current year. The analysts normally will want information on all activities being planned in the budget year but the focus will be upon the program changes from the current year.

Internal audit: Designed to address the board concepts of legality, effectiveness, and efficiency within the agency.

Issue Assessment: A written presentation which identifies and describes the major features of a significant issue facing the government. The assessment is only a few pages long, but it clearly sets out the ingredients which would be considered in preparing a major issue study.

Journal: A chronological listing of transactions, setting out the date of the transaction's occurrence, the dollars, and a brief explanation of the transaction.

Legal reserve requirement: A third tool of the Federal Reserve (Fed) for economic stabilization. The Fed can tighten the money supply by requiring a greater reserve to be maintained, thus normally shrinking the loan amount available. The converse normally increases the money supply.

Liabilities: Include accounts payable and payroll taxes payable.

Lien: A claim upon property arising from failure of the owner to make timely payment of a claim.

Management by Objective (MBO):   A technique for establishing specific objectives for agencies as well as requiring regular periodic reports on the progress toward achieving those objectives.

Method of averages: Revenue forecasting technique conducted by averaging the revenue generated over the last three to five years. A growth trend in the tax source and the economy is assumed.

Miller-Orr model: Method of determining the proposed cash balance. Focus is on the upper dollar limit needed for cash purposes. When the cash balance touches the upper boundary, then a predetermined amount of securities are automatically purchased. When the cash balance touches zero or an amount slightly above zero, then a predetermined amount of securities are sold, thus increasing the cash balance.

Mortgage bond: A type of bond which uses property to secure the debt obligation without transferring the title.

Muckrakers: Popular newspaper and book writers who advocated government reform around the early 1900's. Due to their efforts, reforms in budgeting were successful especially at the municipal level.

Nonguaranteed debt: (moral debt) Consists of a long-term debt payable often from earnings of revenue-producing activities, from special assessments, or from specific nonproperty taxes. The government does not guarantee its assets and earnings in support of the debt.

Open-ended expenditure forecasting: These estimates are based upon work plans often detailed and involving months to be prepared or quick judgments involving a few minutes' preparation.

Open-market operations: The most important tool of the Federal Reserve in economic stabilization. A committee frequently meets to decide to buy or sell government bonds or bills. Selling results normally in tightening, and buying normally results in expanding the money supply.

Operating budget: The budget which deals with the everyday activities. In most cases, these expenses are depleted in a single year.

Outcomes: In a systems model, these are the resulting benefits to individuals and society.

Outputs: In the systems model used in this book, these are the specific units produced by a governmental unit.

Performance budgeting: The budget material is arranged so that the existence of economy and efficiency can be ascertained easily. The budget is classified in terms of performance units and detail. The keys are accomplishment and linking achievement to resources.

Planning-programming-budgeting (PPB): An attempt in the federal government and some state and local governments to bring more analysis into the budgeting process. It is not an analysis itself but stresses the use of analytical tools in deciding budget related public issues. It attempts to apply the rational model of decision-making into the executive branch's policy-making process.

Policy letter: Used in government to convey executive guidance and budget ceilings to the lower levels in the executive branch. Issued to agencies and departments to inform them of Presidential or Office of Management and Budget decisions on the executive budget.

Productivity: A measure of efficiency usually expressed as the ratio of the quantity of output to the quantity of input used in the production of that output. Usually it focuses upon output per man hour of change or changes in cost per unit of output.

Program and Financial Plans (PFP): Summary tables of the budget categorized by major programs and activities. In the federal government, the PFP includes both obligations and disbursements; but obligations or expenditure can be sufficient for some state and local governments. The information covers the past year, current year, budget year and budget year plus five additional years. The PFP should reflect any policy changes, and it is particularly useful prior to budget call to forecast possible agency requests.

Program budget: Arranges the budget material in such a way as to aid the executive and legislator to understand the broader policy implications of their decisions.

Property tax: A revenue source for local and some state governments. Property is normally assessed locally. Then a tax rate is determined and applied on the basis of property value.

Quality indicators: Show characteristics, duration, content, extent, or degree in evaluating outputs and outcomes.

Ratio indicators: Show the quantity of service in some larger perspective such as population or area.

Rational decision-making model: The rational approach emphasizes: (1) setting goals and objectives (2) defining alternatives (3) analyzing alternatives and (4) selecting best decision based upon the established goals and objectives.

Reactive budget decision model: It is based on a stimulus response pattern. The budget calendar and the request govern the proponent of this model. Little thought is given to shaping events or making a difference through the reactor's product. The job is merely a task to be done as defined in the job description or job demands.

Registered bonds: This type of bond provides more protection to the bond holder, as the ownership is registered on the books of the issuing government or its paying agent.

Repurchase agreement: An innovation of government security dealers who recognize the selling potential of securities tailored to specific short time periods. Dealers agree to repurchase a security at a specific future date, thus increasing the number of transactions and the resulting total fees from those transactions.

Revenue forecasting: Systematic approaches used by governments to estimate the levels of revenue they can anticipate in future years.

Risk control: The reduction of risk or loss through careful procedures and practices in security, personnel safety, fire prevention, auto safety, product safety, environmental protection, and emergency planning.

Risk funding: Providing for sufficient funds to meet loss situations if they occur through the most effective use of internal and external financial resources.

"Rule of Penultimate Year": A technique for forecasting calling for the forecaster to use the last completed year as a basis for the revenue estimate. This technique is based on the assumption that there is growth in the economy and related revenue source.

Safety stock: It is the level of inventory which should be maintained for effective operations. It is where the total of holding costs and expected shortage costs are minimum.

Serial bond: The most common type of bond. It has maturity paid normally every year.

Sunset legislation: The concept is that government programs should automatically expire unless positive action is taken to renew them every few years. In many cases, the sunset provisions permit the program to remain on the law books but the legal authorization for funds expires.

Tax anticipation notes: Emergency borrowing by local governments against future anticipated tax revenue.

Tax certificates: This is a form of tax lien on property for delinquent taxes. They are negotiable securities and can be sold as they represent a debt which must be liquidated before a clear title can be given. At the sale of property, certificates on the title are given and the owner normally has one year to redeem them. If not redeemed, the property goes to the holder of the certificates.

Term bond: Matures at one time and a sinking fund is normally used to accumulate the necessary funds over time.

Transactions: Financial decisions such as obligating money, deciding on disbursement, and setting aside funds for a purpose.

Transfer payments: Often they are built-in automatic stabilizers for the economy. These payments normally rise substantially during periods of recession and fall during prosperity. For example, the unemployed receive unemployment compensation and eventually may receive welfare and food stamps as well in recessionary times.

Trend line approach: An expenditure forecasting technique which uses the activity's historical date, by developing and extending a trend line of expenditures from the past into the desired forecast period.

Volume indicators: Display the quantity of service such as the number of graduates in a university.

Voucher: A document which confirms the fact that a financial transaction has taken place.

Warrant: A banking service in which a draft is payable through a bank with the express permission of the government. It is used to slow and control disbursements. When a warrant is presented for payment, the bank will not pay until the warrant is accepted by the government.

Wise budget model: Proponents of this model recognize that politics is extremely important and sometimes of overriding importance. They also believe analysis has its limitations but it can often greatly help in decision-making situations.

Zero Base Budgeting (ZBB):   An approach to public budgeting in which each budget year's activities are judged totally with little or no reference given to the policy precedents or dollar amounts of past years.

Index

A

Accounting system design, 171
Accrual method of accounting (*see*
    Financial administration)
    statement of revenue, 172
ACIR, 29, 255 (*see also* Budget
    reform)
Agency Budget Office, 92
Allotments, 148
Alternative budget (*see* Expenditure
    forecasting)
Anti-Deficiency Act (*exhibit*), 100
Appropriation and expense ledger, 173
"Arbitrage" bonds, 224
Assessment cycle, 264
Auditing, 181–82, 188–207
    external audit, 182
    internal audit, 182

B

Backdoor spending, 38–39
Balance sheet, 177
Beard, Charles (*see* New York Bureau
    of Municipal Research)

Benefit-cost analysis, 282–86
    discount rate, 286
    externalities, 286
    intangible benefits, 285
    primary benefits, 285
    secondary benefits, 285
Bond anticipation rates (*see* Short-term
    debt)
Bond issue, 224–28
    call provisions, 224
    coupon structure, 224
    serial bonds, 224
Bond prospectus, 225
Bond ratings, 228
Bonds (*see* Government debt)
Budget:
    cycle, 6
    definition, 5
    estimate, 5
    operating, 5
    presentation, 8
    time period, 5
Budgetary process:
    control approaches, 9–10
    management approaches, 9–10
    planning approaches, 9–10